Defiance

DEFIANCE

*The Extraordinary Life
of Lady Anne Barnard*

STEPHEN TAYLOR

W. W. Norton & Company
Independent Publishers Since 1923
New York   London

For information about special discounts for bulk purchases, please contact
W. W. Norton Special Sales at specialsales@wwnorton.com or 800-233-4830

Manufacturing by QUAD Graphics, Fairfield

ISBN: 978-0-393-24817-3

W. W. Norton & Company, Inc.
500 Fifth Avenue, New York, N.Y. 10110
www.wwnorton.com

W. W. Norton & Company Ltd.
15 Carlisle Street, London W1D 3BS

1 2 3 4 5 6 7 8 9 0

To my daughter Juliette

Contents

CONTENTS

Illustrations

[ix]

Maria Fitzherbert, by Sir Joshua Reynolds
  © National Portrait Gallery, London
William Windham, by Sir Joshua Reynolds
  © National Portrait Gallery, London
The Morning After Marriage, by James Gillray
  © National Portrait Gallery, London
Andrew Barnard, by Sir Thomas Lawrence
  Private collection
Lady Margaret Fordyce, by Anne Mee
  Courtesy Peter Barrett © Philip Mould & Company
Lady Anne Barnard, by Anne Mee
  Courtesy Peter Barrett © Philip Mould & Company
George Macartney, after a portrait by Ozias Humphry
  © National Portrait Gallery, London
Platteklip Gorge, by Anne Barnard
  Reproduced with permission
Church Street, Stellenbosch, by Anne Barnard
  Reproduced with permission
Homestead in the Breede River valley, by Anne Barnard
  Reproduced with permission
Lady Anne Barnard's Pool, artist unknown
  © Iziko Museums of South Africa, Social History Collections

Prologue

Right to the last months of her life Lady Anne Barnard stayed tied to her desk in London's Berkeley Square. Her stomach pain was acute and she knew as she scratched away to a much-loved nephew that her time was short: 'I am beginning to burn and put my papers in order,' she wrote, 'but fear I shall not accomplish it.'

Her misgivings were natural. Banked around her was one of the most formidable collections of papers compiled by any woman of letters of an age that counted Jane Austen and the indefatigable Fanny Burney among its number. Piled on shelves and in cabinets stood letters, journals, memoirs, diaries, poems, sketches and watercolours – along with reams of what Anne called her 'scraps'. Just what these amounted to before she started to cast them into the flames is unclear, but the task did indeed remain incomplete. The surviving papers still extend to something like a million words.

Soon after her death, her nephew returned to the old house. James Lindsay had lived at 21 Berkeley Square as a young guards officer before going off to war, then again while convalescing and, since Waterloo, whenever he was in London. Colonel Lindsay walked with a stick these days, the mark of his wounds, and entering the dark house, emptied of the society that once filled it with music and hilarity, brought on the sense of a past age. The long drawing room with its portraits by Gainsborough and Lawrence was shrouded by drawn curtains. Anne's pianoforte stood silent. Her mounds of papers gathered dust.

James wandered upstairs, to the room he had occupied at what he used to call 'kind Aunt Barnard's hotel'. The nine bedrooms were rarely empty in those days, with guests who ranged from another dashing army officer – one esteemed a hero by Wellington no less – to a mysterious young girl of African origin whom Anne called 'my protégée of a darker complexion'. The circle of characters to be encountered downstairs was just as eclectic – literary and artistic, political and royal; among Anne's most intimate friends were London's oddest couple, the Prince of Wales and his secret wife, Maria Fitzherbert.

As a sixteen-year-old boy from Fife, an ensign with the First Regiment of Foot, James had entered this world with awe. After surviving the disaster of the Walcheren Expedition, he returned a worldly warrior, able to take his place at his aunt's table and enjoy what he recalled fondly as her benevolence, 'a readiness to share with others her purse, her tears, or her joys – an absence of all selfishness'. Often in the years that followed he observed her sparkle at the centre of Regency society, noted how she could 'change a dull party into an agreeable one . . . make the dullest speak, the shyest feel happy and the witty flash fire'. With it all, she mixed as easily with the lowly as the high-born, with servants as well as aristocrats.

'I loved her as a mother,' James recalled, 'and so did all who dwelt under her roof.'

Because of their intimacy, he was also able to see the paradoxes within. When asked after her death to describe her character, he stepped carefully over awkward terrain. It was, he said, 'no easy matter to draw the portrait of one whose charms and weaknesses were so intermingled, where shades and sunshine chased each other so rapidly over the landscape.'

In a more candid age it might have been admitted that kind Aunt Barnard was always seen by some of their family as dangerously unconventional, a character too colourful for propriety. Her sins were usually put down to the wilfulness she had shown as the young Lady Anne Lindsay and although the details were never very clear, some light was cast on the subject in her later years when James was drawn into a family dispute. Anne had largely withdrawn from society by then and, assisted by her young protégée, was writing a personal memoir. She had always been a compulsive chronicler and so absorbed was she by the task that she became a virtual recluse. 'The sagacious hint I am turning Methodist,' she reported gleefully. Meanwhile, the reputable side of the family watched in consternation, fearful of what Anne might surprise them with next. Finally, she was urged to stop. It made no difference that she insisted her memoirs were intended purely for relatives. Her youngest sister, married to the prominent and respectable Lord Hardwicke, said that with her history there was a real danger they would be stolen and stories which should never see the light of day made public. So Anne turned to James and another of her nephews for support.

Eight years on, James found himself back with her papers, and her story – the six volumes of memoir bound in calfskin, along with diaries, journals, literary works and a vast collection of letters. He was their custodian.

Dipping into Anne's archive transported him to another time and other worlds – to the era before revolution and war, when conflict was limited to debates over philosophy and ideas, to the conversations of men such as David Hume and Adam Smith. Anne had grown up in the brilliant milieu of Edinburgh during the Enlightenment, engaging with local intellectuals and demonstrating, as James Boswell used to relate, that she could hold her own in exchanges with Dr Samuel Johnson. On moving to London she became a leading society figure, sharing her wit and dining table with the high-minded – Edmund Burke was a friend – as well as the dissolute, among whom the young Prince of Wales was only the most prominent. The women who attracted her company and activated her pen included the Duchess of Devonshire and Emma Hamilton.

The tone of Anne's memoirs was intimate, addressed in authorial voice to her 'gentle reader'. At times they were confiding: 'These anecdotes have remained unseen to this day. I think you have a very tolerable chance of being entertained.' Yet frequently she wrote of the dramatic and clandestine events to which she had been party as a series of light-hearted frolics, and with a touch of mischief.

The voice became darker with disclosures about her romantic life and, as the volumes progressed, more confessional. As well as setting down a record of her life Anne had evidently seen it as part of her task to guide young female relatives away from her own mistakes, and explain some of the mysteries attached to the widow of Berkeley Square.

Here, too, among the mounds of her papers, James found records of events for which she had some fame. Her adventures in Africa – 'living with the Hottentots' as her London friends used to jest among themselves – were well known. She spent four years at the Cape of Good Hope from 1797 as official hostess during the first British occupation and, on wagon journeys to the interior, kept notes and drawings which captured another world, of frontier peoples, fantastic creatures and epic landscapes.

But there were revelations too, by a single woman negotiating her way through the scandals of a wild age, about the drama that threatened the monarchy and took her to Europe, and of her experiences of France during the Revolution; James had been Anne's fondest and most regular correspondent over the last decade of her life, and he knew her to be a vivid writer as well as a spirited woman. When she promised to entertain the reader, it came as no surprise that she did. Even James, though, had cause for astonishment at her unflinching self-exposure, at discovering the scope of a kindly aunt's hinterland.

Perhaps, by the time James set her papers aside, he had found an explanation for the enigma of Lady Anne Barnard – the outsider who wanted to belong, a woman defiantly independent yet always on a quest for love and understanding.

The archive did not stay at Berkeley Square. In time, General James Lindsay (as he had become) inherited Balcarres, the sixteenth-century ancestral hall in Fife where Anne was born, and the collection was taken there, to the library overlooking the Firth of Forth where her early learning had been shaped by a fond father. Here her papers were to remain, as they do in large part to this day. Whether, in passing again over her memoirs in later years, James contemplated what the outside world might learn from them, whether he was tempted to open these volumes to others, he left unsaid. As custodian, he was party to the vow she had given her family: they were never to see the light of day. 'As far as a departed person can debar any thing,' she had written, 'I utterly debar the publication now or ever of any work of mine.'

I knew enough when I asked the Earl of Crawford and Balcarres for access to her papers to realise that exploring them would be a serious undertaking. Since her injunction, the journals and letters from the Cape had been published (and mined by historians) and they alone run to four volumes. These were a personal starting point. Having been born at the Cape, I came to her writings after leaving South Africa as a young man, and found her hope and vision for the country where she landed in 1797 poignant as well as prophetic. But when setting out for Balcarres, I had no real notion of what to expect from the six volumes of memoir, still unpublished and virtually unexplored.

What follows is the life story of Lady Anne Barnard, as related by those memoirs. It is told here for the first time.

PART ONE

I

The Black Broth

1750–1768

'The wife for you is Lady Anne Lindsay,' Hester Thrale informed a wealthy member of her literary and intellectual circle in Streatham in 1779. 'She has birth, wit and beauty, she has no fortune and she'd readily accept you; and she has such a spirit that she'd animate you, I warrant you!' Dr Johnson's friend was not the first to see Lady Anne's marriageable qualities, nor the first to note her aptitude for handling spendthrifts. 'O, she would trim you well!' Mrs Thrale told William Seward. 'She'd take all the care of the money affairs, and allow you out of them eighteen pence a week. That's the wife for you!'

Attempts to match Anne – witnessed in this instance by the novelist Fanny Burney – reached a new pitch that year and crossed the spectrum of London society.[1] Similar confidence was being expressed by relatives of the dissolute Viscount Wentworth who had identified her as his saviour. Meanwhile a wild set of aristocratic mistresses offered other candidates for her hand in the belief that she had 'kept her virginity rather too long'.[2] What they shared, both prim bluestockings and racy courtesans, was a conviction that this clever and spirited woman would make an excellent wife. She was, to top it all, brilliant in company.

Anne Lindsay may have been born for companionship. She certainly had it thrust upon her. As the eldest child fathered by an earl in his sixtieth year, she began life at the dark old hall of Balcarres on the coast of eastern Fife in virtual solitude. The house soon turned into a nursery of mayhem; Anne was followed by ten more children, born at home within fourteen years of one another into an intensely socialised form of isolation – almost, as she observed, like castaways. Balcarres was distant enough from any other world to require a household of governesses, scholars, servants and hangers-on; and raised high above the Firth of Forth, it was surrounded on one side by trees and presented on the other with the sea. 'If we had supposed ourselves to be islanders we should not have been much mistaken,' Anne wrote. 'We were completely secluded.' There was, however, more than a hint of ambivalence in her memories of the place. 'Though our prison was a cheerful one, yet still it was a prison.'[3]

She could recall, as if it were an idyll, gambols with siblings and barking dogs across Balcarres. Field ran down to coast in what was, in part, an Eden. Among the landscapes of Scotland, the wildernesses and turbulence of highlands and glens, this low green aspect of Fife has a pure loveliness and cultivable soil that had attracted a branch of one of the country's oldest clans. John Lindsay, Lord Menmuir, acquired some 800 acres here in the 1580s and 'built a house to the skies'. More than 150 years on, his descendants – these young inhabitants – were still paddling in muddy pools, rambling across the estate and looking out to Bass Rock, which Anne saw rising from the sea 'like a great whale'.[4]

Yet this same gentle pastoral had a more forbidding aspect. The house resembled a bastion, standing high on the estate and rising over four levels in austere, castle-like tiers to towers like turrets with croaking rooks. Balcarres had been at the heart of a century of conflict. Alexander Lindsay, the First Earl of Balcarres, served as a royalist officer during the Civil War and died in exile. Colin Lindsay, the Third Earl, was imprisoned for his Jacobite sympathies before joining the 1715 rebellion against the Hanoverian monarchy; placed under house arrest, he died at Balcarres in 1721.

Insurrection cost the family dear. Scottish aristocrats had always been less affluent than the English among their Palladian mansions, sculpted lawns, artificial lakes, mazes and follies. Balcarres was an austere seat to start with and by the time Anne's father, James Lindsay, became the fifth of his line, the estate had been reduced to a state of self-sufficiency, its riches the food on his table. The house was bleak, a statue of Venus in a pond an isolated symbol of wealth.

James was a bookish, kindly former army officer who had failed to reach senior rank because of his Stuart sympathies.[5] These remained passionate, but at the defining moment of the second Jacobite rebellion in 1745, which broadly divided Scots between the Gaelic-speaking Highland clans and the landed and professional classes of the south, he prudently kept to his library, even after Bonnie Prince Charlie's forces entered Edinburgh. A solitary man, he seemed likely to end his days a bachelor among the books which, Anne recalled, 'had made chemists and philosophers of all the moths in the castle'.[6] Away from the army, James was content: 'I dine alone and find the sentiments of the dead much more instructive and entertaining than the fellowship of the living.'[7] The Stuarts had been extinguished at Culloden and he was fifty-nine when he visited the spa town of Moffat and met Anne Dalrymple, aged twenty-one. Naturally she refused his proposal, for the Dalrymples were a distinguished family, her father a knight, and even in those times a marriage between a man and a woman separated by almost forty years was a curiosity. Just such a ceremony nevertheless took place a few months later at Balcarres; for when Miss Dalrymple's father had died soon after their meeting and the earl offered to settle half his estate on her, she was pressed by her brothers to accept. The young bride came to Balcarres burdened with resentment.[8]

On the new Lady Balcarres falling pregnant expectations were raised of a first-born male heir who, according to prophetic oracles, would help to restore the Stuarts, so the birth of Anne Lindsay two weeks before Christmas in 1750 came as a profound disappointment. Lady Balcarres was with child again within four months, this time a boy, Alexander. A second daughter, Margaret, followed a year later. Nothing loath, the earl continued to father offspring on an almost annual basis. By the time the last was born, he was seventy-three and he had a complement of eleven: eight boys and three girls.

Their isolation was relative. As the crow flies, the city of Edinburgh lay little more than 20 miles across the Firth of Forth, although it was almost twice that by road and ferry and the obstacles of high winds and contrary tides ensured journeys were occasional. Arising from this seclusion, however, and enforcing it, was what Anne called 'a sort of creed in our family . . . that it was impossible anyone at Balcarres could wish to be anywhere else'.[9]

Her own feelings about home were always more ambivalent. This had nothing to do with the frugality of their existence, for while the children of English lords rode horses on their family estates, Anne Lindsay would laugh at the memory of how she used to dig up turnips and jog about on the back of a pig. These rustic early years were typical enough among landowning Scottish families and it was combined at Balcarres with an easy familiarity towards common folk, such as the shepherd Robin Grey. On Sunday they would all, family and servants, walk two miles to church 'and listen with reverence to all we understood, and with smiles to the horrid discords with which a Presbyterian congregation assails the ears'.[10]

Yet although Anne grew up without the usual affectations of class, she bore another burden. This arose partly from being the eldest, a girl among a rabble of boys, a thoughtful, sensitive child and, being clumsy too, conspicuous in any hunt for wrongdoers. In an ordinary home this would have mattered less. But with the austerity of Balcarres came a disciplinary regime that was nothing short of severe.

'Had my mother been married to a man of her own time of life ... I am convinced she would not only have been a more complying wife but a tenderer mother,' Anne recalled. As it was, harnessed to the sixty-year-old earl when their first child was born, and sustained in an almost constant state of pregnancy, Lady Balcarres vented her discontent as much on her growing brood as on her husband. This was a subject which Anne wrote about with some guilt, consoling herself with excuses for her mother's coldness and emphasising her rectitude and honesty. The fact remained that Lady Balcarres 'was not naturally fond of children – they annoyed her'. She slapped them freely and frequently in order, so she said, 'to fit us for the hardships of life', but in reality, Anne believed, out of bitterness.[11]

Adding to the Gothic aspect of Balcarres was her mother's entourage. While the earl lived among his books, his wife surrounded herself with female companions who competed for her favour, including her cousins, the Miss Keiths, a trio of sour spinsters who visited often. The dark, central figure in a gallery of curiosities, however, was Henrietta Cumming, small, eccentric and hysterical, with a fondness for laudanum.

Henrietta came to Balcarres in her mid-twenties as governess to the Lindsay girls, having passed herself off as an ill-fated gentlewoman descended from a Highland chief and cited by Edinburgh society as a creature of exalted mind. In reality she was modestly educated but bountifully endowed with cunning. She refused quarters below stairs by staging a hunger strike, then settled in the heart of the family where she nestled like a viper.

Fantastic in her dress, and naïve in her manners, her countenance was pretty, her shape neat and nice; but in that casket was lodged more than Pandora's Box contained – of sorrows and of ills to demolish mankind.[12]

Henrietta's rival for Lady Balcarres's favour and the girls' affection was another member of the household, Sophy Johnston, the natural child of a debauched local laird. Sophy, as Anne observed, was a woman of Amazonian stature. 'Nature seemed to have hesitated to the last whether to make her a boy or a girl ... She worked well in iron, could shoe a horse quicker than the smith, made excellent trunks, played well on the fiddle, sung a man's song in a bass voice, and was by many people suspected of being one.'[13]

The tensions within this bizarre circle were felt particularly by Anne, aged about ten when Henrietta was appointed to cultivate the sisters' manners, morals and accomplishments. Henrietta noted early on that if Lady Balcarres showed any indulgence it was for Margaret; and because she regarded Sophy as an enemy, and saw she had a partiality for Anne, she turned against the older girl with an 'aversion which met me in every turn of my progress thro' the early stages of life'.[14]

It became Anne's way to make light of her childhood. She could write amusingly of Balcarres as:

A little Bastille, in every closet of which was to be found a culprit. Some were sobbing and repeating verbs, others eating their bread and water, some preparing themselves to be whipped, and here and there a fat little Cupid who having been flogged was enjoying a most enviable nap.[15]

But there was real darkness too. With 'everything done by authority and by correction' the displeasure was constant, the spankings were severe.[16] Anne was often left confused and frightened. Why could her mother not be kind like Sophy? As the eldest, she felt exposed. Once Henrietta's malice was brought to bear she became even more vulnerable as, for reasons that defied her understanding, the governess set out to turn others against her. Having established what Anne perceived as 'an ascendancy over the mind of Lady Balcarres', Henrietta became increasingly hostile until it became not so much common ill will but 'the malediction of an evil genius'.[17]

Rarely did Anne abandon the wit and irony of the memoirs written late in her life, so it is evident the scars from Henrietta's spitefulness and the lack of love from her mother ran deep. Reflecting then with horror on the damage done by severity to children *'for their good'* and the depressing effect this could have in adulthood, she became an advocate for the French writer and educationalist whose pioneering ideas on gentler child-raising had won approval in Britain: 'Long live Madame de Genlis if she can make youth happier and better without the birch!'[18] Almost the first lesson Anne drew from her own childhood was a 'great dislike of making others unhappy' which, as she said, was a negative virtue. But it went deeper than that. Behind what became a constant desire to please lay a real dread of disapproval, of being misunderstood. The girl with the brightest smile was always on a quest for affection. Balcarres she called, only half in jest, 'the Black Broth of Sparta, seclusion and correction'.[19]

Like many an unhappy child, she took refuge in books. And here at least the dark broth contained light, for the library at Balcarres was a treasure trove: the basis for what became the Bibliotheca Lindesiana, one of Britain's great literary collections, was started by the Lindsay family in the seventeenth century and contained poetry and philosophy, Classics and history, along with theological works.[20] Words became the wisdom, the comfort, of Anne's lifetime; and it may be concluded, too, that in these early years they fed her with ideas, strong beliefs and even notions of romantic love.

There was no formal education system for the earl's vast brood. In theory the pupils were formed in two age divisions, the first composed of Anne, Alexander, Margaret, Robert and Colin, the second – arising from a two-year gap when the countess failed to produce a single child – consisting of James, William, Charles, John, Elizabeth and Hugh. In reality the boys had an occasional male tutor, Mr Small, while the girls were given a haphazard blend of lessons from Henrietta and Sophy. As one of the family recalled, young women were taught no language besides English, and in addition to that only a little arithmetic and cookery.

> But Lady Anne and Lady Margaret were not to be so satisfied; they studied and read together, working out instructions for themselves; and their example was followed in time by the third sister. This struggle of the intellect against difficulties drew forth the energies of the three sisters.[21]

Anne's first surviving literary effort, from her twelfth year, a poem entitled and dedicated *To My Pocket Book*, is revealing of the private, confessional world of words which became her retreat.

> Of all the friends that can be named,
> For Secrecy and Prudence famed,
> I hear thou art the very best,
> For in thy Breast can secrets rest,
> Thy chattering tongue will neer reveal,
> What we require thee to conceal.[22]

The black broth had other warming elements too, notably the old earl himself who provided some of the affection lacking in his wife. When he thought her treatment of the children too severe, the former army officer would remonstrate: 'Odsfish, Madam! You will break the spirits of my young troops. I will not have it so.'[23]

Along with fondness came the intelligence of an exceptionally well-read man. Anne especially enjoyed his company in the library where he would reach down a favourite volume, declaring: 'You must have books.' James Lindsay's learning – and his collection of rarities – brought guests of real eminence to Balcarres, including a giant of Scottish letters, the philosopher and historian David Hume, and Alison Cockburn, writer, literary hostess and Edinburgh's 'romantic old lady of genius'.[24] Anne's early reading often consisted of verse. In time she moved on to Plutarch's *Lives* and Spenser's *Faerie Queene*, and thanks to Rollin's multivolume *Ancient History* 'became acquainted with the exact height of the pyramids and how to make a mummy'. The earl encouraged a love of music too and as Anne and Margaret were taught the keyboard and singing by Sophy, he would ask them to perform for him, savouring the 'soft sownds from a pair of fine lips, the sweetest of all musick'.[25] As she told her beloved nephew James many years later, if a single source can be identified for fostering the liberal, questing mind of the woman who became Lady Anne Lindsay, it was her elderly father.

On a more pragmatic level, he exerted political influence – guiding his 'troops' away from the Jacobite sympathies that had deranged the clan's fortunes, and urging reconciliation in the light of the prosperity that Scots in the Lowlands, mainly the urbanised Edinburgh–Glasgow region, were starting to enjoy under a new king, George III. 'You my children are born after the Union,' the earl declared. 'Scotland is no more, and likely never to revive.'[26]

But the principal comfort of Anne's childhood, the companion with whom she shared a bedroom at the top of a dark, spiralling stone staircase, who would grow into the soulmate of her adult years until family and society alike saw them as virtually indivisible, was her sister Margaret.

In a house teeming with male siblings it was natural that two girls should have formed a particular bond. Margaret, roughly two years her junior, was the prettier and more favoured by her family. In later years Anne was so overwhelmed by recollection of their shared lives she could scarcely comprehend how this tragic figure could have loved her so deeply, 'with a tenderness which no arts of Henrietta could undermine, or partiality of Sophy destroy, so foreign was discord or jealousy to our united hearts'.[27] Margaret she declared to be her superior in almost every way, from beauty to enlightenment. So deep was the love between them that Anne felt compelled to admit the strains, the quarrels and the guilt that went with it.

Anne was the principal target for feminine vindictiveness at Balcarres; Margaret was the favourite. Yet Margaret had 'a tendency to self-distrust', and deferred instinctively to her elder sister whom she secretly envied.[28] Anne believed it was 'as if she left me, whom she loved, to think feel and act for her'.

> Nature had given her a sensibility so acute to ridicule or blame that it was difficult to find words so tender as not to hurt her feelings or alarm her pride – she needed my cheerful careless view of things, the hope and hilarity of my self-content to reassure her respecting herself.[29]

The need, in fact, was mutual. Insecurities vanished when they were with one another. They shared gaiety and what Anne attributed to Margaret as 'the brilliancy of harmless wit'. During the day they sang, painted and read together, and when they retreated to their bedroom at night they performed together. 'By the embers of a fire we sat talking, imagining and laughing, till we could laugh no more. How often have we not made a theatre of our apartment . . . There we acted plays, farces and harlequin entertainments till we almost brought down the old house about our ears.'[30]

Affection for their swarm of brothers was naturally diffused. Alexander, reserved and seemingly burdened by his birthright, became a distant figure quite early on. Anne was closest to the next two boys, of whom she recalled:

Robert bought a knife for sixpence, used it for three months and sold it to Colin for a shilling. Colin discovered this and complained in terms so judicious that the whole family pronounced Robert must be a merchant and Colin my Lord Chancellor. Robert was forthwith destined to go to India as a writer and Colin was bred to the bar.[31]

In fact, the Lindsay brothers might have served as standard-bearers for that generation of Scots who carried the Union flag across the globe and, for good and bad, shaped Britain's empire. The saga of the laird's sons, forced by primogeniture to leave the land and make their way through opportunities created abroad by English mercantile interests, is intrinsic to Scottish history and it could have been written with the Lindsays in mind.[32] Of the eight boys, only the eldest could inherit the title and estate. Four would enter the army, two went to sea and one joined the East India Company. Just one entered the Church. Among the earl's last productions was a third daughter, Elizabeth, thirteen years Anne's junior – too young to have fully joined her sisters' indivisible circle.

Their first insights into a world beyond Balcarres began with visits to Edinburgh. Anne had just entered her teens when she and Margaret spent six months with their maternal grandmother, Lady Dalrymple, a kinder soul than her daughter, who provided a beacon of warmth. 'She loved me,' Anne recalled. 'I was her god-daughter and her sworn friend.' Moreover, the old lady held court in the quiet, antique corner of Hyndford's Close, described by Sir Walter Scott as a retreat where 'worth and talent and elegance were often nestled'. Along with receiving dancing lessons, the girls were taught the forte-piano and harmony by an Italian exile named Pignatelli, reputed to have murdered a Venetian noble who had seduced his wife.

By the time of their next visit Anne was a sparkling fifteen-year-old and starting to engage with the kind of circle that would become her natural milieu. Intellectuals gathered at Lady

Dalrymple's table for what were called 'Dinners of the Eaterati' by one of their number who promptly collapsed at his own wit. David Hume was counted among the guests here too. Less renowned but a great favourite for his enquiring intelligence and bonhomie was Sir Augustus Oughton. Anne thrived in this good humoured environment, to which she and Margaret were encouraged to contribute.

On one occasion Hume, recalling previous meetings at Balcarres and Edinburgh, reminded Anne of a particular conversation.

'Do you remember all this, my little woman?'

'I was too young to think of it at the time.'

'How's this? Have not you and I grown up together?'

I looked surprised. 'Yes,' added he, 'you have grown tall and I have grown broad.'[33]

Behind such inconsequential banter lay a significant fact. Anne spent her formative years in one of the cleverest places in the world. The intellectual blossoming of Scotland's Enlightenment produced philosophers, economists, writers, scientists and lawyers of a brilliance out of all proportion to the size of the population. Men like Hume and Lord Monboddo, a jurist and philosopher in whose company she also learned to sharpen her wits, were leading figures in a movement which had far greater impact on the immediate environment than its equivalent elsewhere in Britain; Adam Smith, the moral philosopher and economist, seems to have been one of the few she did not meet until she was in her twenties, after publication of his landmark study, *The Wealth of Nations*. The stimulating effect such men had on this teenage girl is hard to exaggerate, especially as they had encouraged her to express herself. The Scottish Enlightenment was advanced in other ways, ascribing to women a progressive role as agents of social change; the literary hostess, Alison Cockburn, another familiar from Balcarres, persuaded Hume to offer Jean-Jacques Rousseau a refuge from his European persecutors and would be an early admirer of Anne's talents. (The young Walter Scott was among Mrs Cockburn's later protégés.[34]) That is not to say early feminism was in any way general; Anne would suffer deeply from conventional opinion in Edinburgh.

One man on the fringe of this intellectual circle had a more sinister aspect, and pernicious influence. William 'Sheriff' Cross, as he was known by the family who regarded him as an old friend, was a poet and traveller, and – although in his fifties with an ill-fitting bushy wig – a roué. Cross insinuated himself with the Lindsay girls and became infatuated with Anne. 'Though not an absolute Beauty, you are very handsome,' he wrote, 'and you know well how to give that handsomeness all its effect.'[35] Her literary interest provided the necessary connection: he bombarded her with letters and Classical allusions, to Horace and Euclid, and she was flattered.

But she was also repelled. There were 'the unholy glances that his wanton little eye shot from under the shade of his wig' which 'too much resembled the Anacreon of antient [*sic*] times; they inspired me even then with a Frisson I could not account for.'[36] From her confusion, and aspects of their correspondence, it is evident that in their early teens both girls were molested by Cross. Anne came close to spelling it out in her memoirs:

> He delighted in Margaret's company and in mine, and always took care to pay his visits when our Grandmother was from home ... He got acquainted with the extent of our abilities and the force of our arms from romping and reasoning with us.[37]

Conflict between the pleasure of his intellectual attention and revulsion at its physical aspect added to her ambivalence. 'I loved Sheriff Cross when he was absent, but I hated him when he was present.' Influential as he was within the family, there would have been no question of challenging him openly, and in an age when teenage girls were married off to older men as a matter of course, his 'romping' would have attracted less revulsion than it does in ours.

That Cross had a significant influence on Anne's development is clear. Many years after his death she prefaced her memoirs with a series of admonitions, citing Cross as the author. The first, spelling out what she had clearly come to recognise as her own greatest weakness, went: 'To the Young: Beware of Indecision . . . It neutralises every virtue.'

Another was a virtual confession by Cross of his own sin. 'To the Mature: Beware of retaining for the education of youth persons of eccentric character . . . They are unsafe. The world is full of coal-pits and wastes into which the young colts and fillies tumble and are lost.'[38]

Anne continued to correspond with Cross until his death, mostly without rancour but also with a forthrightness rare in her – as if knowledge of his flaws dispelled her usual need to please – and in one instance with venom; her letter to him does not survive but his reply makes this clear: 'You say you hate me sometimes, and I can partly guess at the reason but I defy you to hate me, and I laugh at the menace for *I love you*.'[39]

The effect on Anne of what must appear in today's light as sexual abuse at the hands of a family friend is a matter of speculation. She did, however, show certain symptoms: the blend of reverence and resentment towards Cross, and a confusion over how to respond to men. The wariness that she would demonstrate during many courtships, to the point of appearing incapable of commitment, was sustained by a belief in true love and a spirit of independence. But it appears to have had two catalysts. Observing her mother's bitterness at being married off to a titled old man was one. Damage from Cross's twisted love may have been another.

*

Soon after receiving what Lady Balcarres called 'the Finishing Stroke' of their Edinburgh education, both girls came down with measles – so seriously in Anne's case that her life hung in the balance for a week. Even then it appeared that the results might leave her face disfigured. Looking at herself in a mirror she thought: 'As on Belshazzar's wall, so a finger on my cheek proclaimed "Anne thou shall't never be married" and that no man of delicacy or pride would have me.'[40]

That was a fate Lady Balcarres had resolved should not befall her girls. As the earl grew frail, keeping to his library in a gown and slippers – with holes slashed in the toes to relieve his gout – the financial infirmity of his estate became equally apparent, and whatever his wife lacked in warmth she was handsomely endowed with flinty resolve. Her sons were being prepared for military careers. Her daughters, at least the two eldest, had to deploy their rank and beauty to save Balcarres by marrying fortunes.

The first attempt at matchmaking occurred in Anne's seventeenth year with the proposal from a retired merchant by the name of Alexander, relayed from Edinburgh by Anne's old bête noire Henrietta Cumming. Although almost fifty and ugly with it, Alexander had a fabulous income of around £4,000 a year.

'You must be sensible that you are not very young,' Lady Balcarres said in relating his offer.

> You are past 16 and, everyone must allow, a woman to all intents and purposes. You also have to consider very calmly whether you would be contented to find yourself at 50 an old maid like Sophy Johnston, your old friends dead, on a scanty income, which would scarcely afford you a bone of mutton and potatoes.[41]

Marrying Mr Alexander, on the other hand, would leave her comfortable and respected – and provide 'the support of your brothers and sisters in case of your father's death'.

Anne's response was clear and direct. She would not accept Mr Alexander, she said, having heard that he was 'frequently deranged in his intellects'. At this point Lady Balcarres volunteered that she had heard similar reports. Rather more to her credit, she accepted Anne's decision and pressed the matter no further.[42] Henrietta's acid comment was that it required a mind of a certain kind to appreciate Mr Alexander's true worth, and she could not resist expressing a hope that Anne would not end up doing worse.

A time of change was at hand. The eldest Lindsay boy, Alexander, had just left for Europe, having entered the army as an ensign. Robert and Colin were sent away to school. The winter of 1767 was approaching when Lady Balcarres, who 'seemed to grow more bitter and displeased with all we said or did', announced that Anne and Margaret must prepare themselves for a return to Edinburgh to be presented to society. While staying at Hyndford's Close, they would rejoin their grandmother's circle for introduction to potential suitors.

Almost the first young man Anne met appeared an ideal match. Lord Deskford, son of the Earl of Findlater, was tall, stiff and 'resembled a young Van Dyke lord with a Roman nose'.[43] They went to a ball followed by a concert, a breakfast, a dance, a walk and a play, at which point Anne and Lady Balcarres were taken to meet his parents. 'We want no fortune with Deskford's wife,' his father said. 'Youth and good connections are all we require.'[44]

Thus were matters neatly poised when a letter arrived from Balcarres, addressed to Anne but meant for both sisters. It was from their father and it had the tone of a valedictory:

My Anne, your father is now no more but the ruin of an old building that never had much beauty in it ... Men love companions as can help to make them gay and easie. For this end fair Nymphs should provide chains, as well as nets to secure Captives. You must have the

Muses as well as the Graces to aid and assist Nature, which has been very good to you.[45]

There was an exhortation to continue their learning: poetry was cheering; history showed man at his best and his worst; and philosophy would bring consolation should they be condemned to life as old maids. Finally, as if holding up the example of his wife as a warning, he urged that if they did marry they should be amiable to their husbands: 'It's the best instrument to have power, as he will have more pleasure in pleasing yow than even himself.'

They hastened back to Balcarres, to find him on his deathbed. 'Have my girls left any lovers behind them?' he asked weakly.

Lady Balcarres accepted his end in February 1768 with fortitude. The troops were assembled. 'We shall all do perfectly well,' she declared, 'by making up our minds to what we have to do.'[46]

The little sea of faces confronted Anne in stark terms with her responsibilities. Six of her siblings had not yet reached the age of ten: her youngest sister Elizabeth was four and Hugh just three. Barely seventeen herself, she would feel a natural fondness towards them all; but her primary role as the eldest child now must be as a provider.

2

Edinburgh's Coquette

A brisk sense of purpose left little room for mourning that winter. The Lindsays of Balcarres were left with an ageing house, an income of £350 a year and the interest from sums of £600 placed in trust for each of the children. The estate might feed them but it would not provide the resources necessary to launch eight boys into the world. With austerity beckoning, Lady Balcarres decreed that Anne and Margaret must return to Edinburgh to resume their quest for wealthy suitors.

Anne's initial response gave every cause for optimism. A week after the earl's death, Lady Balcarres could write to her brother: 'My daughter, thank God! cast down and depressed as she is, behaves like a woman of good sense and principles. She looks forward to her great charge.'[1] A sense of family duty was Anne's principal inheritance. That and a desire to please her mother, or a fear of her displeasure, gave an appearance of compliance.

She may of course have been anticipating the handsome match that seemed in the making. But weeks went by without word from Lord Deskford – no letter either of enquiry or condolence – until another note came from Edinburgh: he had been taken with a fever, his life despaired of, and though now out of danger doctors had recommended his removal to a Mediterranean climate.

In the meantime, brother Alexander had returned home as

the Sixth Earl of Balcarres, bringing a friend from his regiment, a fellow ensign. Anne observed that Charles Gordon 'enter'd the old drawing-room with the figure of Apollo, the manners of a Prince, and the light heart and heels of a young man without a guinea in his pocket'.[2] This proved sadly true, for although a half-brother of the Earl of Aberdeen, the young spendthrift had dissipated a small fortune of £6,000 on high living at the courts of Europe. He was charming with it, managing to ingratiate himself even with the icy lady of the house; and while Anne recognised him as 'a complete puppy', she was taken. Young Gordon had hastily to reassure Lady Balcarres that he had no designs on 'either of your dear little girls'.

An extended family circle now provided the network that would connect them to a world beyond Edinburgh. Alison Cockburn, the poet and hostess, wrote enthusiastically to David Hume: 'Lady Balcarres and her lovely lasses are in town for the winter.'[3] They spent a week at the Hermitage, home of the Miss Keiths who had been frequent visitors to Balcarres. Their father, Sir Robert Keith, a former ambassador to Saint Petersburg, was welcoming and he had a fund of anecdotes about life at the court of Catherine the Great. His daughters were less convivial, particularly Anne Murray Keith, who, like Henrietta Cumming, was in her thirties, single, sour and determined to take charge, 'particularly of the young folks, whom she loved so much she thought it a pity we should not be perfect'.[4]

At Caroline Park, a grand house on the outskirts of Edinburgh owned by Sir Adolphus Oughton, the welcome was unreserved. An army man, Sir Adolphus was typical of an era of Scottish gallants who brought learning to their military careers. Dr Johnson said of him: 'You will find few men of any profession who know more. He is a very extraordinary man; a man of boundless curiosity and unwearied diligence.'[5] General Oughton had married into the Dalrymple clan and with his stepson Captain Hew Dalrymple, would escort the Lindsay sisters in Edinburgh society.*

Anne delighted in Oughton's company. Military connections ran in her family and Sir Adolphus became a paternal figure. He was among the first correspondents to remark on her literary style. 'Critics said Congreve was a bad economist for having lavished on one play [*The Way of the World*] as much wit as might have served for a dozen. Did I not know, my dear Lady Anne, that your fund is inexhaustible, I might say the same for one of your letters.'⁶ For a seventeen-year-old just starting to make her way this was inspiriting stuff. So was a sweet verse which he addressed jointly to Anne and Margaret.

> No conquests you'll make while together you dwell.
> With beauty, wit, figure and voice
> All others in charms you both do excel,
> But together you puzzle the choice.

The transition had begun that saw Margaret turn from a diffident girl into one of the true beauties of the age; Anne's description of her, auburn-haired inclining to red, with an aquiline nose and wide mouth, matches the grand, full-figure portrait by Thomas Gainsborough.

Her general form and stature had the fulness of youth's first bloom, while her skin and complexion had lustre and delicacy; but the turn of her face and throat! . . . it was Grecian beauty's own self.⁷

Though Anne felt overshadowed, she too was counted a beauty.

---

* The young captain went on to a distinguished military career as Lieutenant General Sir Hew Whitefoord Dalrymple until a falling-out with his junior, Lieutenant General Arthur Wellesley, led to his recall from the Peninsular campaign in 1808.

What emerges from contemporary accounts is not so much any special purity of her features – though the eyes stand out in Richard Cosway's portrait – as vivacity and warmth; while the eyes invited, her personality proclaimed a pleasure in company. Margaret, it was said, could light up a room with her beauty; Anne, as if to compensate with another quality, animated it with expression.

Simple wardrobes reflected their meagre circumstances: a single hard-wearing brown dress for daily use; a satin negligee, as Anne called it, for balls and other social occasions; and 'a black silk sack' for solemn events including church-going and 'as assistant to the others during the fatigues of their offices'.[8] Indivisible as they were in dress and charm, the Lindsay sisters were equally so at musical evenings, performing on the forte-piano and harp, and singing. Margaret's voice, according to Anne, had 'that natural *affettuoso* which often surprised tears from the listener, he knew not why'. In fact, although they delighted audiences when singing together, Anne's musical talent was the more generally acclaimed. It was suggested that she might sing with the castrato Giusto Tenducci for the Edinburgh Musical Society during his visit in 1768;[9] and Fanny Burney would remark on the sweetness of her voice at London salons.

Anne was still thinking of Lord Deskford, who was due to return from Banffshire on his way to Italy, when she met a young military officer.

He presented himself at Caroline Park, heralded by young Captain Dalrymple, who gave a light-hearted warning that Anne would never manage to please the handsome, high-minded and elegant colonel of his regiment. Such were the attributes of the Comte Rudolph de Bentinck, a Dutch officer serving in the army. The sisters tittered at the very idea . . . an elegant Dutchman?[10]

Count Bentinck, it turned out, really was refined and handsome, tall with a shock of curly dark hair and, far from being indifferent, he was smitten. Soon after his arrival, Anne received a note. Even the date proclaimed its passion: 'Saturday morning, four o'clock'.

From the first evening I had the satisfaction of being in your ladyship's company I was struck with the idea of a Most Perfect model of all the requisites for procuring the highest felicity in a connubial mate ... My enterprising genius imboldens me to offer myself as a candidate for the most admirable of her sex.[11]

Prolixity aside, Bentinck appeared a real catch. He had dashing exploits to his name – capture and escape from certain death at the hands of American Indians – along with rank and connections; he was a distant cousin of the Whig politician, William Cavendish-Bentinck, the Duke of Portland. The female circle at Caroline Park, which at this point included the Miss Keiths, became animated, and a week passed in company with singing and dancing before the military men departed to rejoin their regiment some forty miles away.

Among other suitors gathering in Edinburgh for the winter of 1768 were Lord Deskford, still frail but smiling at the sight of Anne, and Charles Gordon. A new face, Lord Lindores, had barely arrived before he started to send amorous notes: 'I dare not ask with whom you danced last night for jealousy is a mighty disagreeable passion.'[12] Following a series of entertainments described by Lindores as 'operas, plays, assemblies, levees, formal visits and song parties', another rival appeared when Bentinck returned to town for a ball.

Lady Balcarres was savouring the attention being paid to her eldest daughter; but the ill will of others had become noxious. Henrietta Cumming declared every suitor unworthy; meanwhile Anne Murray Keith made it her business to enquire about Colonel Bentinck among local gossips, and reported back with relish that the fellow was a charlatan: no fighting in America; no capture by Indians; even the connection to the duke was in question.[13] 'Thank God, Anne, you have learnt this in time,' her mother declared. Miss Keith was praised for her indefatigable pursuit of the truth.

Anne could not reconcile her open-faced lover with the alleged impostor. She was nevertheless beset by doubts. At this point a letter of proposal came from Bentinck. In reply she wrote a letter which still made her cringe years later. 'I called it a rejection; but it was a rejection so much afraid of hurting him, so grateful for his partiality, so unexplicit in its phrase, that I pity myself when I read it.'

Anne's vacillation arose from a desire to please. Subjected to different voices, challenged with contrary opinions, she was paralysed by choice. Whom to accept? Whom to please? The need for approval rendered her more indecisive and, in leading her to deeper waters, had the very effect she sought to avoid. Horrified by the thought of causing pain or offence, she would hesitate to declare herself, injuring many who professed love and doing opinion of her much harm. The letter of rejection remained undelivered when she went to a ball, intending to hand it to Bentinck.

The evening was a disaster. Bentinck danced with her while plainly distressed that she had failed to declare herself. Other admirers were gathering like Highland stags. Charles Gordon cornered her and said that whatever assurance he had given her mother, his heart burst at the sight of such innocent gaiety. Across the room, Bentinck's eyes were on fire, seemingly ready, 'to call out Charles Gordon – to shoot himself, me and everybody around him'. At this point, Lord Deskford came over, having decided that he wished to dance with her, rather than Margaret with whom he had spent the evening. When she refused he asked: 'How come you to be so barbarous?' She was then joined by Anne Murray

Keith. 'Dance, dance, for the love of God,' she whispered. 'The eyes of the whole room are on you.'[14]

Bentinck disappeared, to be found by Hew Dalrymple who explained how he had been traduced. Persuaded to return, he spent the rest of the evening muttering darkly that a foreigner commanding a regiment of jealous Scots was not in want of any other enemies. Finally, Anne, after what some saw as a virtuoso act of coquettishness, passed him her note.

Matters did not end there. Having denounced him as a fraud, Lady Balcarres was informed that Bentinck was indeed who he claimed to be and really was related to the Duke of Portland. It followed that as a handsome, well-bred man with a comfortable income and excellent connections, he was thoroughly acceptable. Anne, confused to start with, now had no idea whether she loved Bentinck or not. He, hoping that she might have changed her mind now the truth had been resolved, asked to see her again, a last opportunity before his regiment marched for Europe.

On the eve of his visit Lady Balcarres set down her own feelings. As one of the few surviving letters from this volatile woman to her daughter, it bears quoting at length:

> As you are to converse with Col Bentinck tomorrow on a very important subject I think it of consequence to tell you I leave you intyrely to your own free mind. I have as was my duty represented to you the inconveniency of this match and . . . the risk of going abroad with him if he is your husband & I have always said if your heart was not much interested now was the time to crush it in the bud. On the other hand if giving him up will be a severe shock to your feeling don't give up your own opinion even to please your mother. You are less a child than any person I know of your years. I have a better opinion of Col Bentinck than of most young men. I have seen his passion for you from the first.[15]

Mixed though the message was, had it been expressed earlier Anne might have been in a less confused state when she was interrogated by her mother that evening. As it was, asked about her intentions, Anne whispered that she could not accept Bentinck. This started an outcry. Miss Keith called her an artful little minx, Henrietta looked on with satisfied contempt. Anne began sobbing aloud and Lady Balcarres ordered her from the room.[16]

Bentinck duly called in the morning. 'Blessed angel,' he said, kissing her hand, 'do you prefer me to all those who are paying you their court?' All she could reply with certainty was that 'I liked him better of all the men I had ever seen on my little list'. Still Bentinck was glad, declaring: 'It is sufficient.' As his regiment marched south, it could have been thought that they had some kind of agreement.[17]

Any hopes that the family's fortunes might be repaired by the attentions Lord Deskford briefly showered on Margaret faded when he left town, ostensibly for a tour of Italy. Anne concluded: 'We had counteracted each other, as Sir Adolphus's couplet prophesied.' Her dark muse, Sheriff Cross, joked: 'See what you have done, foolish hussies, scared away this young peer and all because you will be witty!' Deskford, he related, had said the sisters were too clever to make good wives.[18] As it transpired, neither explanation accounted for Deskford's reluctance. Although it took years for the details to emerge, he was, in fact, homosexual and had gone into exile not for his health but to avoid scandal. Two years later his father, who had encouraged a match with Anne, committed suicide.*

* Deskford was briefly married before settling in Carlsbad where he became a local patron and landscape gardener. He died in Dresden where he is buried with his partner Johann Fischer.

Events that winter left their mark. Anne may have recalled the season for her agonised dithering but it is clear that she had been quietly exhilarated at finding herself a belle; and being presented with a range of suitors had opened her eyes to the possibility of choice, which was never likely to spur a hasty decision. Then there was Margaret. The question of marriage had forced the sisters to face the prospect of separate lives, and they had embraced and wept at the very thought.

It was in the nature of contemporary society that courtships, structured as they were around formal gatherings, were intense but brief. When another beau, Charles Gordon, went back to his regiment as well, Anne and Margaret picked up the threads of life as it had been, sewing and making music, and for a while contentment was restored. Margaret once wondered why, with a careful marshalling of their resources, they should care about marrying at all. Anne went further, voicing unease at the way they were being set out as wares for wealthy spouses, recalling their mother's tart observation that, 'goods which stick long in the market prove themselves to be unsaleable.'[19] While sorry that Lady Balcarres could not understand them, could not bring herself to join their little circle – 'what happiness might she not have given to herself' – Anne came to a conclusion, remarkable for the time, that:

> The desperate determination of marrying anybody amount[s] to marrying nobody except that somebody who had not presented himself.[20]

Respite was brief, the autumn of 1768 signalling the onset of another season, the appearance of fresh suitors. As another old admirer wrote years later: 'I remember that winter I saw you in Edinburgh, the women were all setting their tops at Swinton and George Home. You carryed them both off . . .'[21]

The first gathering took place at Leuchie House, a mansion east of Edinburgh owned by the Dalrymples where a trio of Anne's uncles held court. These were not men she felt comfortable with:

> ... loving what was called a bottle of good wine and that dastardly style of conversation called *double entendre* which I look upon as the murder of the innocents; for no assassination can be more cruel than to attack the ears of a modest, sensitive young woman with what she must not understand and dare not resent.[22]

Among the guests was Henry Swinton, a merchant in his late thirties, a bulky figure with a sombre manner given a little lustre by the princely fortune he had made in India. The cost had been his right arm. The nabob had an artificial cork limb, fastened at the wrist to his waistcoat. His infatuation with Lady Anne Lindsay turned into one of the darker episodes of her life.

Swinton came as the companion of his aunt, the Edinburgh poet Alison Cockburn, who had set her sights on matching him with her favourite Lindsay girl, and initially Anne 'thought it a little duty to be good to him'. She cut his meat and did nothing to temper her usual outwardly bright spirits – and was then mortified when Mrs Cockburn announced triumphantly a few days later that Mr Swinton was headlong in love with her. Here was a new dilemma. How was she to reject a man 'so kind, so unfortunate, so sensible of it'? She asked Lady Balcarres to intervene by writing a letter to put him off before he could propose, but her mother refused: it would be imprudent to reject so wealthy a suitor out of hand.

Still only eighteen, Anne was not so unworldly nor so innocent as she liked to suggest. She could be wickedly observant, as she demonstrated in describing the nabob:

> There is a light prance which men who are endeavouring to make themselves agreeable and who are conscious of not being much so by

nature, affect, which suited ill with his ungraceful and colossal figure; the inflexible arm too was inconsistent with the prance, and the brown hand without its two joints was rendered still more horrible by the large uncut ruby set round with diamonds which adorned one of the remaining fingers.[23]

Fortunately, regular movements between households with occasional returns to Balcarres did not make for sustained courtship. Lady Balcarres, however, began to rebuke her daughters for an 'immoderate love of dissipation' which she said made them 'justly regarded as girls who were not likely to make good wives'. Miss Keith's sour verdict was that Anne and Margaret (she just sixteen) were beginning to be aged.[24] An intervention by Henrietta Cumming at this point changed everything.

Margaret had become captivated by one of Edinburgh's milder spirits. James Burges was a year her senior, educated, a poet and the son of a prominent local family. Nothing stood in the way of marriage other than his youth and Lady Balcarres. He was accordingly despatched to start legal studies at Oxford and Margaret was distraught.

Henrietta had meanwhile been growing 'more discontented, more wretched, more yellow' when, out of the blue, she acquired in her mid-thirties an admirer of her own. James Fordyce, a Scottish clergyman, had won renown in London with his sermons against 'the folly, infamy and misery of unlawful pleasures', and as the author of an unlikely best-seller, *Sermons to Young Women*.* His brother Alexander was a character of a quite different stripe yet still greater fame – an investment banker with a magic touch and fabulous wealth. As he was buying an

* This is the same volume cited by Jane Austen in *Pride and Prejudice* as the favourite reading matter of Mr Collins, the sanctimonious cleric who, like Dr Fordyce himself, believes novels utterly unfit for young women.

estate in Scotland, nothing would do but that he should be introduced to the Lindsay girls.

Margaret was still mourning the loss of Burges when she met Alexander Fordyce. Coming from a family of Aberdeen hosiers, the idea that he might seek the hand of a Lindsay would once have been thought preposterous. Yet the mercantile class was on the rise, and as the man whose early intelligence of the peace of 1763 enabled him to make investments that earned a fortune, and yet more fabulous wealth when East India Company stocks soared a year later, Fordyce had transformed himself. Now the senior partner at the bank of Neale, James, Fordyce and Down, he was the most sought-after financial adviser in the City. Fordyce was forty, Margaret, it bears repeating, was sixteen, and by the time he returned to London it was clear he saw her as his next prize.

Anne had her own plate quite full. Letters arrived from Colonel Bentinck addressed to 'that most bewitching of all Human Creatures'.[25] At the same time the one-armed nabob was pressing his suit – 'Mr Swinton begs leave to wait on Lady Anne Lindsay with a heart as much devoted to her as ever' – when he heard of the existence of his rival and dashed off a letter: 'It was not till this fatal day that I rightly understood ... the state of the affair that stands in the way of my most ardent hopes of the greatest Felicity that life can afford.'[26]

To top it all, Charles Gordon came to Balcarres before sailing with his regiment for the West Indies and spent his last night trying to persuade Anne to elope with him to Jamaica where, he said, even a mere ensign might make a fortune from sugar. Although he did so 'with the eloquence of Cicero', it ended there at eleven o'clock when 'we each took our candle and pursued our road above stairs to our separate cells'.[27] Departing in the morning, Gordon pressed on Anne a ring and a love-letter in twelve verses of which the following is a fairly restrained example:

Ah wretched is the youth that loves, but trembles to declare
The flame his ardent passion moves, to his Beloved Fair.[28]

Swinton made his way to Balcarres as well. His cause was vigorously promoted, not only by Lady Balcarres but her brother, Charles Dalrymple. Anne continued to resist. Indeed, she 'was tempted to exaggerate my love for Bentinck the more to annihilate hope in [Swinton's] torn mind'. To Margaret she admitted that the sight of his cork arm brought on an involuntary shudder, and when he pressed money and diamonds on her, she declined them. Uncle Charles was furious. 'You are a stone! Had you a heart you would not behave as you do.'[29]

Compiling her memoirs some fifty years later, Anne cautioned herself at this point against allowing her narrative to descend into 'a mere novel'. She was less inclined to reflect why she might have gained a reputation as a coquette, though accompanying Gordon upstairs near midnight, and tossing him a handkerchief with a lock of her hair in farewell, would have been thought forward. Whether being courted by Gordon, Deskford, Lindores or Bentinck, she had savoured the attentions of young men. Swinton, understandably, was another matter. To modern sensibilities, Anne was showing a proper feminine spirit. In her time and circumstances, she was seen as defying family as well as convention; and had her father still been alive, indulgent and loving though he was, it is unlikely she would have been permitted to continue as she did.

Ties of blood to money were almost invariably arranged. In England the aristocracy had formed itself into what has been called 'a tight self-reproducing oligarchy of the extraordinarily wealthy and influential, a club exceedingly difficult to join'.[30] In Scotland membership was easier because the titled class was poorer, and therefore more open to the likes of Fordyce and Swinton; a new rank of capitalist Scots had grown prosperous by throwing in their lot with the English, yet still sought feminine youth and beauty among their own. On either side of the border, however, youth was paramount. The acidic remark by Miss Keith that at eighteen Anne was 'starting to be aged' was not quite as absurd as might be thought. A sample survey of the female aristocracy among Anne's contemporaries shows the majority to have married while still in their teens: to take a fairly typical selection, Dorothy, Duchess of Portland, was sixteen; Georgiana, Duchess of Devonshire, was seventeen; whether Jane, Duchess of Gordon, was eighteen or nineteen is unclear; but Frances Villiers, Countess of Jersey, was seventeen, Elizabeth Lamb, Viscountess Melbourne, eighteen, and Henrietta Ponsonby, Countess of Bessborough, nineteen. To set this focus on youth in context, the mean age of marriage for women of all classes during the second half of the eighteenth century was twenty-five years.[31]

A charitable interpretation would have put down Lady Anne Lindsay's resistance to fancy or a romantic imagination. There were perhaps elements of both – a literary education combined with an austere upbringing gave her a perspective unusual for a young woman of her class. Living frugally and owning just three dresses did not concern her. When she said, as she did, that simple pleasures brought the greatest delight, it was without affectation. When she said that marriage must go with love, it was with conviction.

There were, of course, other, less visible, factors. The fumblings of Sheriff Cross had made her wary; and her mother's example was no encouragement for any young woman to marry an older man. Yet, paradoxically, although Lady Balcarres intimidated her daughters she did not coerce them. Their opinions were subjected to fire and disapproval, but it was now clear that the decision as to whom they married was theirs. Such was the case even in the courtship of Lady Margaret Lindsay by the tycoon Alexander Fordyce.

3

Auld Robin Grey

1770–1771

The most powerful investment banker of the age made his intentions towards Margaret clear from the outset. Alexander Fordyce's first visit to Balcarres lasted barely a morning but once an inspection confirmed reports of her beauty, he started to move the pieces of his campaign into place. In the weeks that followed, Uncle Charles Dalrymple wrote to Lady Balcarres of the noble grapes sent by Mr Fordyce from his hothouse, his admirable Stilton cheese. Mrs Dalrymple declared Fordyce 'a devilish handsome fellow' and extolled his 'princely country house near Richmond, his chapel, his riding house'.[1]

Practised at getting what he wanted, Fordyce also made a point of ingratiating himself with the person closest to Margaret. 'If fame reports it fairly,' he wrote to Anne, 'you, Madam, have had more lovers than your sister.' He followed with further flattery: 'You seem to be one of the few females in your world who will not, cannot, be spoiled by the approbation of your friends.' And addressing his reputation for ruthlessness: 'I have sometimes, at the expense of being thought cold-blooded and frigid, kept myself from loving my friends too well.'[2]

The fact was Anne had an aversion to Fordyce from the start. He was, she agreed, good-looking, despite a pate as smooth as a billiard ball, with long locks that curled down the side of his head like a Stuart monarch and an imperial nose; but she shivered to see how he gazed at Margaret with a level-eyed insolence, as if

[40]

she was to be won with a wave of his handkerchief. She was not alone in her dislike; but whereas Edinburgh gentry objected to the former hosier on grounds of class – 'a low fellow, a mushroom, a bashaw, a citizen!' declared Robert Keith – Anne thought his manner crass, his heart unfeeling.*

He returned to Balcarres in the spring of 1770, arriving in his own coach, packed with trunks and trailing servants. On emerging to be met by Margaret, he looked disappointed and declared: 'Good God! How much this lovely woman is changed since I saw her last!'[3] No less disturbing to Anne was the way her sister appeared in awe of him. When Anne voiced her fears about what she perceived as Fordyce's vile temper, they had a rare spat. Having tried to speak her mind, Anne then felt compelled to make it up by saying she was sure he was also generous and clever.

Fordyce was to spend three weeks at Balcarres during which, convention dictated, he would make himself agreeable and win Margaret's family to blending her blood with his money. He presented himself in outfits that included a pea-green coat and pink silk waistcoat embroidered with silver, and walked out alone, impressing inhabitants of the earl's village of Colinsburgh by handing out coins. He flattered Lady Balcarres, Henrietta and, above all, Anne, though she was clear that: 'I could not have married him had he possessed the Universe'.[4]

The one female of the household who did not receive his particular attention was Margaret; and, as Anne noted, her sister's usually acute eye for human absurdities was in this case blind – 'or by some compulsion [was] resolved not to see'.

Lady Balcarres appeared surprisingly neutral. Anne even perceived something of a mellowing in her. She remained a stern

---

* Mrs Thrale used to relate a story, possibly apocryphal, that Fordyce sent a rank haunch of venison to Margaret, who was warned by Anne, 'Have nothing to do with this fellow, he begins with both bribery and corruption.'

matriarch, ever ready with reproof, but she had acknowledged Margaret as an adult too; and though she saw how Fordyce's fortune would benefit the family, she was not ready to compromise – as became clear one evening as they all sat drinking tea in the drawing room. Her mother was in good humour, Anne recalled, when she declared:

'Tomorrow, ladies, I will go to the church.'

'Will?' repeated Mr Fordyce. 'Will, my good Lady Balcarres? Shall if you please, we always say so in England.'

'Do you so, Sir?' cried she, her face kindling. 'Do you so? Then to shew you that in Scotland we know the meaning of Shall as well as Will, know you that you neither Shall nor Will have my daughter . . . There Sir, take your answer and take it to England with you as soon as you please . . . Arrogant, insolent fellow,' muttered she to herself.

'As to your sentence that I Shall not have your daughter, Madam,' replied he, smiling disagreeably, 'I should be very sorry for it, but when you say I Will not have your daughter, you are very much mistaken . . . Do not be so keen, Madam,' said he attempting to take her hand. 'By heavens! I did not mean to offend your Ladyship, but I find we shall never agree in the English language without the aid of Dr Johnson.'[5]

This telling row was still fresh when Margaret came to the one person whose advice she could depend upon, and asked whether she should refuse what was plainly an imminent proposal. While Anne never explicitly took responsibility for her sister's marriage to Fordyce, she always felt a profound sense of guilt. Margaret, having in the past deferred to her, was starting to assert herself; yet she was still only seventeen and – on the verge of the biggest decision of her life – out of her depth. She needed, Anne reflected, to be 'properly piloted thro' this gale'.[6] Caught between her own misgivings about Fordyce and perhaps with their own recent quarrel still in mind, Anne was indecisive at the crucial moment.

'You would have me refuse him, would you?' Margaret asked.

'I dare not say it,' Anne replied. 'I know not what I would recommend, but look into your heart my dearest sister, and if it does not go along with your hand, oh, do not give it.'[7]

They embraced and a servant appeared to announce that Fordyce awaited Margaret in the drawing room. An hour later he emerged, his lips trembling, declaring: 'I am the happiest of men.' Lady Balcarres found it within herself to forgive and Anne took him in her arms 'with a fervency that proved my love for [Margaret] more than for him'. For the time being she cherished the hope that she might have been wrong.

One final issue remained to be resolved – the marriage settlement. At the insistence of her mother, a paper was drawn up which settled £500 a year to be paid by trustees to Margaret, irrespective of any debts of Fordyce's. Lady Balcarres may stand out as one of those Edinburgh women said by James Boswell to have had 'a too-great violence in dispute'; but as her daughters always said, she had common sense with it.[8]

The marriage took place at Balcarres soon after Margaret's seventeenth birthday and the summer equinox of 1770.

> The servants were assembled, the company met, the old Presbyterian clergyman appeared in his bands. Mr Fordyce looked handsome, very handsome, dressed in gawdy colours as he was, like the proud falcon unhooded to gaze on the Sun and pounce on his prey.[9]

Any bright sense to the occasion was overshadowed by the separation it heralded; and when the moment came it was so agonising Fordyce felt constrained to come between them. 'Come, come, Margaret,' he cried with forced gaiety. 'I shall be jealous if you are so sorry to part with your sister.' Anne watched her step into his coach: 'We did not cease to strain our mournful eyes to gaze on each other till its wheels had conveyed her out of sight.'[10]

*

Balcarres grew darker still. The Black Broth never provided a recipe for joy and with Margaret's departure it became miserable. Anne would climb up to their room alone and as summer turned to autumn the place infected her with gloom . . . 'the old rooks with their melancholy note, the company of the parson and his wife our only jubilee, the whistling winds tuning their dreary notes thro' all the turnings of our winding staircase'.[11]

Separation opened up the correspondence that, though intermittent, fed both their souls and lasted Margaret's lifetime. Most of their hundreds of letters went up in the bonfire Anne made of her papers towards the end of her life – possibly as an act of censorship, in the same way Cassandra Austen burnt or cut up large quantities of her beloved Jane's correspondence, to preserve the image of a perfect sister.[12] Those that survive, however, testify to the intimacy of these exchanges. They wrote in the florid style of the period, declarations of love, support and loneliness which turned into prolonged conversations renewed by each exchange. Margaret's letters from this time have an especial intensity.

> I feel the want of you! I wish for your company, for your conversation. I can get neither, and the knowledge fills my eye with a tear. You were never in your life half so dear to me as you are now.[13]

'Oh, that I were with thee,' she wrote when Anne was under renewed pressure to accept Henry Swinton. 'They none of them understand thee thoroughly but myself.'[14] In brighter vein she urged Anne to 'seize upon some General Scot or other, make a Benedict of him, clap him into a coach, whisk him up to London, and let us make a quartet'.[15]

As later became clear, Margaret's letters were an outlet for the love absent in her marriage. But to start with, Anne thought them 'affectionate and gay and I could not resist thinking she was happy'. With a fine home in Richmond and fast becoming a figure in London society, Margaret, it seemed, had been 'transported at finding herself mistress of a thousand things she never had before'.[16]

Quite when Anne's melancholy set in train the work that brought her literary fame is unclear; from this point her pen was her companion and as well as being a dedicated recorder and letter-writer, she would 'scribble away poetically and in prose till I made myself an artificial happiness'.[17] What we know is that separation from Margaret sent her back to a song they used to sing together and which provided her with the metre for a ballad she began around 1770, a lament of love entitled 'Auld Robin Grey'.*

They had been taught the song by Sophy Johnston, the eccentric Amazon, who – as Anne told Sir Walter Scott many years later – used to render an ancient Scottish melody with '*very naughty words*'. (Perhaps reflecting that this might seem to lack rectitude or sufficient disapproval, she went on to call them 'coarse and odious'.) Here is evidence that while not yet twenty, Anne was more worldly than most well-born young women as, although the exact words sung by Sophy are not known, most versions of the song 'The Bridegroom Greets (When the Sun Gaes Doun)' concern a man's sexual inadequacy.[18] Her own lyrics were of a quite different order. 'Auld Robin Grey', named after the shepherd from her childhood at Balcarres, tells the tragedy of a country girl's love for a lad named Jamie who goes to sea, intending to return and make her his wife. In his absence her family falls on hard times and is supported by old Robin Grey who woos her until, pressed by her mother and believing her long-absent lover to be dead, she marries him – only for Jamie to return. It ends:

> I gang like a ghaist, and I carena much to spin,
> I dare no' think of Jamie, for that would be a sin;

* The song has since become generally known as 'Auld Robin Gray', but in Anne's hand it was always entitled 'Auld Robin Grey'.

But I will do my best a gude wife to be,
For O! Robin Grey, he is sae kind to me!

The theme of 'Auld Robin Grey', of poverty driving a young woman into a dutiful but loveless marriage, arose from Margaret's loss of her first sweetheart and subsequent courtship by a richer, older man: James Burges, sent away to acquire a profession, is represented as Jamie while Fordyce, then still capable of being idealised as kindly, is Robin. But the subject was universal and 'Auld Robin Grey' went on to win fame, both as a popular ballad sung to the original melody, and as a verse admired by Scott, Wordsworth and Hardy.[19] It retained a place in folk culture, being passed down orally – not least to Scott who heard it first as a boy in Edinburgh from his grandmother – before being anthologised for Victorian readers. More recently it has been cited for its subversive character, 'showing how duty and virtue as defined by conventional morality lead to human misery', along with a suggestion that Anne also had in mind her mother's marriage to an elderly man.[20]

Anne, while professing herself mystified as to how 'Auld Robin Grey' gained renown, had set the process in train by singing it herself at music evenings, from where 'somehow it got into the world'.[21] Among those impressed was Mrs Cockburn, who had written another enduring example of the Scottish ballad, 'Flowers of the Forest', published as early as 1765 and admired by Robert Burns as well as Scott. (Both Alison Cockburn and Anne Lindsay opted for anonymity as poets, the condition seen as proper for their sex and one which Anne, as we shall see, persisted in maintaining almost to the end of her life.)

After the household was transported from Balcarres to Edinburgh for the winter Anne became a bright spark at literary evenings in Mrs Cockburn's parlour where she resumed her engagement with the local intellectual order. Mrs Cockburn and

David Hume both championed Rousseau – Hume to the extent of helping the French thinker to a refuge in Britain – and they seem to have introduced his writings to Anne.

Two other well-known Enlightenment figures, Lord Monboddo and Lord Kames, were also regular guests. Monboddo, whom Anne had known since her youth, encouraged further progressive thought with the incredible statement that 'men were derived from monkeys'.[22] Kames was a more forbidding figure, an essayist and judge noted for robust sentencing and his frequent use of the term 'bitch' from the bench.[23] Even in so relatively enlightened a society, women walked a fine line. When Anne Lindsay crossed that line it led to an agonising rupture with Edinburgh's gentry and flight to England.

A lull in courtship had been a relief. Count Bentinck continued to write from Europe but did not long remain a contender once his patron, the Duke of Portland, insisted he had to marry a woman of fortune and connections. Bentinck wrote that he continued to love Anne, but did not know how to refuse the duke. At first she was furious at what she called 'this false, unmanly reasoning'; but on hearing that his father had threatened to disinherit him as well she dried her eyes, reflecting ' 'twas better to be jilted than to jilt' and that 'I had still my liberty and had not shown Bentinck that attachment which entitled me to expect much sacrifice on his part'.[24] With young Gordon off in the West Indies that left Henry Swinton.

Mrs Cockburn was quick to inform 'my much lov'd friend Mr Swinton' of Bentinck's abdication, and just as quick to convey to Anne his revived ardour. She wrote: 'How different is the real passion of love in one person and in another. If you had seen what I lately have, the swelling joy of learning that a rival is no more, checked by the tender sorrow for what a beloved object might be suffering . . .'[25]

Now that Anne was back in town Swinton could call almost at will. He was not alone. Another proposal came from the son of a rich lawyer, of whom Anne remarked with unusual cynicism: 'The father had been a complete miser, but a dead miser is not a bad thing . . . I rejected his suit without any modifying words.'[26] Then there was George Home, son of Lord Kames. She thought Home pleasing, well-dressed and a perfect gentleman. But Swinton was relentless.

Sometimes she tried 'to get the better of myself and endeavour to make everybody happy – to marry Mr Swinton in idea, to sit down by the cork arm, caress his hand without the forefinger, stifle in myself all little disgusts – in short to be a heroine if I possibly could'.[27] Her real feelings were better revealed to Sheriff Cross, her clutching old muse, who asked whether she preferred Swinton to Home – to which she replied: 'I am sick of them and will have nothing to do with them, or with you.'*

Here, in a flash of anger, she spoke with a too rarely heard spontaneity. She was caught between two forces: on the one hand, her need for approval; on the other, resentment at the demands being foisted upon her. Inadvertently, perhaps because Cross was one of the few (possibly only) individuals to whom she could give vent to anger, she had taken him into her confidence. Cross was no simple predator but one of Edinburgh's minds, whom she and Margaret had dubbed Anacreon, after the Greek versifier of love, infatuation and bacchanalia, and who, as she saw it, understood her as no other man did. He once told her:

---

* Cross's response amounted to a further act of physical interference. Anne wrote: 'He replied, "Very well then Madam, I will kiss you, 'tis the only way to make a young woman listen to reason." This incensed me, a struggle ensued, my hands were tied behind my back and to my great resentment I was kissed till tears came while he laughed ready to kill himself and eventually I was forced to laugh too.' (Memoirs, vol. 1, p. 197)

'Your judgment is strong and brilliant, but it dazzles itself with its own light, for confess now, does not fancy place so many sides of every question before you that you are puzzled how to act?' (Oh, how true thought I!) 'You remind me,' continued he, 'of your friend Hume's father, who was an excellent lawyer but a very indifferent judge. Do what you like, Anne, and follow your nose without ambling after systems and trying to please all the world. As for finding a man as perfect in everything as I see you hope for, do not expect it.'[28]

It was good advice. But she was sick of suitors, sick of courtship, and sick of the code that dictated she should act 'in the common, dull way which is the best for women to proceed in – [or be] liable to misrepresentation'.[29]

Had she been equally forthright in Edinburgh's drawing rooms, not so desirous to please, she may have been less misunderstood. To others, however, her prevarication had become plain coquettishness. Henrietta's accusation that she was 'teazing everyone around you and keeping [Swinton] on the rack to gratify your vanity' came as nothing new. But a vitriolic attack by Lord Kames left Anne stunned. Convinced that she was toying with his son George Home, the judge burst out one night: 'There she sits looking so good humoured and naïve. What a veil she draws over her heart! You witch, you little she-devil. No sooner do you gain a heart I am told than you tear it in pieces. But have a care Miss how you treat some I know.' Anne recoiled in shock but Kames persisted: 'You assume any shape you please – You look like an angel till you gripe [*sic*] us fast, and then like a serpent you destroy us!'[30]

She was still digesting this onslaught when one of her disagreeable Dalrymple uncles called one morning to announce that Swinton had been taken off to a sanatorium. 'The man is done, his health and spirits broken and they have ordered him there as a last resource. If he dies you have made an end of him.'[31]

Swinton had, it seemed, attempted to take his life.

Feeling herself 'entangled like a poor fly among cobwebs' and just turned twenty, Anne lost the power of resistance. Swinton might be old, ugly and maimed, but his devotion was beyond doubt. On a night when Lady Balcarres arranged to be at the theatre, he presented himself, proposed and was accepted.

The climax of a courtship deeply damaging on both sides was orchestrated by the Dalrymple clan. Having impressed on Anne her duty to bind herself to Swinton's fortune, Lady Balcarres and her brothers Charles and Hew started to have doubts when it emerged that this treasure was less substantial than first thought. The nabob had returned from India with debts as well as capital, much of which he then spent on an uncultivated estate, Kimmerghame, about forty miles east of Edinburgh. That left him with an income of a mere £200 a year. While he was blissfully happy at the prospect of a rural idyll and reassured Anne, 'We will farm a little and you will have your poultry, your dairy, your music and painting,' Lady Balcarres now saw him as a far from appropriate match.

Anne was torn. Swinton had actually gone up in her opinion: 'He was poor but he was estimable. He demanded nothing of me but what was right.' Marry him 'and the balm of self-applause would shed its soothing influence over my heart'. Moreover, she felt betrayed by the relatives who, 'awed by the reputation of his Indian property, had been afraid to ask questions!'

Lady Balcarres and her brothers presented Swinton with an ultimatum: Kimmerghame must be sold. Swinton returned to Anne, saying that no man of honour could submit to such terms. Money was 'a subject unworthy of hearts and fit only for heads such as your mother's'. At this point Lady Balcarres entered the room and a furious row broke out, with Anne trying vainly to restore calm.[32] A few days later a letter came from Swinton:

It is not to be expressed with what regret I resign any pretensions to a treasure I have never ceased to aspire to for these two years past. But as I find neither my fortune or plans can render Lady Anne Lindsay happy, it would be doing her infinite injustice to prosecute them further . . . I can never cease to remember Lady Anne with that esteem and admiration which her numberless perfections so justly entitle her to. I pray Heaven to shower upon her its choicest blessings.[33]

When Swinton's advocate Mrs Cockburn came to call, her frostiness turned to anger, and though she was not so savage as Lord Kames, Anne was again accused, and now by a woman friend, of using feminine wiles to torment a decent heart. Mrs Cockburn apologised the next day, writing to say that she had been hasty and having since realised 'that your mother and uncles interfered to stop your marriage' she wished to patch up their friendship. 'My temper thoroughly irritated, I threw out some sarcasms, for which Lady Anne I ask your pardon,' she wrote, concluding warmly: 'God Bless you, my child!'[34] There is no record of any answer and, from the ripostes Anne added in her notes on the letter, the episode evidently continued to rankle long afterwards.

Instead of replying to Mrs Cockburn, she wrote – as always in a crisis – to Margaret, in this instance in the third person.

Wretched, wretched Anne, into what a labyrinth of sorrow and difficulty the desire of making others happy has led thee! As to me, Beloved Margaret, happiness is nowhere in view![35]

As ever, her sister responded with reassurance: 'Good God! What motive can that man have to give up a heart like my Anne's? . . . Had I been with you, you could not have been agitated so . . . Thou art a blessing my Anne, and shall be a blessing to some other man whom thy Creator will give thee as a reward for the virtuous part thou hast acted here.'[36]

Swinton went on to marry a young woman he thought resembled Anne but who became alarmed by his mental state and fled naked from the house one night to seek refuge with neighbours. Anne's mother wrote: 'Amongst all the pieces of good fortune that has befallen you, none is the more worthy of grateful acknowledgment than your amazing escape from Mr Swinton ... Some months ago he became disordered in his senses.'[37] Despite financial difficulties, Swinton proved his devotion to Kimmerghame by clinging on to the estate, Anne noted, until 'He died, in peace and sanity.'[38]

But Anne had been damaged too. Confidence in her own judgement, never robust, had been profoundly shaken. 'I am a weak, foolish, unfortunate creature,' she reflected. 'My heart is good, my head is bewildered.' There would be a good deal more in the same vein, along with what became a growing tendency towards self-pity.

She might have spared a little more compassion for Swinton. A man who had demonstrated love, simple values and steady principles would be described in her memoirs as a 'great spider who had caught me by the throat and was dragging me to his nest'.[39] Nor did she show much consideration for Mrs Cockburn. The older woman had doubtless played matchmaker with zeal, but so had Lady Balcarres and her brothers until Swinton's modest means were revealed. Mrs Cockburn came far closer to Anne's own way of thinking than her family when she wrote in her letter: 'I hate the questions of people who live upon the excrements of the human race and whose constant chase is a pursuit of malignant stories of their poor fellow creatures.'[40] Mrs Cockburn was in many ways a kindred spirit; but Anne was not used to being rebuked by one of lower standing, and there may have been a hint of the grande dame in her response.

The upshot of this disastrous affair was that Anne resolved to have no more to do with lovers of any sort. When George Home

– perhaps her most suitable admirer yet – asked to see her, she refused. That only tended to reinforce a view now widely held in town: Lady Anne Lindsay was a complete coquette. Home's father, Lord Kames, was among Edinburgh's most powerful men – not merely a judge but also the author of such opinion-shaping volumes as *Essays on the Principles of Morality and Natural Religion*. His speech was earthy, sometimes coarse, and his judgments were harsh. He sentenced an old chess partner Matthew Hay to death for murder with the words: 'That's checkmate to you, Matthew.' It may be assumed that if Kames was prepared to call a lady of quality 'a witch and a she-devil' to her face, he would have said as much to others too.

Anne could not understand how she had been so maligned. As she wrote in a parting letter to Swinton, 'I am fond of amusement because I am young and have tasted so little of it that it has not lost its relish yet.'[41] She told Margaret she felt like Rousseau when he said he was being misconstrued by everybody. Indeed, at times she seems to have suffered something approaching the paranoia that afflicted the philosopher. 'As one who had risen every morning with the desire of being on charity with all mankind, to be confronted with cold looks and eyes of distrust threw a thick fog over the sunshine of life.'[42]

Suddenly it became important to 'get out of the cruel circle and a country where I experienced that prosperity alone is virtue, where innocence was oppressed by envy'. At this moment of despair, Margaret extended her familiar, loving hand:

Come to my bosom, my dear, my generous gentle noble creature, come to my sisterly bosom and repose all thy griefs with me. My soul flys to meet thine and to pour the balm of consolation into thy torn mind ... The town to be sure will talk. Let it talk – leave it and its animadversions. Come to me. The sooner you leave Edinburgh the better ...

How I long to have you once more with us. You shall divide your
vexations with me and you will be once more the Anne Lindsay who
can captivate hearts as well, and better than anyone I know, and then
perhaps we may not be again divided. But hush Margaret – lest my
Mother should hear . . . That is not her plan. It is natural to be sure for
her to wish you fixed near herself.[43]

So it proved. Early in 1771 Anne was on a coach bound for
London. Her hopes for a fresh start might have been brighter had
Lady Balcarres and Henrietta Cumming not been seated beside
her.

4

The Great Crash

1771–1772

The luxury promised by Fordyce's riches was not immediately apparent on Anne's arrival in London. Her brother-in-law had arranged to buy one of the new mansions being built in Grosvenor Square and owned a palatial country house seven miles from town at Richmond where he and Margaret spent weekends entertaining business associates. The Lindsays, however, had been directed to another address and a week after leaving Edinburgh their coach passed up narrow, muddy lanes and sharp bends before halting at a small door in Holywell Lane, just north of the market at Spitalfields.[1] Servants received them with word that the Fordyces were expected from Richmond the next day and ushered them into a small, gloomy room lit by two candles on a table. When the Fordyces' coach arrived and Margaret burst in, Anne 'took her in my arms and bathed her in my tears'.[2]

Her instinctive sense that the gaiety of Margaret's letters had been contrived was quickly confirmed. Even now, though, Margaret refrained from expressing her misery. Having found out too late that she and her husband were totally unsuited, she would have to endure it. The fortunes of her family had become inextricably linked with Fordyce's and when in his company Margaret simply withdrew, as if 'putting aside what she could not contemplate [and] refused to see her own misfortunes'.[3]

Fordyce presided at table – the food and drink at least were excellent – like an emperor, 'bizarre when in good humour, indelicate when in spirits, and brutal when out of sorts'.[4] His mood towards Margaret swung from petty unkindness to disdain, with bouts of generosity when he would load her with 'bales of goods she did not want, purchased in bad taste'. Anne reflected: 'There was an insecurity in his company that we dared not confess to ourselves and still less to each other.'[5] Even Lady Balcarres was inhibited. She soon came to detest Fordyce, yet would bite her tongue because he held also the future of her sons in his hands. Robert, the second-born, had obtained a post as a writer, or clerk, in the East India Company at Fordyce's behest, and more of the Lindsay boys were destined for India.

Fordyce notwithstanding, London opened Anne to the world beyond her unhappy childhood in a way that Scotland never did. She made light of this life-changing event: 'Happy was it that the Black Broth of Sparta, seclusion and correction to which we had been accustomed made ensuing existence so full of luxury to us.'[6] In fact, luxury had little to do with it. London was the centre of the intelligent world. It had the stimulus of Edinburgh without any of the small-town constraints. It exposed her to excitement, opportunity and adventure. Moreover, it provided a new platform on which her abilities, particularly musical, could be presented. Anne was infuriatingly reticent in describing the artistic side of this new life. What we know is that as a talented singer and keyboard player she would have attended concerts at the Almacks and Hanover Square assembly rooms where Johann Christian Bach performed and championed a new instrument, the pianoforte. London loved music, and Anne and Margaret, singing in duet or accompanying one another on the harpsichord, were soon being encouraged to perform publicly.

As Scottish ladies they stood out as novelties. The time had yet to come when, in Anne's words, 'Scotland like a volcano threw out her eruption of great men which thundered down over all our little island and carried everything before them'.[7]

Hostility among some of the English endured: she remarked on the virulence of John Wilkes's pen and the public letters of the mysterious controversialist Junius; but antagonism towards all things Scottish, a hangover from Jacobite times, was waning – due largely to a king, George III, now a decade into a reign in which healing between the two nations played a significant part.

The first important step was being presented at court, a ritual for persons of status on coming to London, 'it being reckoned improper to be seen anywhere in publick life till their Majesties had had the first glance'. Margaret made a dazzling impression in a gold gown woven with scarlet carnations, her head crowned with an ostrich feather plume and jewels. Anne was restrained by comparison in pale pink satin trimmed with point lace. The king, extending a Hanoverian hand of friendship, asked Margaret why a Scotswoman would live in London: was it for pleasure, comfort or economy? 'Please, your Majesty,' she replied, 'we citizens sum up all in one word – *convenience*.'[8] Anne thought Queen Charlotte 'the plainest and best of queens', her only fault being that 'she set her faithful subjects a'sneezing with the quantity of snuff she took'.[9]

Soon society was coming to them.

Some much-dressed animated young men with looks of fashion attached themselves to us as if they wished to make an early property of us. We were invited to many places, all eyes dwelt on us with pleasure and many hands disputed the honour of taking care of us to our carriage, various wishes were expressed to know where we might be met with the following day. When we stepped into the splendid coach of Margaret with her three well-powdered footmen behind it, and it wheeled us back to our low, dark, dirty, dismal den in Holwell [*sic*] Lane, it had no power to flatter the gay spirits we brought home with us.[10]

Margaret mesmerised this world much as Georgiana, Duchess of Devonshire, did a few years later. She had a particular impact in Bath, the favourite resort of English society, where Fordyce took the sisters and their mother in November of 1771. Here, among stylish mansions set along crescents against a lush backdrop of Somerset hills, the titled and rich – for Bath was unusual in making parvenus like Fordyce as welcome as gouty aristocrats – went to escape the mud, smog and grime of London, take the waters and, as the social historian Roy Porter put it, 'ogle the exquisite, haggle matches for their daughters and, above all, gamble'.[11] Fordyce found them a clean, handsome and well-furnished house, which made a welcome change from Holywell Lane, and set out to display his own exquisite trophy for ogling by the envious.

Among those who saw her at a ball was the young Richard Sheridan. The Irish-born playwright and politician had begun his literary adventures with poetry, among the earliest examples being *Cleo's Protest*, which was dedicated to Margaret and first published a few weeks later in the *Bath Chronicle*. Like Horace Walpole, who used to refer to Margaret's 'quarter-of-a-yard-long eyelashes', Sheridan was struck by her eyes:

> Mark'd you her eye of heavenly blue?
> Mark'd you her cheek of rosy hue?
> That eye in liquid circles moving,
> That cheek abash'd at man's approving,
> The one love's arrows darting round,
> The other blushing for the wound![12]

Anne did not escape the young poet's attention, although she seems to have impressed him less with her looks than her lack of self-importance.[13] He spoke of 'gentle Lady Anne Lindsay who disdains the pomp of praise'; but the lines devoted to the sisters together are comparatively prosaic:

Remark, too, the dimpling sweet smile
Lady Marg'ret's fair countenance wears;
And Lady Anne whom so beauteous we style
As quite free of affected fine airs.

It was probably also during this visit to Bath that Fordyce commissioned Gainsborough to paint portraits of himself and Margaret – his a restrained head-and-shoulders showing off his smooth pate and curly locks, hers a full-length extravaganza.

While Anne celebrated Margaret's beauty, and acceded to its superiority without hesitation, she would have been less than human had she not sought to match, even outshine, her sister in some other way. Margaret was described by another admirer as 'quiet, gentle and elegant'; Anne was emerging as a character – gay, unaffected, accessible and animated. These characteristics, and her wit, were Anne's means of making up for what she perceived as her eclipse by the younger sibling said by Elizabeth Linley, the singer and a beauty herself, to be invariably the loveliest woman in the room.[14]

For the time being Anne was content simply to be with Margaret and in company. Still wary after the Swinton courtship, she would have been reluctant to acknowledge the interest in her being shown by Fordyce's associates, particularly as he surrounded himself with other risk-taking financiers. James Boswell made plain his disquiet at the rudeness of Fordyce and his cronies: 'They are doing all they can to destroy politeness,' he wrote. 'They would abolish all respect due to rank and external circumstances and they would live like a kind of literary barbarians.'[15] Viewed in this light, and their uncomfortable residence at Holywell Lane, Fordyce's treatment of the Lindsays may be seen as a form of class vengeance. Lady Balcarres did not stay for the Grosvenor Square house to be completed before returning to Scotland.

Two of Fordyce's associates did not conform to the usual criteria. Henry Hope, the American-born scion of a merchant banking family in Amsterdam, had met Anne at Bath, started to visit, danced with her at balls and sent verse hidden in a basket of pears with a nosegay. He was about thirty-five with a luxuriant black beard, and though she tended to disqualify anyone described as a merchant, she was taken with his humour and what she called a 'sort of squirrel vivacity, curling up his little nose in a way that made me laugh as fast as he'.[16]

Richard Atkinson was slower to declare himself. A partner in a West India merchant house, he was in business with Fordyce and shared his lowly beginnings in trade, being from a Westmorland tanning family, yet with an innate gentleness and none of his associate's vulgarity. Atkinson became a part of their circle, a family friend and regular dinner guest, long before it became evident he was in love with Anne.

Occupied with matters of the mind rather than the heart, she savoured the company of London's intelligentsia and alighted briefly on its racy side. The Duchess of Queensberry, a warm-hearted and eccentric patron of the arts, took a great shine to her, welcoming this Scottish spark into her circle and her box at Covent Garden. She gave a ball for the sisters, commanding, 'Chickens, if you do not look handsomer than anybody I will whip you.' Margaret was partnered with the queen's brother, Prince Ernest of Mecklenburg, and Anne with the king's brother, the Duke of Cumberland, who had recently been ordered to pay £10,000 in damages to the husband of Lady Henrietta Grosvenor after being found in bed with her. The duke seems to have restrained himself with Anne, but Margaret suffered Prince Ernest's hands all over her before she retreated, pleading a sprained ankle.[17]

Others of this circle were Lady Elizabeth Luttrell, a notorious gambler, and her equally colourful sister, Anne, a widow who had confirmed their family's reputation for opportunism by coaxing Cumberland into marriage some months earlier. A bright acquaintance between the Lindsay and Luttrell sisters would blossom into friendship. Here was to be seen a carefree, vivacious Anne, as she had explained herself to Swinton, 'fond of amusement because I am young'. At Vauxhall Gardens she met Horace Walpole, and heard his description of France and its splendours.

She had not long been in the capital, and her mother had just returned to Scotland, when she was reminded of all she had hoped to put behind her.

Late in 1771 Charles Gordon sailed home from the West Indies and, given his previous ardour, it was assumed he would call. A curious silence was followed by news that he had died. It transpired that Gordon had already been ailing, but Anne was mortified to be told that he had also heard malicious accounts from his half-brother, the Earl of Aberdeen, about her treatment of Henry Swinton.* 'That he should die without my having seen him again – die believing me changed perhaps – oh, 'twas hard.'[18]

A letter from Sheriff Cross revealed what had happened: 'Unluckily, you are superior to most women in parts,' he wrote. 'These good qualities entitle you fully to the hatred of the world, at least of your own sex. You have been vilely traduced, and traduced by a friend, which always gives to slander a Strong Colour of Truth.' According to Cross, another source of the gossip still doing the rounds in Edinburgh was Henrietta Cumming.[19]

Henrietta had recently been married, to Fordyce's clergyman brother James, so was no longer part of the household when the breach occurred. 'We found it beneath us to expose the madness of a person [after] 17 years of intimacy,' Anne wrote. 'We were silent therefore on this family feud.'[20] But ostracism did not

* Anne could have been excused a particular resentment towards this defamer. The Earl of Aberdeen, or Lord Haddo, was also known as 'the Wicked Earl' for his treatment of his tenants and innumerable mistresses.

silence Henrietta. She wrote to friends in Edinburgh how Anne
had brought about a rift between her and her beloved friend, Lady
Margaret Fordyce. Now living in London, she had the capacity to
spread poison here too. Richard Atkinson, who observed her at
work, described her as 'a little viper stinging poor Lady Anne in
the bosom of her friends'. Henrietta Cumming won modest fame
as Scotland's first governess of note, a reputation embellished by a
hagiographical memoir published on her death in 1823.[21] Despite
her continued provocations, the Lindsays remained silent.

Still, the harm done was lasting, for there were now those in
London as well as Edinburgh who had heard Anne Lindsay to be
a heartless coquette. She developed a phobia, or at least an acute
sensitivity, about what others were saying about her, and what
she perceived as knowing looks and whispered asides. Above all
it pained and bewildered her to find herself 'the victim of that
most erroneous opinion, that it is impossible to have a gay mind
and a feeling heart'.[22]

In a rare letter, Fordyce suggested she needed to be more robust:

> You are a silly girl for being so just. Men don't expect it & are
> disappointed when they find a woman simple and sincere.[23]

It would be simplistic to say Anne's response to men changed
at this point. She had been dismissive of suitors before; but in
Scotland she had failed to understand why that might be seen
as unfeeling, failed to accept that a willingness to befriend men
rather than marry them flew in the face of convention. By now
she may have felt there was no escaping the stamp of a flirt; and
her mother's return to Balcarres had come as a form of liberation.
'I must own,' Anne admitted, 'that I was delighted to be left
behind.'[24] In England, she began to live up to her reputation.

One confession of cruelty was dropped almost casually into
her notes. Henry Hope, whose squirrel-like vivacity had charmed

her out of an aversion to 'merchants', was quickly set aside when a young man of 'melancholy sweetness' appeared at a ball. Anne wanted to comfort him, while 'the assiduities of Hope became irksome'.

> I endeavoured to mark by the carelessness with which I received them, the small value I annexed to them . . . The more I maltreated him the more he doubled every fidgety attention. Hope asked me incessantly to be his partner in spite of the contraction of my brows, pursued me into corners where I had escaped [and] handed me teacups and chairs till I foreswore drinking tea and sitting down.[25]

A wealthy Norfolk squire received equally dismissive treatment. Anne thought John Norris so ugly 'I was afraid to look at him at all for fear of hurting him', and when he proposed, not once but twice with the offer of £6,000 per annum (almost £1 million at today's values) she told Margaret: 'What a noble little creature it is. How well he deserves to be loved, and how impossible it is to do it!'[26] Squire Norris met with a more receptive eye in the daughter of the Dean of Norwich a year later and was remembered for his generosity as a benefactor to lost souls.

There may actually have been an element of throwaway defiance in remarks so at odds with Anne's usual air of cultivated kindness. She went on to note ruefully that accepting Norris – or Hope, whom she called a 'worthy Croesus' and who went on to transform Hope & Co. into Europe's leading merchant bank – could have saved her and Margaret from the disaster about to descend. But then, as she added, 'we cannot be young and old, prudent and senseless at the same time!'[27]

For the present, even Margaret had misgivings about her sister's behaviour. In condemning 'the inexcusable coquetry . . . of the woman who endeavours to make men love her merely to try her power', Margaret wrote:

You have a great deal [of charm] and no dissimulation, so all the world sees how you are flattered by the admiration you are receiving ... Coquetry of this sort is more a weakness than a fault.

If you cannot conquer the desire of pleasing – which carried to a certain length I call a little troublesome sort of coquetry – conceal it better from others.[28]

Then, with the wit of their common currency which passed straight over this good advice, Margaret added: 'Voila! – a woman respecting sincerity advising dissimulation!' The Scottish sisters, still so young, were learning fast in the dissolute world of Georgian London.

The city's sophisticates were delighted to have Anne and Margaret in their midst, but drew the line when it came to Fordyce. While he was just about tolerated in a gathering, few hosts were willing to have him at dinners or musical evenings.[29] A form of selective exclusion persisted after the household moved to Grosvenor Square, where the neighbours included three prime ministers, past and present, Rockingham, Grafton and North.[30]

Fordyce was more comfortable at entertainments of the kind made fashionable by Madame Cornelys. This entrepreneurial spirit, an opera singer and former lover of Casanova, had turned impresario since arriving from Venice and won patronage to promote concerts and public revels, striking a particular chord with masquerade balls renowned for their extravagance. There was a risqué aspect to these occasions as assorted bizarre characters mingled in disguise, flirting and making assignations. Processions of harlequins and goddesses, cloaked knights and shepherdesses would make their way to Madame Cornelys's residence of Carlisle House where, a contemporary source observed,

Soho Square and the adjacent streets were lined with thousands of people whose curiosity led them to get a sight of the persons going to the Masquerade; nor was any coach or chair suffered to pass unreviewed, the windows being obliged to be let down and lights held up to display the figures to more advantage.[31]

Anne and Margaret entered gleefully into the spirit. One night they dressed as a pair of Greek statues – not, it should be said, in the manner of Elizabeth Chudleigh, who once made a semi-naked appearance as Iphigenia. But after having their trains trodden by the crowds, Anne made a change the following evening when she 'found the mask of a withered old hag, put on a straw hat and went as a fortune-teller from the Highlands'. She was delighted to find the guise 'led me to be much more talked to than when I was a beauty. Everyone pressed to have their fortunes told.'

That night she received a marriage proposal from Henry Hope. The Amsterdam banker was set up in a silk outfit as a blue domino with a mask, and Anne's account of her rejection might have come from a period farce. 'Alack-a-daisie,' she said. 'A husband to such an old woman as me? Look at me kind Sir. I might be your Grandmother!'[32] Hope's was the first overture to be deflected in her best flippant manner. A more studied response found its way into her private scraps: 'An immense fortune where I could not use it in the company of those I loved was of no value to me.'[33]

Anne's Scottish familiars perceived these early London forays in different ways. The old Amazon from childhood days, Sophy Johnston, was thrilled:

My dearest Pupil . . . my dear Lassie . . . Of all the entertainments in and around London the Masquerade is the one would take my fancy most. I make no doubt but you was pretty bonny. 'O my Dear Lady come dance to my Jigg.'[34]

Her grandmother, Lady Dalrymple, could not conceal her alarm: 'I tremble for you Dear Child when I see you venture out as ye do Amongst a Crowd of Strangers in this Corrupt Age, whilst your inexperience and I will say some *conceit* may lead you into mistakes that terrifie me.'[35]

The corruption of the age was in fact far closer at hand than Anne realised. The life of free-spirited independence that had fallen to her since coming to London, that made it possible to reject so blithely a moneyed husband, was fragile. She was twenty-one and Margaret still nineteen when what seemed the secure walls of their world came tumbling down.

Fordyce's business affairs had always been a mystery to both sisters. From early in 1772 he became increasingly ill-tempered, but as his disposition was so frequently sour this was not cause for particular note and when he told them he needed privacy at home, sending them to the Richmond mansion 'to be in the country' for a while, they leapt at a respite.

In the first week of June, his associate Richard Atkinson arrived looking haggard. Anne's first thought was that Fordyce must be dead.

'No,' replied he, 'but total ruin! All is gone. Last night determined everything. After every exertion, he has stopped payments. Bailiffs will take possession of the house.'[36]

The banking crash of 1772 set a pattern for the kind of financial crisis with which the world has become familiar. Then as now individuals drunk on wealth and power gambled with investments entrusted to them and precipitated the collapse of one powerful institution, which spread panic across the financial spectrum. The equivalent of Lehman Brothers was the bank of Neale, James, Fordyce and Down; and the man who brought it down was Fordyce.

Fordyce's reputation as a financial wizard had been made when inside knowledge of the 1763 peace treaty enabled him to reap his first fortune. Further windfalls came from investments in the East India Company. Hubris led him into heavier gambling, and the start of heavy losses during the 1771 crisis over the Falkland Islands. But his downfall was precipitated by selling Company shares in anticipation of a fall that never materialised; if what Atkinson told Anne was true, Fordyce had been betrayed by the chairman of the Company, Henry Crabb Boulton, in their private speculations. In any event, Fordyce started to use his partners' resources until these ran out and the Bank of England withdrew its support.[37]

At this stage the ramifications were lost on Anne and Margaret, who knew only that bailiffs were about to descend and would seize the Richmond and Grosvenor Square houses with the contents, from Renaissance art to Chinese porcelain. Fordyce had disappeared into hiding and all his property was seemingly lost, even Holywell Lane. They gathered up what possessions could be loaded into a hackney carriage and were taken to a house in Sackville Street owned by another of Fordyce's brothers, William, a physician. It would have been remarkable if they had not been petrified. As Anne reflected on this new calamity to have befallen Margaret: 'Ten short minutes had beheld her despoiled of everything and flying to whatever asylum would receive us.'[38] Gone in those moments were the splendid coach, the well-powdered footmen, every trace of their new lives – for Anne shared to a large extent her sister's fate. They had virtually no money, and no resources other than friendship to call on.

In the days that followed, Atkinson was a rock. Although himself a victim of Fordyce's machinations, he called to offer reassurance and shield Margaret from the full shame of what her husband had done. He insisted that 'we who know [Fordyce] know how incapable he is of a dishonest action'. But within a week the magnitude of the calamity became clear. On 10 June Fordyce's partners suspended payments and a pall fell over London. Runs on associated institutions spread and ten banks collapsed in as many days. The city was in uproar. One of Fordyce's partners went out of his mind, the wife of another cut her throat with a razor. Atkinson told Anne: 'Each man in business grasps the hand of his neighbour as he meets him and asks if he is still safe . . . The Government must interfere.' As he said:

> A madness of security has existed for some time. Public credit went too far. The first stone of the edifice which failed brought down the whole.[39]

What had started with one man's folly precipitated the biggest financial crisis of the century, dwarfing losses during the more notorious South Sea Bubble crash of 1720. By the time Lord North's government stepped in and forced the Bank of England to act, the unravelling of the credit system had spread to Scotland and Holland. Even the most eminent houses, Drummonds and Coutts, had been affected and the *Gentleman's Magazine* reported: 'Many prominent London families are in tears.'

Fordyce was universally excoriated. Atkinson, whose own merchant house had lost £40,000 in supporting him (the equivalent of about £6.5 million) was the exception in declaring: 'He who first plucks off the mask from the delusion is reckoned the author of all the evil.' Horace Walpole wrote: 'Will you believe that one extravagant and rascally banker had brought Britannia, Queen of the Indies, to the precipice of bankruptcy!'[40] According to one story, Fordyce applied to a wealthy Quaker for help and received the reply: 'I have known many men ruined by *two dice*, but I will not be ruined by *Four-dice*.'[41]

Of their own predicament Anne recalled: 'When a sudden misfortune is not of a nature to melt the heart it sometimes has the effect of bracing the nerves to any exertion; but this goes off when the call for that firmness is over.'[42] The extent of their fall was brought home by the visit of Mrs Butler, a dressmaker who, on being told they could not pay a bill for £38, took a large pinch of snuff, suggested they send other customers her way and tried to press money on Anne. She burst into tears at this blend of humanity and their humiliation.

What little comfort she drew arose from her sister's fortitude. Margaret, who was as much a victim as any investor, forgave rather than blamed her husband, seeing his fall as an opportunity to rebuild their marriage. 'No wonder he made us unhappy, with such a dreadful load upon his mind,' she said. Anne might not have agreed with the reasoning yet she honoured the sentiment; and she marvelled at the letter Margaret wrote to be taken to him:

> I hope you know me well enough, my dear Fordyce, to be convinced that I can live with as much content on a small fortune as on a large one ... Perhaps we may not be able to live in this country. Well then my dear Husband, we will go to another ... O Fordyce! Had I known that your mind had had so great a calamity to struggle with, how I should have tried to soothe it, and instead of having been hurt at any little start of temper, I should rather have wondered at there being so few.[43]

Fordyce proved hopelessly unworthy of her loyalty. Facing debtors' prison, he remained in hiding while plans were laid for his flight to the Continent. He emerged just once, making a clandestine visit late one night to the house in Sackville Street and astonishing them with a display of bravado. 'Any new lovers Anne?' he asked; and when this levity produced no response, demanded: 'What the devil is the matter with you all?'

'God Almighty,' was Anne's thought. 'Can he suppose this to be fortitude?'[44]

Strains flared up. When Fordyce indicated that he wanted Margaret to join him for a few hours at his hiding place, Anne objected that this was imprudent. Fordyce bristled: 'You choose to spirit up a wife against the commands of her husband.' In the end it was agreed the couple would be left alone, but that Margaret was not to leave the house. When she reappeared some hours later she was speechless with misery.

The next day Atkinson told them that Fordyce had escaped to France.

Anne was left with twelve guineas, Margaret with four. Otherwise, they each had gifts of £50 from their grandmother and inheritances of £600, held in trust by their brother, of which they were entitled to the interest alone. The marriage contract purportedly guaranteeing Margaret £500 a year would, it was said, be claimed by Fordyce's creditors. Anne's only possession of any value, apart from a collection of clothes – enough silk, satin, velvet and dimity to last the rest of her days – was a watch valued at twenty guineas. We might remind ourselves that she was twenty-one, Margaret nineteen.

One early thought was to 'take a couple of foolish names to serve our purpose and make a happy family of well-educated peasants abroad'. Anything seemed better than being pitied and patronised by society. Once news of Fordyce's flight became known, the likes of Lady Mary Hume took the earliest opportunity of calling with their condolences, as Anne recalled in her best ironic style:

> Lady Mary was one of those circulating beings who pique themselves on being the first to pay the necessary *devoirs* on all occasions, whether of joy or sorrow ... a wedding or a death ... a child born or a sprained ankle ... a fortune lost or acquired. All was a matter of enquiry to Lady Mary.[45]

The Duchess of Richmond invited them to stay, but reasoning that the duke was a roué who cast lecherous glances at Margaret, they agreed it would be best to decline. So Anne wrote to one of their uncles, Hew Dalrymple, asking if they might use one of his two London homes while planning their next move. He refused: 'All the plate is locked up and the Butler is with me in the country.'[46] Matters were becoming desperate when Lady Anne Erskine gave them a room in her Hanover Square house and the kindly old Duchess of Queensberry sent Margaret a note for £100 (worth about £16,000 now).

Less welcome was a letter from Henrietta, offering shelter in the unctuous tones of a sermon by her husband, and delivered in the evident hope of luring Margaret from Anne:

> Now that she who was once the beloved gem of my heart has discovered how little *real greatness* there is in the Glare of Wealth . . . and now that feelings of remorse have led her to regret the undue Contempt with which she once treated what she was pleased to think Inferiority, the arms of her Henrietta are open to receive her . . . We are all equally undone my Gem . . . Believe that past injuries shall be forgiven by Henrietta Fordyce

Margaret replied with a magisterial disdain in which Anne's hand may be discernible:

> As I never felt myself unduly elated by prosperity, Madam, so it is not adversity that can humble my mind to accept of that place in your bosom which I have long resigned my claims to. In the constant and calm friendship of my Sister I have had that support which my heart values . . . If you have lost money by Mr Fordyce I regret it sincerely. I wish to God I had been the only sufferer in this misfortune . . . Had I injured you I would have accepted of your forgiveness with gratitude, but as I and others have only shewn too great a forbearance on all occasions when passion got the better of reason, keep that forgiveness

for a better occasion, as it is of no use to, Madam,

Your obliged servant, Margaret Fordyce[47]

The fact remained that they were undone and the news relayed by Atkinson offered nothing by way of hope: Fordyce was living in a village near Boulogne; his debts amounted to about £325,000. Horace Walpole was not alone in his opinion that the prejudice against bankers was likely to last twenty years. With Lady Balcarres urging them to return home, the two young women had no option but to look north for sanctuary.

'I am ruined, you have been tormented,' Margaret reflected philosophically. 'Things may mend with both.'[48]

5

Return to Sparta

1772–1776

Scotland's welcome was slow in coming that summer, and frosty even then. A coach journey from London to Edinburgh could take less than a week, but in July of 1772 the Lindsay sisters spent twelve days on embroidery and gazing out of windows before reaching the Hermitage, home of the Miss Keiths, once quick to disapprove of Anne.[1] Now it was the ruined Margaret and her connection with a man on the run from creditors that caused their noses to turn up, their mouths down. No hugs were bestowed, no kindness was offered. 'This is not a place for me,' Margaret whispered. The next day a ferry took them across the Firth of Forth.

Outwardly Balcarres was unchanged. 'The rooks sang us their hoarse welcome,' Anne wrote, 'Venus in the pond was heard streaming as we had left her, the old coachman stood ready to open the door.'[2] But two years on the house seemed relatively empty, the cavernous space silent. Brother Alexander was a captain in a Highland regiment soon bound for America. Colin, studying law at Glasgow, would also join the army. Robert, since sailing to India as a clerk, had begun an ascent to riches as collector at Dacca. The second division of Lindsays too was destined to wander in pursuit of fortune – James and John soldiering in India, William and Hugh as seafarers. Among those still at Balcarres was the third sister, Elizabeth, now ten years old and with a distance from the elder two that was to prove a blessing.

The chill persisted after a return to Edinburgh. Fordyce's speculations had damaged Scotland's banks in particular and Margaret was ignored by the society in which she had been celebrated. 'No offers were made by those with carriages to take her to little airings,' Anne noted indignantly.[3] Margaret soon had further cause for misery. Heavily pregnant when they arrived, she gave birth to a daughter, Euphemia, named after that faithful friend, the Duchess of Queensberry. The baby was frail and died within weeks.

Whereas Margaret preferred seclusion to public shame, Anne did her best to rejoin their former circle. It was not long, however, before she heard the past summoned against her. Once more local society was heard to sniff that at twenty-two the eldest Lindsay girl was too difficult to please, 'as I had a great many lovers and fancied none of them good enough for me'.[4] Another echo of the old refrain returned as well. 'You have been accused of avarice and art in the affairs of Mr Swinton,' an acquaintance confided.[5] Her reputation would endure while she remained in Edinburgh or until she took steps to remedy it by marrying.

Why did she not? Just before leaving London she had received a second proposal from the Norfolk squire John Norris, who thought Fordyce's ruin might make her reconsider. Back in Edinburgh she met an English baronet named Sir Michael le Fleming who formed a 'hasty but decided liking'. Norris she again rejected; Fleming – warned of her arts – fled.[6] She was warier of commitment than ever. On top of the anxieties and confusion of her youth, she had witnessed much marital misery over the past year. Being with Margaret she had been confronted daily with wretchedness. London society was strewn with other casualties – titled but lonely women acquired, in effect, for the purpose of breeding by aristocratic families and who, in their loneliness, sought solace with other aristocrats who used them for pleasure. It was a bawdy age. A number of those married into titled families when they were little more than girls went on to take lovers, and some became quite notorious, among them Frances Villiers, Lady Jersey; Elizabeth Lamb, Lady Melbourne; Lady Elizabeth Foster, and Henrietta Ponsonby, Countess of Bessborough. Anne had met a few of them, would know others and, now a relatively mature twenty-two, had set herself against that fate.

It was also the case that she had been unfortunate. Of her two most appealing suitors, one was dead and the second had been forbidden by his father to marry. Another was homosexual and two others, including Swinton, had been mentally unstable. Norris, though a generous patron, was a man of unattractive appearance and gloomy disposition. But at least two more she had simply dismissed, including George Home, son of Lord Kames and a thoughtful, educated man who had recently departed on a grand tour. Edinburgh society's verdict, that Anne had a great many lovers and fancied none of them good enough, was facile but not altogether wide of the mark.

Initial relief that at least Margaret's sufferings at her husband's hands were over proved premature. As the financial storm began to abate, Fordyce sent out feelers and by September was back in London, appearing before a commission to answer for himself. Astonishingly – 'by some chicanery' it was said – he escaped a bankruptcy order, even though his debts remained unpaid. Moreover, no proof was produced that he had acted corruptly or recklessly and should be disqualified from practising business again.

Whether Margaret's financial state influenced her next decision is not clear. The marriage settlement of £500 a year from Fordyce was, it turned out, not worthless, but it was dependent on her living with him. When she received a letter stating that although severely ill, 'a spectre, scarcely to be known', he was trying to satisfy his creditors and rebuild a career, she announced her return to London. Anne, they agreed, would not go. If any rebuilding of the Fordyces' marriage was to take place, it could only be in her absence.

For all the pain a second, and this time prolonged, separation may have been to Anne's benefit. She was not, for almost the first time since her father's death, responsible for her sister or anyone else and, perhaps because of Margaret's calamitous marriage, was no longer under pressure to find a rich mate. She could circulate socially, spreading wit and ignoring the mutterings of the mean. She may even have charmed a few out of their malice.

One genial host was the renowned physician and scientist, Sir Alexander Dick, a distant relative who included Anne at gatherings in his Edinburgh home. Among other regular guests were the composer Thomas Erskine, Lord Kellie, a bibulous bon viveur with a taste for coarse humour and bad puns (he it was who coined the term 'Dinners of the Eaterati' for these gatherings) and another old friend of the Lindsays, the philosopher David Hume, who called almost daily when she was in Edinburgh.[7] She was also reintroduced to Hume's intellectual sparring partner Lord Monboddo, who championed frugality, fulminated against modern decadence and exercised naked outdoors.

A witty young lady of quality had proved herself worthy company for these figures of the Scottish Enlightenment. It was only to be expected, therefore, that when the celebrated Dr Johnson came to Edinburgh, one of those to engage him in verbal jousting was Lady Anne Lindsay.

Johnson was sixty-three and thoroughly prejudiced against all things Scottish when his young friend and admirer James Boswell took him to the Highlands and islands, and on to his native Edinburgh, in 1773. There one night Sir Alexander Dick organised a concert and dinner at Prestonfield attended by Anne, whose exhilaration was still evident days later when she described the event in a letter to Margaret.

The figure of the Doctor is a mountain of deformity and disgust, without any point about him being crooked. His colour is sallow, his motions paralytic ... his manner self-sufficient, his sentences pronounced to be repeated. He was silent for the first hour and a half, till he had fed the animal part, which he conducted nastily. That over, he assumed a more 'questionable shape'. Someone asked him if he had seen the fine new house of Lord Findlater at Banff? Boswell replied hastily that the Doctor never looked at new houses ... old castles, lakes, mountains and inhabitants pleased him better. On this the Doctor quoted the reply that a French Comte had made the preceding summer to a question of that sort – that he had not left France to go to Scotland to see a fine house.

The company laugh'd at the jest, as people do who are in the hopes of getting more. Now for rousing the Lion (thought I) and in a quiet way I said that the most remarkable part of that speech in my opinion was that it had been made by a Frenchman. The Doctor squinted at me thro' the curls of his bushy wig and, playing with a knife awkwardly flourished in his hand, opened on the subject of French politesse ...

Having now stirred the beast, who was evidently disposed to be sulky, I wished to give him a little flattery to quiet him. He told us that the old Countess of Eglinton always called him 'Son' as he was born the year after she was married. 'No,' said Boswell, 'the year before, Sir.' 'Had that been the case,' said Johnson, 'she would have had little to boast of.' 'Would not the *Son* have excused the *Sin*, Doctor?' said I.

The dose took. He became excessively agreeable & entertaining (and I saw Boswell steal to the window to put down the *Jeu de mot* in his commonplace book).*8

Having managed to disarm the Great Cham, Anne joined in an impromptu concert, switching between an ill-tuned

---

* The quip found its way into Boswell's account of the tour as a compliment which Johnson never forgot and which gratified him so much that when in good humour and in search of an anecdote of their journey he would say, 'Boswell, what is it that the Young Lady of Quality said of me at Sir Alexander Dick's?'

harpsichord and a French horn with an ensemble of string players and managing to produce what she thought a respectable sound, despite the sawings of Sir Alexander on his 'detestable Cremona'. And as the doctor continued to answer questions she sketched his likeness, noting how he 'seesawed with his person when preparing a reply'. There was, she concluded at the end of the evening, something vulnerable about this 'poor bear' who was said to have a thousand enemies and could offend the nerves and senses in twenty ways, yet had a palpably good heart.

Art joined writing, music, reading and embroidery among her pleasures. She had begun to draw as a girl, usually portraits of siblings and friends, and although without formal instruction believed she had a natural talent for 'seizing the characteristick air of the person I drew [which] is of more importance to likeness even than the features'.[9] This declaration of her own abilities notwithstanding, Anne's art remained unseen during her lifetime because of a 'fear of levying from [friends] the Tax of Praise which I had heard paid to others with a benevolent awkwardness that would have demolished me'.[10] Her drawings and watercolours remain at Balcarres, the majority unseen.

Stimulated though she was by intellectual company, Anne was just as content to be alone with her 'occupations'. During this separation she and Margaret wrote to one another almost daily and it became Anne's aim to entertain as much as to comfort. The family's hopes for her improvement had been raised by her reading the New Testament and Cicero, she reported, and a welcome warming had taken place in one particular quarter. 'My Mother is really becoming a different creature! She has been very kind and companionable with me. Do not be jealous.'[11]

Margaret could be a sharp observer too. Of James Dalrymple, one of Lady Balcarres's thoroughly miserable set of brothers, she wrote: 'I hope he has a heart. If he has it is a very small one. Naturally of contracted materials, he is rendered more contracted by his domestic unhappiness, which leaves him that sort of patience which is but the virtue of an ass.'[12]

Occasionally the letters from London were touched with hope: 'Fordyce has plans by which I think our fortunes may be considerably bettered . . . Our excellent friend Atkinson has been indefatigable in assisting Fordyce's endeavours to mollify the creditors.'[13] More often, though, Margaret confessed herself to be wretched, sunk in depression, her looks frightful, 'my face all over with a kind of rash, a fine purple below my eyes'. A glimpse of her previous sumptuous way of life – visiting the old mansion at Richmond, 'looking at Raphael's cartoons and the Great Room' – was excruciating. For months she and Fordyce lived with his brother and she was desperate for 'a snugg house of my own', however humble.[14] When he fell ill again, Margaret went off to stay with Lady Erskine, a pious, kindly woman of whom she could say: 'She really loves me, I believe, which in my present state of mind is a cordial drop.'[15] Fordyce felt aggrieved at being neglected.

Anne reached out as lovingly as she could. 'My best of good creatures and first of philosophers . . . O! May you soon have an end to all your troubles my beloved.' Often she would chatter about pastimes, of eking out odds and ends to embroider a coat for her brother, Alexander, 'for 'tis well to make pleasures of anything we can, and squeezing resources out of ingenuity is no contemptible one'. But a passionate outpouring was never far away:

What a thousand pities it is, that you and I, sent into the world – you with beauty [and] solid parts, I with superficial ones – both with feeling hearts . . . and with benevolence to share the good things we might possess – that you and I should have nothing for it, but to moralize with one another – and to curb our young and natural wishes that we may protect our happiness!

To become wise at 20! O! Margaret, it is hard, hard – but if we can bring it about to be contented with all as it is, perhaps we are in fact as happy as our more prosperous contemporaries amongst the ups and down of this wicked world. [16]

Anne had indeed found a form of wisdom. Around this time her old intellectual and physical sparring companion Sheriff Cross died. The memory of his wandering hands lingered but she had, in a sense, prevailed over the dark aspect of that legacy, not by beauty but in mind, for this was how Cross had come to appreciate her; and she chose to remember what she called his misty philosophy and the gentler aspect of his infatuation, which he expressed touchingly in a final letter:

My Dear Daughter, I cannot add Pupil for I really think you are become my Preceptor; your letters please me so much that I begin to be afraid to answer them . . . Your mind is fast advancing while your person shews nothing but the bloom of spring in its full perfection. [17]*

Two of Scotland's notable men were drawn to her during this period. One was a glamorous wanderer who made a dazzling if brief appearance in Edinburgh. The other was a hard-bitten giant of public affairs who transformed British political life, and altered the course of Anne Lindsay's too.

When James Bruce returned from Africa in 1774, his discoveries were initially seen as overshadowing those of Captain James Cook and Sir Joseph Banks in the Pacific. In locating the source of the Blue Nile, Bruce had penetrated deep into a region hitherto thought too alien for European exploration, and Fanny

---

* This was one of four letters from Cross that Anne withheld from the bonfire of her papers. After his death she asked Cross's daughter to return her letters to him and, for reasons she did not go into, was furious on being told that they had already been burned. (Memoirs, vol. 2, pp. 160–1)

Burney and Horace Walpole were among those to remark on the sensation roused by his accounts from Abyssinia.

On meeting him at a dinner Anne was impressed, finding Bruce 'horribly handsome' and, at six feet four inches, 'far above the common stature'.

> His black eyes gleamed with the lustre of self-sufficiency, and his smile was a fortune to anyone who was so lucky as to obtain it. All-perfect in his own opinion, full of intellect & conversation, insolent and jealous, he was hated by the men, I perceived, as he allowed of no competition . . . Mars looks like a poltroon beside him.[18]

And Bruce, according to his biographer, was won.[19] He sought permission to call on her and presented a drawing from his travels. 'It seems to me that I fit his vanity somehow,' she wrote to Margaret.

Yet clearly though Anne enjoyed these attentions, there was something sceptical, even offhand, about her response to strongly masculine characters like Bruce. With the exception of Fordyce, it was rare that she thought anyone a downright blackguard; her inclination towards forceful types was rather to observe their weaknesses – in satirical form. With Bruce about to return to London, Anne entrusted to him jewellery to be delivered to Margaret, along with a letter of introduction:

> Receive your jewels by the hand of Mr Bruce. I can be answerable for their safety as no man will find the courage to rob him . . . I hope he will not propose for me; for if he does and should I not accept, which I certainly should not, there would be an end of me. He would swallow me up at a mouthful.[20]

There was further drollery: the suggestion that she might be cut into thin slices while alive, an allusion to Bruce's account of

Abyssinian nomads carving the flesh from live oxen. It was all quite frivolous and harmless – but it showed a mocking side that could antagonise vain and powerful men. The frisson between Anne and Bruce ended there – it was unlikely to do otherwise as he remained in London – although Fanny Burney wrote after meeting the explorer how he threatened, in similarly light-hearted vein, to murder another of Anne's admirers, the Earl of Rosebery.[21]

Henry Dundas was the second of the Scots to show interest in Anne at this time – another rugged, manly figure who had just embarked on the political career that made him a power in the land. He had grown up near Edinburgh and practised there as a lawyer, so their paths may have crossed before Anne's first mention of him, at the Duke of Buccleuch's country house at Dalkeith after Dundas's election to Parliament in 1774.[22] He was in his early thirties, a man of shrewd talents and limitless ambition. He had once been extremely wealthy too, thanks to an heiress whom he married when she was fifteen, but lost a vast sum in the banking collapse. Seeking to repair his fortunes, he was among the ablest of his countrymen to see that opportunity in the imperial age lay not in Scotland but the united destiny of Britain.

Homes of the great and powerful were political as well as social gathering points where, over dinners, musical evenings, countryside walks and some very late nights, influence was exerted, deals made and consensus reached. Among the guests at Dalkeith, some of whom would spend up to a month there, was the old Duke of Montagu, whose wife had just died and who 'was walking about dejectedly with her little dog Perry under his arm, barking at everything which could look like a successor to his departed Mistress'.[23]

Anne was an ingénue among what she called 'this cabal where old favourites tremble for new ones and try to prevent their success' and her variety of little accomplishments tumbled out without art. She conversed, she amused, especially the Duke and Duchess of

Buccleuch, and made a friend of Jane, Duchess of Gordon, whose zeal as a reforming agriculturist on the estates of her husband has tended to be overshadowed by her influence as a political hostess. In the evening Anne would sing for the company, notably her ballad 'Auld Robin Grey', and it was from this time that the song began to circulate publicly. Who first copied the words is not known but it may well have been Lady Frances Scott, herself a woman of letters who went on to encourage Walter Scott, then a young author. (They were not related.) Frances wrote to Anne after hearing her sing 'Auld Robin':

> No words can express how much we all delighted in your Epic Poem. Without flattery, it is generally allowed to be much the best thing of the kind that ever was written. If I did not love you, I certainly should hate you from envy. You have, as you see by the enclosed, inspired another poet.[24]

The enclosure was from another guest, Lord William Gordon, whom Anne thought 'mad to that point which is often more agreeable in society than the contrary'.[25]

> Dear Anne, Since Sappho to the present time,
> No dame has ever equalled you in Rhyme!

The attentions of Henry Dundas were more significant. 'He formed a partiality for me,' Anne recalled. 'It was a hearty, serviceable, admiring, gallant goodwill, such as was in his nature for all womankind, old and young, tho' more particularly for the young.'[26]

This is a rather sanitised version of Dundas's partiality. His marriage had been among those doomed matches of blood and youth – his titled family with the fortune of Elizabeth Rannie, the fifteen-year-old daughter of an Edinburgh merchant. Ten years on Elizabeth had in all likelihood taken even more lovers than he, and attracted further propositions and leers while they were at Dalkeith.[27] Not long afterwards she eloped with a Captain Faukener. Dundas, though hearty and gallant, was also a libertine and after divorcing Elizabeth began a long courtship of Anne.[28]

Dundas occupies a curious place in Anne's writings. Late in life, when compiling her memoirs, she did not shrink from revealing aspects of various turbulent love entanglements – was agonisingly remorseful over her treatment of one devoted man, and full of anger towards two others at whose hands she had suffered. Even then, however, she was relatively silent about Dundas, despite an intimate association of almost forty years. Perhaps Anne felt the complexity of their friendship defied ready explanation; but she had grounds for guilt too. She had always known Dundas to be a womaniser, blamed him for his wife's fallen state on the grounds that he had 'first corrupted her mind – her modesty at fifteen thrown down by his passionate fondness for her beauty'.[29] Yet she encouraged him, attracted by a rough decency even as she recoiled from what she saw as his coarseness and hard drinking. There was another aspect to his appeal – a natural air of authority. From the outset, Anne recognised a coming man. With Fordyce a spent force, the younger Lindsay boys would soon be in need of a new benefactor and Dundas had admirable potential for the role. In time she would exploit shamelessly his power to confer favour.

It may be asked whether Anne – increasingly worldly and in her mid-twenties – had yet become sexually experienced herself. She was no prude, had lingered on a staircase late at night with at least one suitor, and was without strong religious convictions. She also had quite advanced notions about physical intimacy: in an exchange with Margaret at around this time as to whether a married couple should sleep in one or two beds, Margaret said two, which was natural enough given her experiences of living with a brute, while the ostensibly virginal Anne opted for one, 'because many little differences which occur during the day would be more easily made up'.[30] Despite her liberality, however, it would appear that Anne still believed chastity was to be preserved until marriage; and her conviction had not yet been tested by real love.

Whatever occurred between them at Dalkeith, both Dundas and Anne had recognised qualities in the other. Dundas was about to return to Westminster where he would forge an Anglo-Scottish alliance in politics that turned him into the 'uncrowned king of Scotland' in Pitt the Younger's first ministry. He had noted the social gifts of his countrywoman and marked her as a possible partner in his endeavours.

The parliamentary Union of Scotland and England created in 1707 was always marked by cultural differences and resentments. In simple terms, the Scots lost sovereignty while gaining access to the wealth of England. Benefits to the English were a secure northern border and manpower. Both nations had diehard enemies of Union and the English mercantile class were bitter at what they saw as an erosion of their privileges. Yet both nations boomed. Scotland enjoyed a 300 per cent growth in overseas commerce between 1750 and 1800; England's was still a hefty 200 per cent. Men like Alexander Fordyce had been among the early wave of traders, producers and professionals to seize the opportunities opened up by Britain's expanding empire. They were followed by other adventurous Scots of all classes – especially the soldiery. Over the second half of the eighteenth century, it has been said, 'the tail was beginning ever so slightly to wag the dog'.[31]

The Lindsay clan was at the edge of the imperial saga. Anne would be swept up in the tide herself and, although born only five years after Bonnie Prince Charlie led his Jacobite forces in an invasion of England, became an ardent agent of 'King and Country'. It is possible to see this as a reaction against the unhappy associations of her native land, but she had seen real virtue in the

English too. There was also, it may be added, a pragmatic aspect to her zeal – evident in her advice to her oldest brother Alexander, who sailed for America in command of an infantry battalion when the War of Independence broke out in 1776. During the conflict she wrote a gentle admonition to 'Bal' as she called him, an abbreviation of the Balcarres title which became his nickname among the family:

> Forget not, My Dearest Bal while you have friends amongst the Scots men, the higher one forms one's connections of intimacy among the English is of the greater consequence – and John Bull is a noble fellow.[32]

Other brothers were also venturing abroad, following Robert who had prospered in India where many other enterprising Scots would make their mark. That same year Anne received a description from him of the practice of suttee, written in awe of how a composed young widow had mounted a pyre and lain beside her dead husband while their son set fire to it: 'I was not affected with grief but admiration.'[33] Such tales from distant parts stimulated Anne's imagination, just as she was gripped by the dramas which engaged her siblings. Of the eight brothers, one was drowned at sea, one died of wounds in battle, and another on military service, one was wounded and taken captive in America while another endured years in a dungeon in India, all as part of the imperial adventure. Only one of the eight stayed at home – Charles, who entered the Church. By the time Anne went to the frontiers of empire herself, she had no illusions about the risks.

For now, though, she was seeing the years passing with no prospect of change. London beckoned and she longed to return, but money remained an obstacle. Meanwhile Edinburgh's transformation by the rise of the New Town – 'pure white stone' connected with the Old by 'a giddy young bridge' – only made her feel ancient.³⁴ Her mood soon after her twenty-fifth birthday was reflected in lines to Margaret.

> Adieu ... Adieu ..., A little blue
> But nothing new, Pray how are you?

A first sign of the reunion both longed for was a court ruling that Margaret's marriage settlement was exempt from Fordyce's creditors. He was allowed to resume business, albeit with little besides her £500 a year. As Fordyce had legal control over this and any other money she might be bequeathed, Margaret could only hope that 'experience dearly bought will prevent his setting all on a die'. At last, though, she would get her snug if simple home, with a green carpet, French chairs and a sofa, in Wimpole Street.³⁵ It was within their means, she explained, because there was no person of fashion living on this, the northern, side of Oxford Street.³⁶

Anne's opportunity to join them came with the death of Lady Dalrymple in 1776. The old lady had admired her granddaughter's independent spirit and bequeathed her £300. With the interest from her father's legacy, it was just enough for a frugal and practical young woman to think of starting a life in the English capital. It would involve economising in a way few ladies would have contemplated; but with some help from her mother, she too could find a house near by.

Before leaving Edinburgh once and for all, Anne was at the centre of a final spat with her least favourite uncle, Hew Dalrymple, over yet another candidate for her hand. She was defiant, Dalrymple indignant. Soon afterwards she set down an eloquent and impassioned declaration of her feelings about marriage:

Matrimony I am not ready for thee yet! Is it not hard to find one's artillery bringing down a set of crows, jays and sparrows that there is no putting into a pie with any comfort for life? To say Yes to a proposal that would thwart the heart as long as I existed! To cheat an honest man out of the only fortune he can expect to get with me, a free heart – No, I can't.[37]

Crows, jays and sparrows . . . not for the first time, there was a sharp, even harsh, edge to that steel. The question that starts to arise is, was her independence simply a matter of spirit? Was she a little frightened too? She might have taken heart at having asserted herself – at being about to start afresh, and in London. Yet perhaps she felt the concern of her years too. She was almost twenty-six and, by the standards of the age, no longer young.

6

'Folly, Folly. But in Character!'

_⟶ ᠺᢓ ᠺᢒ ⟵_

1777–1780

For well over a decade, Anne Lindsay occupied a paradoxical place in fashionable London. On the one hand the world seemed to be at her feet. On the other it regarded her warily. She appeared at the centre of society. Yet she was never quite at the heart of it. The Prince of Wales was counted among her many friends and almost everyone declared her delightful company. But there were hints of further scandal, and some thought she had 'not appeared in a dignified or respectable light'.[1] If an insider could be an outsider, she contrived it.

Various factors contributed to her status. There was her origin to start with. Having joined that band of Scots who felt more at home in London than in their native land (James Boswell among them) she was conspicuous for an accent that her friend the diarist Lord Glenbervie called 'a frank, vulgar sort of half-Scotch'.[2] Her lack of money was obvious too, from a small home in an unrefined street to the outfits she wore to the pleasure gardens of Ranelagh or Vauxhall. Anne's dress was the opposite of fashionable. It was an expression of her personality – self-made, colourful and individual to the point of eccentricity. Indeed, the combination of her dress and intelligence might have suggested that she was less a blueblood than a member of that new class of intellectual women, a bluestocking.

The question she must sometimes have asked herself was where was it all going?

She was no longer youthful when she arrived back in London and arguably no longer a catch, at least among her own class. Margaret had married at seventeen while the third sister, Elizabeth, would be eighteen when she married Philip Yorke, the Earl of Hardwicke, five years later. These were typical ages, as we have seen, for titled women to wed. Among Anne's other friends, Jane, Duchess of Gordon had married at eighteen, as had Elizabeth, Viscountess Melbourne. Conventional wisdom held that if Lady Anne Lindsay did not find a suitable man soon she would take up with an unsuitable one. Either that or be left a spinster.

London early in 1777 was a smoggy, sooty, wintry and often filthy place, even in its more refined parts. St James's Square became at times 'a receptacle for all the offal and cinders, for all the dead cats and dead dogs of London', while the streets north of Oxford Street meandered off into fields of what one visitor called, 'a sort of soft and stinking mud which abounds here at all seasons'.[3] Here in Wimpole Street, a short walk from the public gallows of Tyburn, Anne found a house to rent 'at a price to suit our pockets'. She was accompanied by Lady Balcarres who stayed to see her established. Their neighbours were Alexander and Lady Margaret Fordyce. The fallen tycoon, sustained by Margaret's income, had turned from investment to chemistry to repair his fortunes. While he conducted experiments with crucibles and tubes, confident of creating a mystery ingredient which he declared capable of winning the war in America and earning him £20,000 a year, the sisters resumed their passage around social gatherings, and joined the capital's more luminous side – of theatre, opera and dinners.

'In general the world was good to us,' Anne wrote. 'We were prized by many and welcomed like little holidays into society.'[4] The Duchess of Queensberry summoned them back to her box at Covent Garden, saying: 'Children, I must have it filled with everything that is young and pretty.' Kitty, as she was called, proceeded to sing along with the performers before going home exhilarated in spirits and dying soon afterwards, reportedly from an excess of cherries.

Just how the two Scottish women made their way into royal circles is not clear, but at some point they were taken up by two earlier acquaintances, the Duchess of Cumberland and her sister, Lady Elizabeth Luttrell, and, perhaps because they too carried a whiff of scandal about them, became friends. Elizabeth was called 'a roué in petticoats – coarse, boisterous and witty'; and after her sister Anne Horton – regarded as an opportunistic coquette – snared the king's brother, the Duke of Cumberland, they were excluded from court. Elizabeth still ran the gambling room at Cumberland House in Pall Mall with panache, enabling them all to keep up with galloping London.[5] Anne followed the escapades of these companions with awe. 'Never have I known London so devoted as it was at that time to the taste for play,' she recalled. 'Men would lose and gain a fortune in a night.'* For all the propriety of her background, she enjoyed the company of a raffish set, and, as she noted, their dissipation was not itself an obstacle to acceptance because 'the wife of the brother of the King was not so easily voted Nobody'.[6]

The one group to regard her with wariness was the cream of the social whirl, the *haut ton*, or circle of high fashion, arbiters on all matters of taste from the season's dress to the latest theatrical production.

> Tho' some of its very first members seemed ready to adopt us into it, could we have given them our company without tax of any kind

---

* Elizabeth Luttrell herself was ruined by gambling, jailed for debts of £7,000 and driven into exile in Germany where she died in poverty, by some accounts after taking poison.

– such as begging to be called for, having no carriage, which was reckoned extremely odd, 'because it was quite impossible you know to do without it' – yet we found the minor personages terribly jealous of our entrance . . . and willing to shut the door on us.[7]

The sisters' relative poverty was plainly a factor. But there was something else members of the *ton* saw in Anne. She did not quite belong. A baffled Frances Crewe once remarked to Lady Frances Jersey: 'She is so *odd*!'[8] Lady Crewe was a political hostess, Lady Jersey a royal mistress. To such women at the heart of society, Anne would ever be on its fringe. Her eccentric outfits contributed to her image. One lady at a party beheld a most curious figure: 'Lady Anne Lindsay thought she was very smartly dressed. She had on a sort of polonaise of light Irish poplin . . . and a short apron of plain linen with two very conspicuous holes in it. I am sure by their appearance that they were in it before it was washed, but I suppose she thought it would not look well to have them darned and flattered herself that it would be taken for an accident that had just happened.'[9]

For the *ton*'s leading light, Georgiana, Duchess of Devonshire, Anne had mixed feelings. A tragic figure, married at seventeen to a man who made a mistress of her closest friend (Lady Elizabeth Foster, another teenage bride) Georgiana was in the grips of a gambling addiction. Anne thought her 'Hebe in form, her countenance beaming with the lustre of the Promethean torch', while observing with horror her losses at the card table in quinze and faro. Georgiana was far from alone, but whereas notorious gambling men like the Prince of Wales, Sheridan and the politician Charles James Fox, could account for themselves, she was dependent on the duke to settle her losses, and it seemed to Anne that anxiety and debt plagued her. She was less tolerant of what she saw as the over-indulgence of Georgiana, as when they were taking the waters at Tunbridge Wells in 1777.

As there was but little company there, she was happy to catch hold of us, and we were equally pleased to have the opportunity of judging of this pretty creature free from the adulation which generally surrounded her. She was reckoned by her own set to be *remplie de talens* joined with the most perfect naiveté. And to be one of the first poetesses of the age. I was not much struck with her abilities the first day or two with respect to the talents when she was sitting for her picture to me. She yawned and said 'Oh! How I wish I could have my own way at present!'

'Why should you not?' said I. 'Speak, what can I do to amuse you?'

'Go out with me,' said she, 'and let us break all the lamps in the town.'

'No,' said I, 'I won't and what is more you shan't.'

'What? You won't let me? What will you let me do then? May I have a fox chase?'

'Yes,' said I, 'if you will have it in the house.'

'I soon repented when I found all the chairs ranged round the room and the Duchess galloping round them at full speed after the fox, whooping, holloaing and making an incredible noise.

'CHAR-MING, CHAR-MING,' cried Lord Boothby when I repeated the story to him. 'There is nothing like her.'

When everything we do is found CHAR-MING, it is no wonder if fancy runs a little wild.[10]

As two bright young minds, Anne and Margaret might have been thought more suited to the intellectual circle of women known as the bluestockings, who gathered principally at Elizabeth Montagu's house in Hill Street for tea and conversation rather than alcohol and gambling. Anne was acquainted with two regular male guests, Dr Johnson and Horace Walpole, and established a warm friendship with a third, the politician Edmund Burke. Yet, just as she was not of the *ton*, she would never be fully embraced by the bluestockings. Mrs Montagu's set observed a prim rectitude during intellectual engagements with one another and theirs was too critical and too competitive a community for Anne's liking. She observed one bluestocking of her acquaintance as having 'discernment enough to know that fading beauty should be reinforced by intellectual auxiliaries; she drew around her a very excellent circle of men bound together in calfskin.'[11]

When Anne did make more women friends it was with two other unconventional types from a fast set. As a trio they exchanged lively letters and nicknames – 'Grubby' (Elizabeth Fauquier) 'Doodle Doo' (Elizabeth Harcourt) and 'Pee Wee' (Anne). Lady Harcourt was another gambler, her husband a libertine. Elizabeth Fauquier had no obvious titled connections but was a free spirit who felt able to suggest Anne had 'kept her virginity rather too long', and that 'perhaps it has become troublesome'.[12] As Pee Wee, she was stung to respond that she had been flirting with 'Sir Something Poppering and Mr Hamilton O-Something', adding: 'I am amused in a *quiet* way but not transported'.[13]

While she was entering into the raciness of the times, Anne retained a spirit that resonates with feminist ideas to this day. She wrote to 'Doodle Doo' of an encounter with the Duke of Dorset, a notorious seducer (along with Georgiana, his conquests included Lady Mary Coke and Elizabeth, Countess of Derby) and her palpable satisfaction at showing him

for once in his life that debauching all the women who come in his way could be overlooked for men of less importance and better character. He found himself cut and went away. There is a paper in *The Spectator* that mentions the joys of demolishing a prude – but the joy of demolishing a male coquet is I think far more transcendent.[14]

Around this time her friendship began with an elegant and engaging seventeen-year-old Prince of Wales. 'O, what a young man he was then,' she recalled.[15] The future George IV had yet to embark on the path of gaming, drinking and debauchery for which he became all-too renowned, and at the time she was not alone in her admiration. But although generous about the princely exterior – 'he smiled often, his figure was full of grace, he danced to perfection and he sang better than most private gentlemen' – she discerned a damage within:

> The interior was a field less easy to be pronounced on. It seemed to consist of rich ground, but from having had too much manure laid on it, and too little expected from it in return, I saw it might produce a superabundant vegetation of what would be useful to nobody ... He was human and delighted with the feelings of being so, but the passing jest of someone less amiable than himself had the power of reversing all.[16]

She believed that young George, having 'just escaped from childhood, educated in the fear of his father, subordinated to his mother ... was beginning to possess liberty over himself, and to catch at pleasure wherever he could find it'. So it proved. An actress, Mary Robinson, 'Perdita', became the first of his innumerable mistresses in the spring of 1780. Whether he tried to make Anne one of them, she never said. It seems unlikely, and in any event she had a playful gift for keeping amorous men at bay. Instead, a simple fondness developed between the prince and the woman he called 'Sister Anne' which lasted her lifetime.

For the time being she was occupied enough as it was. Returning to London had ushered in a happy, frivolous period, when 'lovers were not wanting', even if they 'started up with zeal, vanished like meteors'.[17] One of these was the traveller and politician Henry Temple, Viscount Palmerston, father of the future prime minister, who pressed a letter of epigrams on her one night at Ranelagh and called at breakfast, only for Fordyce to enter and ruin everything with a crude *double entendre* at finding them together. That baneful family connection still loitered in the background.

*

The theatrical sensation of the summer was Sheridan's satire, *The School for Scandal*. Audiences flocked to hoot knowingly at the stage antics of the Devonshire House set – the duchess represented as the spendthrift Lady Teazle, Lady Jersey as the venomous Lady Sneerwell. Anne and Margaret laughed with the rest while agreeing that music was a kinder form of entertainment.

At Tunbridge Wells the sisters had encountered a figure from the past. James Burges, Margaret's first suitor (characterised as the young lover Jamie in 'Auld Robin Grey'), had prospered as a lawyer and married. Back in London he invited them to join a musical ensemble which performed at his house for audiences that included Sir Horatio Mann, whose real passion was promoting the new sport of cricket. Music became 'a band of concord in our little circle'. Burges played bass fiddle, Thomas Hampden the violin. George James Cholmondeley, a notorious seducer with a rich baritone voice, 'kept them in order with his steady, serious note'. Then there was Lord Wentworth, who played the flute.[18]

Anne was twenty-seven, Wentworth was thirty-two and on top of a boyish handsomeness, she thought 'his figure spoke him more decidedly the man of rank than most men I had seen'. What added to his attraction in her eyes was that this bold deportment was belied by a shyness of manner. For the first time since being courted by Gordon and Bentinck, she was genuinely attracted.

So was he. After one of their early concerts Wentworth wrote that Anne and Margaret 'were the Syrens of the night and sang *à ravir* [exquisitely] . . . We made a true debauch, not having left the table at 2 this morning.'[19]

Thomas Noel, Viscount Wentworth, could be seen as a male Georgiana – beautiful and wealthy, but indulged, vulnerable and a wastrel. As Burges, his brother-in-law, explained to Anne, although good in head and heart, he was in thrall to bad influences '. . . bon vivants who assure him his claret is the best in London, men of fashion, who will ultimately be men of fortune but have not a guinea in the mean time. They have rubbed poor Wentworth all over with bird-lime and they stick to him in a manner that he has not the courage to disengage from.'[20]

The next step had something of the inevitable about it. Anne found that Wentworth's family had identified her as a saviour. 'Could we but get him away from a set who wish to make him their prey,' his sister Lady Milbanke told her, 'what a good and respectable man he would prove in the hands of an accomplished woman.' Wentworth, she said, had confessed himself attracted to Anne. His family now saw her as the one person to have 'given us a gleam of hope'.[21]

Anne might have avoided any obligation to lure a weak man from his circle of dissolute, hard-drinking cronies. What struck her, however, was the notion of redemption – of how the very powers of charm that had once brought opprobrium upon her might now be employed to rescue a fundamentally decent man and find love. It could be said that there was a more practical aspect as well – that with an ever-alert eye to family duty she saw an opportunity to join the Lindsays' destiny with the Noels, wealthy English nobility. But her romantic sense had been aroused. So too, now in her late twenties, had her marital instincts. 'Every motive awakened to make me attach myself to the idea with zeal, and to the person with tenderness.'[22]

Her enemies, as she saw it, were Wentworth's cohort of young lords, 'worldly men who lived for the day and regarded wives as necessary evils, which it was time enough to have when old age and gout came on'. One, Lord Denbigh, whom she dubbed 'the Macaw' for the size of his nose, was heard screeching that it would be madness for Wentworth to marry a Scottish woman of no resources besides a clan of poor relations – that he would be better off losing £20,000 at the card table; to which another replied that he had in fact lost £6,000 just two nights before. Another source of trouble took longer to emerge.

In the summer of 1778 Anne was at a concert at Ranelagh one night when she was approached by a fearsomely florid figure in her mid-thirties:

... large, overdressed, many jewels, and a pint of Port wine to the better. This terrific woman marched up to me and in a voice of thunder pronounced the name of Lord Wentworth in my ear, saying I wished to marry him but that my stratagems should not succeed, and, laughing loudly with her friend, brushed past me. I trembled and was obliged to sit down.[23]

Mademoiselle Vanloo, as Wentworth's mistress was known, had been a family governess to the Noels and acquired a hold over the heir by seducing him in his youth, bearing him two children. On perceiving a threat to her influence, she had gone through his papers, found Anne's letters and 'beat him so violently with the wicked flute which had played soft airs to me that it was necessary to send for a surgeon to tie up his wounds'. Wentworth was later seen wandering around 'with a head like a plum pudding'.[24]

Others watched, fascinated. Lady Hampden was avid for more detail, writing to Anne: 'Pray, let me know everything as soon as you can, and be certain that whatever you write to me is quite safe ... I burn your letters directly.' The best remedy was to rejoin the hurly burly. 'For God's sake, run about, be giddy and above all flirt a good deal. There is nothing like a variety of trifling occupations to divert the mind from one particular object.'[25]

At this point it might be thought that a sensible woman, and certainly one of Anne's past independent spirit, would have done just that. But despite all the evidence, and her own awareness that Wentworth was a sad, useless fellow, she clung on. After he disappeared to his country estate, she continued to believe that 'we might still have our happy WE, in the wilds of Derbyshire on his own acres'. She even managed to persuade herself it would be cruel to give him up: he was, after all, a lost soul – an orphan since his youth, in thrall to malign forces. 'His was a disposition I was sure as easily influenced to good by the person he loved, as to evil when under a worse direction.'[26]

'Folly, folly. Oh, most foolish!' she reflected. 'But in character!'[27]

Catherine Vanloo retained a hold over Wentworth, continuing to live at his London home, pregnant with his third child. 'Her art is consummate,' his sister Judith Milbanke wrote to Anne. 'It is with the greatest concern I have heard of my brother's conduct and most particularly that part which concerns you and your letters.'[28] Had Anne known it, this same woman who hailed her as a saviour was secretly vilifying her. 'I never thought L[a]dy Anne a very eligible woman,' Judith wrote to a family member after the Ranelagh incident, 'but imagined she was good temper'd, had rather a good heart & was much attached to [Wentworth] & tho' she would bring no fortune, would not by extravagance farther involve the small one he has left'. She went on:

> But her late conduct has been forward, foolish and unaccountable [and] seems to me to have more of folly (or rather madness) than anything else, as she must be totally unknowing not to discover that it must disgust beyond measure.[29]

Lady Milbanke was a malign force within the family, a jealous monster remembered mainly for her part in her daughter's disastrous marriage to Lord Byron, and her outrage over the Ranelagh affair appears unbalanced. But she was not alone in seeing it as discreditable; and though Anne chastised herself for folly, a change in her behaviour becomes discernible from this point. The capricious young spirit once seen to toy with supplicant suitors was turning into a vulnerable woman who seemed unable to tear herself away from the wrong men. Age had caught up.

*

As Anne came into her thirties, public affairs were dominated by the war in America. Although not a political being by instinct, she would have come down on the side of Edmund Burke's emollient policies that, had they been adopted by Lord North's government, just might have prevented a conflict disastrous to Britain; Burke was the politician of the day whom she most admired, for his principles as much as his oratory. But once the war began emotion took over. Years of fighting took a toll of the Lindsay clan.

Alexander, or 'Bal', a major in an infantry regiment advancing south from Canada, was wounded at Ticonderoga in 1777 and taken captive at Saratoga on General Burgoyne's surrender. Though offered parole and a direct return home, he refused to abandon his men and consequently spent the next two years a prisoner. Meanwhile, Captain Colin Lindsay, a gentle and eccentric young man beloved by his sisters and known to his men as Don Quixote, went from the American war to fight the French in the West Indies.

While the American Revolution was the defining event of the era, the hardships were still greater for those caught up from 1780 in the Mysore war in which two of Anne's other brothers were serving. Lieutenant John Lindsay, then aged nineteen, was among the third of a force of about 3,000 men to survive a catastrophic defeat by Hyder Ali, Sultan of Mysore, at the battle of Polillur – and then endured almost four years as a prisoner at Seringapatam where many more died and, it was said, still more would have preferred death. John's diary of his captivity suggests that resilience and practicality ran in the family; his sister would have been proud to learn that he helped to pass the time by making and repairing clothes.[30]

John was still a captive in India when another brother, Captain James Lindsay, led his men in storming the fortress of Cuddalore, was wounded, and died a few days later.

Lady Balcarres had meanwhile resolved that Bal, as head of the family, should have a suitable London residence and mustered her resources to buy a house in Portman Square. Anne, living a short walk away in Wimpole Street, was given the task of putting it in a state fit for habitation by the Sixth Earl of Balcarres. From this time dates an engagement with London property in which she took a practical interest rare at the time.

Residents of London's squares had adopted new fashions in decor: floral wallpaper had replaced tapestries; Thomas Chippendale was designing and creating furniture for the entire house, from cabinets to bookcases and chairs in the French, Gothic or Chinese styles; decorative as well as utilitarian ceramics were available from Josiah Wedgwood's rooms off Pall Mall. None of these luxuries was accessible on Anne's budget. So beds were sent by sea from Balcarres; and some old silver plate was melted down to buy second-hand furniture which Anne herself then restored with patchwork. She was pleased with her handiwork: 'the sofas and chairs of white glazed calico, profusely covered with roses and leaves, looked gay'.[31] Lord Glenbervie, however, saw only what he called dismissively 'second hand furniture pieced and patched to look fashionable, or what is called *tasty*'.[32]

Bal duly took possession of Portman Square, and married Elizabeth Dalrymple, a cousin. Anne's eldest brother was becoming an even more distant figure – diffident yet ill-tempered and, according to Margaret, 'really too fat for so young a man' – having developed in military life a coldness that replaced his earlier reserve.[33] Two decades later, as governor of Jamaica, his handling of an uprising by freed slaves earned him notoriety. Anne blamed herself for not doing more while he was in London to charm him out of social isolation, 'to have his heart opened and expanded by the hilarity of our spirits and by the proper self-confidence we should have tried to instil into him'.[34]

Of more pressing concern was finding a place to live, the new house having swallowed up family resources, and Anne was obliged to turn to the Fordyces. Outwardly Margaret and her husband had come to a loveless but functional accommodation. While Fordyce's experiments with chemistry continued, he was back in business and when Margaret asked whether Anne could live with them again he consented. The tenor of their domestic arrangement is apparent from the fact that Anne and Margaret often shared a bedroom. Still, there were no immediate alarms. Anne wrote to her mother:

> Mr Fordyce makes his house perfectly comfortable to me and for that I am very much obliged . . . What he himself is I suppose he cannot help; I wish he had less power over Margaret, but I check myself for fear it might take away any atom of happiness from one who has so little to spare.[35]

While she was living with the Fordyces at Wimpole Street, London was shaken by the most violent episode of civil unrest in its history. On a midsummer day in 1780, an MP named Lord George Gordon led a march by some 50,000 followers in protest against Catholic reform and set off rioting that lasted a week. The Bank of England was besieged. A mob stormed Newgate gaol, freeing prisoners who proceeded to raid distilleries, creating drunken mayhem. The breakdown of law and order spread to residential streets where homes of Whig politicians were threatened or attacked. Three men known to Anne were directly affected: Edmund Burke confronted the looters who had gathered outside his house off St James's Square; Lord Mansfield, the Chief Justice, saw his house in Bloomsbury Square including a splendid library go up in flames; Dr Johnson told Mrs Thrale of his dread at 'the glare of conflagration filling the sky from many parts'.[36]

The trigger for the Gordon riots was an Act to repeal laws discriminating against Roman Catholics. But the spark, and the first violence, had occurred in Edinburgh, where Presbyterians rampaged through Catholic chapels and threatened Protestants sympathetic to reform, before Gordon, himself a Protestant from a prominent Scottish family, carried the mood to Westminster. What started as a protest left 458 people dead or injured. Twenty-one of the fifty-nine culprits sentenced to death were executed.

For once Anne's pen was stunned into silence. That she made no more than passing mention of these events is noteworthy because although her modest street had not come under threat she would have observed the riots with even deeper shock and alarm than most inhabitants. Liberal-minded Scots were ashamed of Gordon and Anne may well have felt the connection more personally: he was a nephew of her early suitor, Charles Gordon.[37]

The Gordon riots did, however, draw her towards politics. So far as she was concerned, the big picture of state affairs was always occupied by the ideal of Union, which had fostered religious and political tolerance rather than dogma. She felt at home in England, citing the novel *Humphry Clinker* by her countryman, Tobias Smollett, in which a Scottish character is 'distended like a raisin by the plum-pudding of English urbanity and happiness'.[38] In this respect she shared common ground with Henry Dundas, another Scot. Dundas had started to make a mark on the national stage as an MP at Westminster. The uncrowned king of Scotland, as he became known, was a reformer who had already begun to act as a bridgehead with England. Of all the men in her life, Dundas was the one to become a true power in the land.

Two years had passed since Dundas divorced his wife Elizabeth and though he had yet to make explicit his desire that Anne should take her place, his partiality was obvious. He held back because he perceived her affections still lay elsewhere.

Wentworth's courtship resumed on his return from some months in the country. His family noted that he had been trying to repair his position, having made Anne 'a great many concessions on account of what happen'd last summer'.[39] And the simple harmonies of musical evenings at Burges's house, where Wentworth's flute was heard accompanying Anne's voice, must have helped. When his mistress Vanloo died in the summer of 1781 while miscarrying twins, another obstacle was removed; and as they appeared in public together again, talk of marriage revived. Wentworth, it was reported by a relative, 'wants to get an Income to Settle, and L[ad]y Anne is the Fair if one may judge from appearances'.[40]

7

'The Devil in Scarlet'

1781–1783

The proposal to elope was subtly couched. As Wentworth explained it, he needed to get away from London – to escape the cronies who had all but gambled away his fortune, and a sister who constantly meddled in his affairs. The idea was that Anne should come with him to Rochester, where his uncle was dean. The hint was that marriage lay at the end of the road. The fact was that to get there they would have to stay at inns along the way, which in the circumstances meant only one thing. Wentworth explained the plan with his usual 'profusion of tenderness, hesitation and agitation'.[1]

Margaret joked that a bawdy adventure might be no bad thing, and Anne could get Wentworth to marry by private licence on the road to Rochester. Her own response was that she would go, 'but not in a manner to degrade him or myself by its indelicacy'.[2] There was a coded message here: bachelors like Wentworth might satisfy their desires with mistresses, but they married virgins and Anne insisted that any union must be conducted respectably. The reply amounted to a no.

Wentworth's younger sister Sophia kept their family informed as his courtship intensified towards the end of 1781. 'All the town says he & Ly Anne are certainly to be married. He goes everywhere she does – to operas, plays, routs, private partys.'[3]

All the while another man waited with patient devotion in the background. Anne had known Richard Atkinson for ten years – as a family friend, the rock who had supported Margaret through

Fordyce's disgrace – and, though slow to declare himself, he had made his feelings plain. He once asked for a lock of Anne's hair which she declined, so it is fair to conclude she had not encouraged him. Eleven years her senior, Atkinson had none of Wentworth's physical attraction, cutting by his own admission a rough, clumsy figure; but whereas the lord was a foolish boy who had dissipated his entire inheritance, Atkinson had transformed himself into one of the more notable financial figures of the day.

When Anne met him Atkinson was a rising merchant, like Fordyce from an artisan family and self-made but with none of the other man's braggadocio; and unlike Fordyce he had gone from strength to strength, culminating in the immense fortune he made as the army's principal contractor during the war in America when he supplied everything from uniforms and horses to rum and provisions. Personal connections as well as his logistical brilliance gained the onetime junior partner in Mures & Atkinson influence in Lord North's administration. Along with vast amounts of capital and authority, he had estates in Jamaica and fingers in the East India Company pie – all of which suggest a certain ruthlessness. In the labyrinthine intrigues of the Company it was the cunning who prospered and Atkinson was London agent for the corrupt Madras nabob Paul Benfield. As for Jamaica, cultivation was synonymous with slavery. But then trade of any sort was rough while empire was on the march, and when it came to the Lindsay sisters Atkinson was a positive philanthropist.

Anne's slender means stirred Atkinson's fatherly interest. He suggested that he might be able to make her small inheritance grow. Surely the amount was scarcely worth his trouble, she replied. 'We must teach it then to become bigger,' he insisted. By using some of his own funds and the same kind of insider knowledge of an impending peace that had profited Fordyce, he turned her £300 into £3,475. Anne did not question what she saw as the benefit of friendship and good luck, but was thrilled by the annuity of £200 it produced. 'This is to be mine?' she exclaimed. 'And without robbing you!'[4] She felt positively rich.

It would appear to have been gossip about an imminent match between Anne and Wentworth that stirred Atkinson finally to declare his love in a long and oblique letter – it is undated, headed only 'Sunday 7 o'clock' but is believed to be from September 1781 – seeking advice on how he might approach the unnamed object of his affection. As he explained it (over many pages and almost 4,000 words) the horrors of the financial crash had demonstrated this lady's virtues and since then his sole concern had been her welfare. He had known financial tribulations himself but now, with a secure fortune, he wondered whether the friendship between a beautiful young woman and a man of forty-two and in poor health might contain the seeds of mutual affection. He would know 'by one look of kindness at our first interview' whether she was about to

extend to me the Golden Sceptre and tranquillise my spirits by that assurance that there is no insurmountable bar to my happiness ... How many blessings does my heart wish to pour on her![5]

Anne's response to what she called this heart-breaking letter was fundamentally honest: the offer of immense wealth from a man both kind and sickly would have tempted many women, especially one past thirty; but the years had not altered her creed; she did not love Atkinson, so could not accept him. With her usual dread of causing pain, however, her reply was as circuitous as the manoeuvres on a ballroom floor. She alluded to a lover – Wentworth was not mentioned by name – who had professed his devotion and how, despite many obstacles, he still intended to marry her. After pages of agonising, she told Atkinson: 'I seek in vain for words to please myself, gentle to your feelings, yet conveying no illusion. Explicit, yet consoling.'[6] She may have conveyed her meaning, but explicit she never was.

As she often did in reflecting years later on her treatment of the man to whom 'I owe everything', Anne combined honesty and guilt with a certain disingenuousness. 'To have confessed that my sentiments for [Atkinson] were not of a nature to make me happy in marriage would have desolated his honest heart,' she wrote. Unable to say as much, she had mentioned the possibility of marrying another to discourage 'a fruitless perseverance'.[7] But ultimately Wentworth remained unnamed because 'he was a man I should have been a little ashamed of confessing I loved to Atkinson'.[8]

Atkinson, fortunately, was too shrewd not to have seen to the heart of the matter. He replied with pithy insight into her character, notably her aversion to painful truths. 'You, my friend, turn over the leaf and try to expel the remembrance of what is distressing by an attention to new objects. I never could do this ... Be the misery what it will, I cannot leave the enemy behind me, but must give battle to my thoughts in the open field ... My *hopes* are *dead*.'[9]

Rejection also inspired dignity:

> I have attempted to show you my whole soul in the most naked sincerity and am incapable of a desire to deceive you ... I feel I can rejoice in your happiness with another & when the proper time arrives can cordially court his friendship ... I wish to watch over your welfare as far as my knowledge extends with a kind brother's care![10]

Anne did feel remorse, confiding in a note to herself: 'To Wentworth I owe nothing but sorrow and disgrace, and yet to him I am attached while Atkinson only wrings my heart.'[11] Within weeks she had cause to reflect on this crossroads, amid the scandal that followed.

At Christmas Anne and Margaret were invited to the great Buckinghamshire country house of Lord and Lady Hampden for one of the gatherings beloved of the English nobility – weeks spent in the supposedly harmless pleasures of idling, dining, singing, drinking, bantering and generally entertaining one another. Wentworth was among the guests and a point had been reached when marriage seemed inevitable. His sister Sophia had recently written as much, while citing further evidence of Anne's habitual hesitation: 'My Brother wrote to me ... *He is certainly* to marry Ly Ann, tho she still denys it to some particulars.'[12]

A few weeks later, after the party had broken up and returned to London, Sophia had a breathless update for the family. Her account of events on a night in January is confusing, but as she related it, Lord Hampden was going around town telling '*such* a story about my brother and Ly Anne that it is quite shocking'.

> It would take up a sheet of paper to tell you the whole of it, but the short of the story is that one day after dinner Ly Anne contrived to stay in the room with my Brother & Mr Hampden after the other ladies had left it. *At last* it came to their being both on the ground & Mr Hampden roll'd them up in the Carpet, put out the Candles & sat by the fire drinking his wine & in *half an hour* he heard Ly A say, For shame my Lord, *how dare you do so!* Upon which Mr Hampden undid the Carpet & they both retired to put their dress to rights.
>
> The next morning my Brother was closeted with Ly Margaret & it is imagined he made some promise.[13]

The details may have been confusing, the implications were clear, and whatever the version Thomas Hampden himself related, to the mirth of his bibulous friends, it was doubtless far earthier.* He and his wife Catherine combined a love of scandal

---

* Hampden seems to have felt remorse over his scandal-mongering. When Anne wrote a reconciliatory note after a silence of more than thirty years between them, he replied: 'I am so gratified for a letter with your signature on it ... I am delighted moreover at the tone of yr note as it is so characteristic of the

with mischief-making, and it may be assumed that she – having recently written to Anne, 'I hope I find you going on in your usual raking way' – was not silent either about the antics on the carpet.[14]

All Anne's anxieties about the power of gossip over reputation returned, and this time there was no refuge. Notoriety had pursued her from Edinburgh to London, and now she had reason to be ashamed. For once she did not leave her own version of the Hampden affair. Keen to set the record straight on so many things, she passed entirely over whether or not – as talk now had it – her virginity had been lost on a drawing-room floor.

Crucially, however, she did not seize the chance, implicit in Wentworth's pledge to Margaret, of binding him in marriage. This could be put down to her usual wavering, which to some extent it was; but her previous doubts would, in any conventional woman of her time, have been surrendered for respectability. Instead, she explained to a friend in weary tones how she found herself at an impasse with 'a partiality which might very probably never come to anything, to a person I did not much approve of, but that it barricaded my heart against other impressions.'[15]

Belatedly, she recognised, too, that she had loved Wentworth not as a man but as a cause – mesmerised by hope in much the same way he and his fellow gamblers were in thrall to the card table. Her need being for approval, she had wanted to prove her goodness could prevail over his weakness. As it was, Wentworth continued to wager nights away with the last vestiges of his fortune.

A few months later he told his family he and Anne had agreed that 'our marrying would be next door to madness'. But of the two, he had actually become the less doubtful. He said as much to one who least wished to hear it, his sister Judith:

Lady Anne Lindsay I was so happy to have lived in the most friendly intimacy and shall always be proud to renew the lease.' (27/4/97)

This I must tell you, that I heartily repent I did not know my own mind sometime ago, for I am convinced that we should have been happy together & that her attachment to me was & has always been real & disinterested ... Was it not for the conviction that misery to both must be the consequence, it would now not be my fault if I did not make her your Sister.[16]

In one regard Judith could take satisfaction. Events at Hampden showed that she had been right all along about Anne, whom she now referred to as 'the devil in scarlet'.[17]

More troubles awaited at Wimpole Street. In the spring of 1782 Fordyce was becoming more boisterous about business and more bullying towards Margaret. Constraint came between the sisters. Anne, living under their roof, was unable to speak candidly, while Margaret, dreading another trauma, was trying desperately to believe in the husband who assured her one more deal would make them rich again. Atkinson warned Anne: 'Our friend has too many irons in the fire.'

Imminent disaster became apparent, as it had before, one harrowing night when Fordyce denounced Atkinson for refusing to invest with him. His former ally was an enemy. Margaret too had betrayed him, by being too proud to ask friends for money. Next Fordyce turned on Anne, shouting that she must use her connections to raise investment. 'I must have it or everything must go to Hell,' he ranted. 'By God, I won't suffer it! By God, I won't!'

A few days later Fordyce returned home 'looking like a man who had been cut down from the gallows, with a grin of convulsion and assumed bravery'.[18] The bailiffs were about to arrive and this time he really was ruined.

Again Atkinson proved the sisters' rock. With Fordyce on the verge of bankruptcy, it was necessary for Margaret to keep her distance, to get away from Wimpole Street. Though Anne had resources of her own, Atkinson stepped in as their guardian and chaperone, renting a house for them at the seaside resort of Brighthelmstone, as Brighton was then known, or 'the nasty fishing town to which nobody goes but the Prince of Wales'.[19]

Anne, as if rising to 'the devil in scarlet' within, turned quite wild and careless, consorting with the renowned lecher George Cholmondeley, who sang *Jolly Bacchus* in her ear, and Tom Onslow, a chum of the Prince of Wales who hurtled around in his phaeton as if it were a horse-drawn sports car. Of a ball at which Anne enjoyed the attentions of a Captain Kaye of the Dragoons, Fanny Burney wrote: 'Lady Anne dances remarkably well and was in every way a suitable partner' for this 'handsome, very tall baronet's son'.[20] When there were no men, she would dance with Margaret, a novel practice seen as rather improper. Judith Milbanke noted with satisfaction: 'Her character being entirely gone, she is spoken of amongst men as slightly as any woman can.'[21]

Anne had come to the point of a dilemma perhaps more familiar to modern women: How old was too old for marriage? What happened to a woman who decided not to marry? When did waiting for someone better to present himself become unrealistic? How she answered these questions is not revealed in her writings. What does emerge is a failure to accept responsibility for the course she had adopted. When she castigated herself it would be for 'foolishness' or some other frivolous (and necessarily feminine) failing, which implied simple innocence. She had become prone to self-pity. One passage in a letter to Atkinson strikes a particularly miserable note:

> The life which a young woman with gaiety, tolerable good looks, a feeling heart but without a fortune passes in this town is more likely to be a mortified than a happy one. If she chances to please ... [she is placed] in the situation of a female Tantalus, with every good held up to her view, & every temptation offered her heart, only to be baulked with disappointment.[22]

Atkinson could not have done more to support Anne over the next two years had they been husband and wife. He demonstrated a gentle devotion she received from no other man. She was content to be a dependant, while aware that he still yearned for more. Years later, when the extent of Atkinson's love became a matter of public interest, *The Times* reported that he had likened himself to the eponymous husband in 'Auld Robin Grey': 'Mr Atkinson used to say that if Lady Anne would take him as a Robin Grey, she might seek out for a Jamie when he was gone.'[23] Atkinson appears to have known his frailty held the seeds of an early death and that the best he could do was to provide for her: 'You can have no objection, till you are under the protection of another,' he wrote, 'to letting me take care of your fortune.'[24] As London's shrewdest investor, he gave Anne the means to comfort and independence.

Margaret also benefited from his generosity. Atkinson used his connections during the final days of the North administration to obtain her an annual pension of £150, granted to 'indigent young women of quality'; and because Fordyce – now subject to bankruptcy proceedings – could lay claim to her money, he urged Margaret to keep this fact to herself. He also secured a pension for the third Lindsay sister, Elizabeth.*

After a season in Brighton and Bath, Anne was back in town where 'gaieties were going on ... the clubs filling ... pockets emptying'. Her own spirits lifted, she being 'ever ready to dance over the moon when I was not thrown flat to the ground by a hailstorm'.[25] Anne 'the Blithe' and Margaret 'the Blue', as they

---

* Thanks to his profits in America, Atkinson's influence in Lord North's government was notorious in so far as the opposition was concerned and attracted attention in the press when he used it on behalf of the Lindsay sisters. The process of obtaining their pensions was complicated, involving Atkinson in buying out an individual, James Macpherson, to whom the government was indebted, but does not seem to have been very improper.

saw their respective temperaments, were spending more time apart and though neither would have seen this as a rift, a cycle of mutual dependency had ended. They were guests in different households and while still living together sporadically would go on to have their own homes.

Anne moved to Portman Square (brother Alexander had withdrawn to Balcarres) and, with an income that for the first time allowed her to keep a carriage and servants, including a maid, Betty, might almost have been seen as a lady of fashion, but for her quirky outfits. On her arrival at a ball, Sheridan's wife, the actress Elizabeth Linley, observed: 'She was so bedevilled by dress that I should not have known her – a thick muslin rondo cap covering her hair, a gypsy hat of black and white chip circles, a black and white spotted petticoat, and over it a black cloth greatcoat and thick muslin handkerchief.'[26]

The Lindsays' status was a little improved by the marriage in the summer of 1782 of Elizabeth, the youngest sister, to Philip Yorke, a politician and heir to his uncle, the Earl of Hardwicke. Aged eighteen, Elizabeth was never fully part of her sisters' union, and the only one to marry a titled, affluent and entirely respectable man. The marriage gave rise to jests that Anne would have to dance in green stockings, a ritual for spinsters seeking husbands, but few took that prospect seriously any more. She had begun a new chapter, seemingly reconciled at thirty-one to her state and relieved that Atkinson was content to act as companion and financial adviser. Although Wentworth resumed visits on his return from the country, she had unshackled herself and was hoping simply to keep him from the tables, in 'a last attempt to save the remnant of his fortune and the wreck of his mind'.[27]

Failure confronted her soon enough. Wentworth arrived late one night, drunk and on his way to the club, then fell asleep, leaving her to reflect 'what an unlovely object is a man in such a circumstance'. He became more unlovely still when he awoke and started vomiting. After she had fetched him a basin, he burbled an apology and went off to sleep again. Her reflection on this episode, that 'a snorer was never to my taste', raises the question whether she had further experience of male snorers, and when it had been acquired.[28]

In January 1783 she received a blackmail letter:

Unless you send a sum of fifty pounds within eight days to the place hereafter mentioned, all your letters, verses &&& to Lord Wentworth will be published in the course of next month. Even all your artful billet doux shall be exposed . . . The world shall then see the villainous art that you practised against her who now sleeps in peace that you might triumph as Lady W . . . I hope your Ladyship will be at no payns to find out who I am as you never will know. I see you very often and yet I am persuaded I am the last person in the world you would suspect.[29]

Anne went straight to her port in a storm. A letter in Atkinson's hand was sent to the address in the blackmailer's letter, Seagoes Coffee House in Holborn.

Your Threatening Letter has been laid before counsel and it appears that by Act of Parlt the punishment for sending it is DEATH . . . You are already in part traced and to push the Enquiry to your complete detection and punishment is far from difficult. The smallest public impertinence will at once fix that purpose.[30]

The culprit's identity was never established, but it is conceivable that Wentworth himself – by now desperate for money – was directly or indirectly involved. As he had returned her original letters, any papers in the blackmailer's possession must have been copies, perhaps made by Vanloo before her death. Anne's reliance on Atkinson is seen in another episode when Wentworth, facing action by creditors, appealed to her for funds to provide for his two illegitimate children. She in turn went to her benefactor, whose contempt for the young lord is evident from his note. 'I saw our friend yesterday with whom nothing in the least degree interesting passed. I paid him £3,000.'[31]

A further revelation in this cycle of devotion came in December 1782. Atkinson had learnt he was dangerously ill, possibly with consumption, and two days before Christmas signed a will naming Lady Anne Lindsay as the principal beneficiary. He sent her a copy, explaining that her fortune would come in the form of estates and holdings, because 'a large and staring legacy in money might excite surprise and foolish talk'.[32]

'Kind, good, unlucky Atkinson,' she would write in penitence, 'to have placed your affections on one so unworthy of them as myself . . .'[33]

Just how much Anne profited by Richard Atkinson's love became, as we shall see, an extremely complicated question. His legacy to her aside, however, it appears that by 1783 his investments had transformed her initial inheritance of £300 into the enormous sum of £20,000 in capital, along with annuities of £200 and £150. Crucially, though, only £9,000 of the capital was banked in her name, the rest being held by his partnership.[34] The reason was to keep her wealth secret from Fordyce and because of what had become her horror of gossip – or, as she put it, 'the misconstruction of those who would perhaps have blamed me for accepting of any advantage from the hands of a rejected lover!'[35] She was none the less happy for 'my zealous friend to act, to decide for me on every point'. And he was, as ever, touched by her apparent unworldliness. 'You are so unlike anyone I ever met with,' he mused, 'so confiding, so incautious.'[36] As a relationship based on trust between financier and investor it worked for the time being; but it was to store up a wealth of woe for the future.

PART TWO

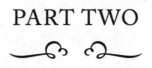

8

Escape to France

~~ ᕲ ᑢ ~~

1784–1785

A great empire had been lost in America, another was on the rise in India and a new era was dawning in British politics. Anne Lindsay's engagement over the next twenty years in domestic and world affairs would have come as a surprise to many, including her younger self. It was not a role for which she had any inclination. 'I am and ever was a poor politician,' she insisted.[1] Like any woman of her time, even the Duchess of Devonshire who campaigned actively on behalf of Charles James Fox, she came to public life through her relationships with men. The connection ran deep none the less. The two men who battled for her heart over the next decade – and the one who tore it to shreds – were both politicians.

By 1783 Henry Dundas had established himself as a power in the land through his influence over Scottish votes – he had made a mark in three short-lived governments, under lords North, Rockingham and Shelburne – when it was suggested that he might ally himself with a newcomer, William Pitt, a twenty-three-year-old MP with little besides a famous name to his advantage. More to thwart his arch-enemy Fox than anything else, Dundas joined Pitt's camp and stood by him that winter as a weakened coalition led by North and Fox clung to office.

Over those months Dundas called regularly on Anne. He had been divorced for four years, was aged forty-one and had much to recommend him. In his conduct towards his adulterous ex-wife,

Anne noted, 'he had been as generous as a Prince ... He was so in all his modes.'

> He had none of the trick of his trade about him. What he could tell he told freely to those he thought well of, and his conversation was not only great in its subjects and interesting in its nature, but luminous by the brightness and force of his thoughts. He knew well how to appreciate talents in men, and how to forgive a few in women, if they were handsome.[2]

Dundas's authority and studied gallantry were less apparent when they were alone together. His weaknesses were women and liquor, and Anne once hinted at the unwelcome advances he made in private: 'He was not in mixed company a brilliant man, nor a comfortable one in a tete-a-tete for other reasons.'[3] She admitted, too, to finding him sullied 'by the coarseness and want of delicacy in his manners'. So there was from the outset a pragmatic – it might be said cynical – aspect to her partisanship.[4] If she had a political ideal it would have been Edmund Burke, a Whig maverick who stood on principles yet put human sympathy before human rights; the Whigs in general she thought 'the cleverest, the pleasantest, and to be honest I fear I must add, some of the most dissipated men in the kingdom' – an allusion to their leader, Fox.[5]

In the end, her political affiliation was defined by personal rather than party loyalties; and she exploited her influence with Dundas shamelessly, on behalf of her family as well as herself. Such was the nature of public affairs, and she did so without the usual admissions to be found in the memoirs when she felt remorse: these volumes of late-years confessional were calculated at times to highlight her lesser sins at the expense of those she camouflaged or concealed; Dundas is far less visible in them than he merits, as is clear from her surviving letters which show just how dependent she became on him as a benefactor.

In turn, she reciprocated with her own services, and took immense pleasure in the journey they afforded her. They carried her across the world and to the courts of Europe, and in the process she showed a daring and relish evident in few women of privilege. She was willing to travel alone and place herself in situations unimaginable to all but the more intrepid of her contemporaries. (As another writer of vivid letters, the redoubtable Eliza Fay comes to mind.) Although best known for her accounts from the Cape of Good Hope, two journeys to France – including Paris during the Revolution when she was in pursuit of love – attracted a good deal of attention, albeit of all the wrong sort. The gay gamine of her Edinburgh days can appear at times wild and desperate. Like Dundas, to whose destiny she hitched her carriage, she became something of an adventurer; and he, as a powerful, tough yet strangely romantic Scot, was an ideal counterfoil.

Anne's first foray into politics set the tone. In the winter of 1783, Fox introduced a bill to redefine the East India Company's charter and curb the money-making opportunities for its servants who went out with nothing and came back as nabobs. Pitt and Dundas opposed the bill. They were joined by Richard Atkinson, whose City interests had made him an influential figure in the Company, in what amounted to a conspiracy to thwart Fox.

Anne had a strong family interest in India. One brother, James, had fallen at Cuddalore. Another, John, was in his fourth year as a captive of Hyder Ali. A third, Robert, was making a fortune in Dacca, a diseased and lonely spot but, thanks to cotton, one suited to healthy buccaneers. She proceeded to help Atkinson in drafting a series of notes, transcribed by Dundas and passed to the palace, which confirmed the king in his loathing of Fox and brought a threat that any peer who supported the bill would be treated as an enemy.* To that extent it might be said that Anne joined in what amounted to a royal coup – for collaborating with George III in his determination to thwart the Whig radical led to the bill's defeat in the Lords. The king's unconstitutional interference brought down the North–Fox coalition and swept Pitt into office.

That early involvement drew Anne into the circle of power, further compromising any resistance she may have felt to the way it was exercised. Dundas was rewarded with responsibilities for the Navy and India and, so far as she was concerned, the capacity to further transform her brothers' careers. As for Atkinson, another of Pitt's coming men, she felt relief that she had been able to 'shew her sense of what she owed him'.[6]

> I was rescued from poverty, the dear Elizabeth was brought to London and happily married, Margaret had a pension. To Atkinson all was owing, and to Atkinson the hearts of our family paid their cordial tribute of gratitude without their exactly knowing the extent to which it was due![7]

Anne would perhaps have further justified herself on the grounds taken by most moderate reformists, that Fox's bill was inspired as much by envy as a desire for sensible change. In the summer of 1784, two months after the election that brought Pitt to power, Atkinson was returned as an MP and, despite what might have been expected of a ruthless agent of the Company, surprised everyone by advocating reforms that went beyond anything anticipated by Pitt or Dundas.

That partnership, the rough Scot and the boyish Englishman, was destined to guide the nation through the storms of war and

---

* Matheson, p. 98. Dundas's biographer also relates that as a result of calling on Anne one night in February 1783 Dundas missed seeing Pitt at a critical point, thus preventing their rise to power for another year (pp. 92–3).

empire for some twenty years. Dundas became Pitt's friend and enforcer (and companion in heavy-drinking binges) while serving as his minister in charge of India, the Navy and, ultimately, the wars with France. 'I feel him to be sent down from Heaven as a saviour to this country,' he wrote. To Anne he once confided:

> I often envy that rogue, while I am lying tossing and tumbling in my bed, and cannot sleep a wunk for thinking of expedeshons and storms and bauttles by sea and laund, there does he lay doon his head in his bed, and sleep as sound as a taup.[8]

Another new MP was about to enter Anne's world, and he was all that Atkinson and Dundas were not – neither a 'noble little creature', nor 'in want of delicacy'. There would be no patronising of one of the most gifted, fascinating and damaged men of his time.

Anne had met William Windham at Tunbridge Wells in 1777 among a party that included the Duchess of Devonshire and two members of the *beau monde*, Brooke Boothby and George Cholmondeley. Windham, it seemed to her, did not quite fit the company. He showed no interest in what Boothby described as their world of 'vanity and folly'; and by the time of his entry to politics, he had emerged as a beacon among his generation.

Windham was born seven months before Anne Lindsay to a wealthy Norfolk family. At Eton he excelled, both as scholar and sportsman – 'the best cricketer, the best leaper, swimmer, boxer, rower, fencer, runner and horseman'. From school he went to Oxford to study Classics and, through his tutor, met Dr Johnson. A thirst for adventure, as well as physical and intellectual gifts, marked him as symbolic of a romantic age. A fearsome pugilist in his youth, he joined a (failed) polar expedition and took to ballooning at the birth of that perilous new technology. Meanwhile he added linguistics, mathematics and philosophy to his learning. Windham was not particularly good-looking. Fanny Burney thought his face 'very pleasing though not handsome'; but she was bowled over by his 'very elegant figure' and his company: 'He is one of the most agreeable, spirited, well-bred and brilliant conversationalists I have spoken with.'[9] Thanks to Johnson, whose beloved disciple he became, Windham was elected to the Literary Club at the age of twenty-eight. When he entered politics, Edmund Burke joined his circle of admirers. An eloquent, fiery orator on top of it all, Windham appeared capable of succeeding either of these great men in their respective fields.

The flaws took time to emerge, but may be traceable in part to his friendship from Oxford days with a man who has lingered for some time in the background of this narrative. George Cholmondeley was one of the ensemble with whom the Lindsay sisters sang and performed at musical evenings. He was a renowned womaniser, but there were many of those and Anne knew how to deal with them. She is unlikely to have been aware, however, of a sinister side that coloured his friendship with Windham.

Anne met Windham again soon after his entry to politics. She would see him at parties given by the Palmerstons whose guests might also include Sir Joshua Reynolds or Sir Joseph Banks and, like everyone else, she was impressed.

His conversation, at once animated and serious, had the happy art of not only rendering every subject interesting but of sending one home particularly pleased with oneself for having drawn the attention of such a man.[10]

Things might have moved faster but for another equally fateful and, historically speaking, more momentous affair of the heart. The setting was suitably melodramatic – a night at the opera early in 1784 when, according to Anne's version of events, a woman entered her box at Covent Garden. She was striking rather than beautiful, which suggests that her proportions and magnificent bosom were carried off by an eye-catching outfit when the Prince of Wales looked across from his box to the friend he called 'Sister Anne' and spotted her guest. The opera's name is not recorded, though Purcell's *Dido and Aeneas*, with its themes of royalty and doomed love, would have been apt. Later the Prince took Anne aside and asked: 'What angel was it beside you in a white hood?' The angel was Maria Fitzherbert, who had been Anne's friend for some years and, now a widow, was starting to make her way back in society.

Towards the end of her life Anne threw off discretion. For almost forty years she had held her tongue over a royal scandal that mesmerised society and in which she had participated to the end. She maintained her silence (apart from a private letter to the Lord Chief Justice) even when it brought accusations that she was driving the Prince of Wales into an illegal marriage. Now she wanted intimates, her closest relatives, to hear her story. 'These anecdotes have remained unseen to this day,' she wrote.[11] 'I shall be no more when you read this.' And, with a hint of vanity at the clandestine events to which she had been party: 'I think you have a very tolerable chance of being entertained by it.'[12]

Maria Fitzherbert met the Lindsay sisters at one of their musical evenings but it was not until the death of her second husband in 1781 that she became part of their circle. Anne and Margaret extended friendship in sympathy for another single woman making her way in an often predatory world. Mrs Fitzherbert was then twenty-five and a magnet for men – sensuously attractive, fiery-tempered and wealthy – while also a convent-educated Catholic. From that point 'Fitz', as Anne called her, 'accompanied us often into public, almost ashamed of being happy again, but glad to be made so'.[13]

Accounts differ as to how she first caught the Prince of Wales's eye. The accepted version has been that she was in Lady Sefton's box at Covent Garden at the time. However, Anne and Margaret had recently obtained their own subscription to a box, thanks to Richard Atkinson – 'an extremely well-positioned one,' the *Morning Herald* reported, 'only a few feet away from the Duke of Cumberland's.'[14] And Anne was clear in recording: 'It was in our box at the opera the Prince first beheld [Maria].'[15] The date was early in 1784. Anne and Wentworth attended a ball together soon afterwards on 10 March, when he observed: 'His Highness is making fierce love to ye Widow Fitzherbert & I think will succeed.'[16]

The prince's infatuation and relentless pursuit of Mrs Fitzherbert mystified many at the time, Anne included, for, despite her physical attractions, the widow's bearing was clumsy, her conversation leaden; Anne, as forgiving of human frailty as almost anyone, thought her not only haughty and secretive, but often heartless. It made no difference to the prince. Though he had a string of willing mistresses, nothing would do but that he should possess Mrs Fitzherbert, and because she was a devout Catholic and resistant to a sexual liaison, his ardour was further inflamed. In public he sought her out. In private he threw himself on his bed, shouting that he could not live without her and threatening to kill himself.

Anne already felt herself to some degree involved when Tom Onslow, the prince's friend, told her he was so resolved on Mrs Fitzherbert there was a danger he might 'throw away the Crown for her sake' – in other words, marry her.[17] Not only was it almost unthinkable for the heir to the throne to wed a twice-widowed commoner six years his senior, it was illegal because of her Catholicism. Anne saw it as time for her to intervene.

She found the widow miserable and bewildered. The prince's attachment frightened her out of her senses. Would it not cause an outcry? Was it not cruel of him to persecute her so when he knew she hated it? Anne sympathised and suggested an escape from London. Bath, they agreed, was not distant enough.

For some time Anne had been considering an escape of her own, partly from Wentworth's dithering, and the prospect of a European adventure presented itself. Laurence Sterne's travel novel, *A Sentimental Journey through France and Italy*, had thrilled her. She was, as she saw it, 'young enough to be gay, old enough to be discreet, great enough to be received everywhere, and small enough to be anyone's equal'.[18] A few days later Maria called to ask, 'Will you accompany me to the Continent?' and it was settled.[19]

Not all Anne's friends approved. It was pointed out that to join Maria's flight would invite scandal, exposing Anne to 'the animadversions of the world'. Philip Yorke, her brother-in-law, made plain his reservations. Atkinson went further, expressing 'great repugnance' at her going abroad without 'any gentleman of your own family', adding: 'The fair young widow makes no chaperon at all.'[20] Though Anne acknowledged that her independence was entirely due to Atkinson's kindness, it made no difference. She persuaded herself that he and his niece, who had taken over care of his needs, would benefit by her absence.[21]

Maria herself was left with little option. The prince became hysterical, resorting to tricks which, as Anne put it tartly, 'however allowable for a lover in modern comedy, were not those of an honest man'.[22] He took physic to make his face pale, threw further bouts of hysterics and, in a final fit of attention-seeking, fell on his sword. Onslow, who reported to Anne that he had 'bled like a calf', was despatched to bring Fitz to his side, with the Duchess of Devonshire as a witness, where he extracted Fitz's reluctant consent to be his wife. Fitz needed only a few hours to reflect on the impossibility of her position before departing for Dover on 9 July.[23]

Anne ordered chests to be packed for what promised to be an expedition of some months and followed, accompanied by her maid Betty and a footman. Her new coach, 'a dark chocolate post-chaise made by Leader with the plain cypher of the spinster', was so heavily laden that 'swinging on to Dover in my fair mansion, the springs were endangered . . . and I was forced into having four horses to draw me up a hill'. In Dover she joined Fitz at the City of London hotel for the first of many dinners and discussions on how they should best proceed. The packet service would take passengers to Calais for half a guinea each, while the cost of hiring their own vessel was six guineas, with another two for each post-chaise. Anne wanted to take the packet but Fitz and her servants were indignant at the idea of sailing in company with 'all sorts of creatures – for her who was running away from being Queen of England!'

That night they departed by a private vessel.[24]

For all the drama that lay behind Anne's first expedition to foreign parts, she treated it as a bit of a lark, and for prolonged spells it was. The fact remained that over the ten months she and Mrs Fitzherbert travelled Europe, from France to Belgium and the Netherlands, she was at the centre of an unfolding crisis involving a matter of state. The consequences were still being felt decades later, and efforts to cover them up continued well after the main participants were dead. The last of these was Mrs Fitzherbert herself, who was seventy-seven when the Duke of Wellington visited her Tilney Street house in 1833 to destroy letters from the late George IV; after several hours of burning he turned to his aide-de-camp Lord Albemarle and said: 'I think, my lord, we had better hold our hand for a while or we shall set the old woman's chimney on fire.'[25] Anne's recollection of events was presented in her usual jaunty style, right up to the point they turned genuinely grave.

France offered a laissez-faire welcome to these visitors from an often hostile land. They had their names noted by police and were asked where they were going. 'How is it possible to tell you, Sir?' simpered Anne in her poor French. 'We are ladies proceeding on a tour to amuse ourselves, and ladies never know their own minds.'

Fitz was keen to revisit her old convent of English Benedictines in Dunkirk where, at the sight of a former pupil, one old nun cried: 'It is our dear child.' The agnostic Anne observed: 'Never did I see religion so cheerful, or sisterly love better preserved'; the convent was 'a haven of peace rather than an imprisonment from happiness'. She sang for the nuns and gave them a rousing rendition of *God Save the King* on the organ.[26]

In Cassel they found 'everything very bad and very dear'; Lille was 'handsome', Ghent 'dirty and uncomfortable'. The first highlight was Spa, with the baths and casino that made it the mustering place of royalty and aristocrats across the Continent – the 'Café de l'Europe' as the Habsburg Emperor Joseph II called it. Here 'the mornings were devoted to bathing, riding, breakfasting and dressing; the evenings to dancing, music, pharo and gaming tables'. In Brussels, where 'the opera house was so dark we might have gone down in our birthday suits', a performance of Gluck's *Orfeo ed Euridice* was carried off by a stout French tenor despite a fit of colic, a Euridice with a hunchback and a one-eyed Amore – both castrati.[27] Anne was exhilarated with it all: 'I am so much in love with travelling', she wrote to her uncle, Sir Robert Keith, 'I am drawing, taking views of everything.'[28]

Along the way Anne and Maria attracted all the curiosity a pair of unaccompanied ladies might have expected. Women wanted to know how they happened to be travelling on their own. Where did their money come from? Did they not have husbands? The unspoken question was whether they were respectable ladies at all. Men were even more intrigued, notably Prince Henri of the German principality of Reuss, who followed up their departure from Brussels with a series of amorous letters to Anne:

Madame, I hate Brussels since the two charming and amiable English ladies have left it . . . Everybody and all the English are lamenting your departure . . . I don't like Paris but I declare that now my dearest plan is to take a trip to Paris to see you again. I sing the Indian song but not quite well. One or two lessons by your Ladyship would have been sufficient for knowing it perfectly.[29]

Fitz, in the meantime, had cast her spell over a Dutch baron who travelled in a procession of coaches and invited the ladies to join his entourage en route to The Hague. The poor besotted baron was treated by Fitz with a mixture of disdain and indifference as he trailed in her wake, sighing longingly over 'my peautiful tyrant'. Anne, indeed, was starting to feel sorry for those who became infatuated by the widow Fitzherbert. 'She is a devilishly overbearing woman at times,' she wrote to Margaret, with 'a haughty contempt [for men] which agrees with them as dogs but not as human creatures'.[30]

Anne and Maria became improbably close. Although the intimacy of the bond with Margaret often stood in the way of friendships with other women, Anne became the person to whom Fitz turned at times of crisis over the next twenty years. She advised her, wrote letters on her behalf to the prince and others, and on occasion acted as an intermediary with the royal family. But the friendship was never easy, often testy and sometimes fractured; Anne's experience was that Maria could be capricious and demanding, and she believed that for all the opprobrium heaped on the prince, his love was genuine, and both parties were to blame for the misery that followed.

An element of rivalry crept in. Anne was still a beauty, more so perhaps even than in her youth. Alison Cockburn, who had known her since she was a girl and saw her in her mid-thirties, thought her 'handsomer than ever – not jolly, but plump, which has greatly improved her looks'.[31] And Maria, aged twenty-eight, used to being the centre of male attention, bridled: 'I wish to God, Lady Anne,' she snapped once, 'that the men who pay you attention would not make it a point to be rude to me.'[32]

All the while a man across the Channel remained a constant if unseen presence. The prince, recovered from his self-inflicted wound, was in despair at finding Fitz out of reach and, in hope of following her, asked the king's permission to live abroad, saying he was deeply in debt (which was perfectly true). Meanwhile he sent emissaries to bombard Fitz with ardent letters. At Spa in Belgium, Anne observed a cohort of young courtiers – Lord Hugh Seymour and various Keppels and Russells – but it was the appearance of a Colonel Slaughter and Edward Bouverie, an aide-de-camp and personal friend to the prince respectively, which signalled a renewal of his siege. Fitz was silent at first before bursting with agitation and reading out a nineteen-page letter in which he declared that the Crown meant nothing to him compared with the possession of her heart. 'Our monarch writes well,' marvelled Anne. 'Cupid's wings make the finest pens.'[33] She was still relieved to be told by Bouverie that he had warned the prince against following Fitz, and the king sealed matters by refusing his son permission to live abroad.

They swept on to Holland. Anne sketched the fortified town of Bois-le-Duc until 'a sentinel walked up to me, letting me understand by a gesture that I should be in danger of being hanged if I did not desist'.[34] At The Hague further diversions awaited – as did an old love, Count Bentinck, now married yet as gallant as ever in welcoming the woman he still called 'the most bewitching of all human creatures'.[35] Another old suitor, Henry Hope, had scarcely received them at his palatial Amsterdam home before asking: 'Why might you not make this yours as well as mine?' Anne's gentle refusal – 'you are well now; don't let us waste time with regrets' – astonished Fitz. 'He cannot live above three years,' she pointed out, 'and to be a widow with £400,000 – what a situation!'[36]

More luxury awaited at court where they were presented to the Prince and Princess of Orange and Anne discovered that Dutch aristocrats were as alert to gossip as the English: Fitz, it was whispered, had 'refused the Prince what she had never refused anybody before; and tho I was a young woman of birth and accomplishments, I was not liked on account of some [other] odiums'.[37]

After four months together, strains had appeared. Apart from her companion being 'devilishly overbearing', Anne was irritated by Fitz's unpredictability, for while the prince continued to write to his 'dearest and only belov'd Maria', she blew hot and cold – waiting impatiently for the next letter to arrive, only to turn sulky when it did.[38]

There was, of course, only one woman in whose company Anne was content to spend prolonged spells and her heart 'had long been famished for want of the food it had been accustomed to through life'. Margaret's arrival in the autumn restored her gaiety.[39] They were to spend the winter in Paris among 'the society 1785, of manners, fashions – all governed with that splendid tyranny of aristocracy which carried all before it'.[40]

Anne's first visit to France – she would return during the Revolution, at the darkest point of her life – was a revelation. Human nature being full of paradoxes, her frugal, down-to-earth side, her dislike of ostentation and pomposity, could be won over by real spectacle; and the ceremonial style of the French court had no rival. What mesmerised her, though, was the contrast of regal grandeur with mass poverty. English society she often found dull and smug. France allowed of no complacency. Quietly she went about observing the corners of misery where few if any of her contemporaries would have ventured, and she was moved.

The news Margaret brought of Richard Atkinson was not good. Years of business and his recent engagement with politics had worn him down to the point that he had suffered a paralytic attack. Still, he urged her, 'amuse yourself well', adding in reassurance: 'All you have to do is double the number of your letters while I am an invalid, as they will be my best medicine.'[41] And so she dosed him with extended accounts of her adventures.

At Versailles 'the society was brilliant, the women handsome and well-dressed' with the 'careless and prodigal' queen at its centre. Anne and Margaret, being from the second rank of British aristocracy, were not introduced to the royal couple, but were invited to observe them at one of their ritual, twice-weekly, public dinners. Anne was surprised to find Marie-Antoinette less attractive than the seductive figure of reputation – not as handsome as Fitz, she thought – but with a flaunting splendour, so that 'while France murmured and hated, it was awed by her pomp'.[42] The king cut a modest figure by comparison but still put on an impressive show at the table where he demolished nine plates of food.[43] Later, observing the royal party in procession to Notre Dame – fourteen state coaches all decorated with velvet, silver and gold – Anne wrote home: 'On such occasions our good George III is, I assure you, a very small gentleman compared to Louis XVI.'[44]

Paris also confronted her with the paradoxes of the 'splendid tyranny of aristocracy'. She and Margaret were given permission to visit the Bastille, described by Anne as 'thou great Prince of Prisons, thou Emperor over all the inferior states of confinement!' but which, despite its notoriety and forbidding appearance, she was surprised to find virtually deserted. The governor, Bernard-René de Launay, was civility itself, throwing open his empty cells to demonstrate it was no place of oppressive despotism.

So contrary was all this to expectations that the sisters behaved like a pair of scamps.

Each having a childish desire to commit a crime in the Bastille, for the pleasure of having it to say we did, Margaret coquetted with the governor while I stole his pen, and I while she stole his penknife.[45]

De Launay lost more than his pen four years later when the Bastille was stormed. While Anne's observations were vindicated and this symbol of repression was found to contain only seven prisoners, a symbolic sacrifice was required. The governor had his head sawn off with a knife, the first beheading of the Revolution.[46]

Mischief was again the order of the day at a chateau where the late king, Louis XV, had retained Madame de Pompadour and Madame du Barry as his mistresses. Anne went, naturally, to the den of royal pleasure, a bedchamber decorated in crimson, green and white damask, and was sufficiently tickled to demonstrate her own risqué side. As she put it in the style she adopted when hinting to her descendants that she was no prim virgin: 'I cannot boast that I have slept with Louis Quinze, yet I mounted the ladder of three steps to the bed and put myself in his place at full length.'[47]

In another chamber Madame du Barry awaited her, 'a middle-sized fat, fair comfortable-looking woman such as one might find in most country societies, no rouge, sweet, twinkling blue eyes and an expression which said "Pray do think me handsome still, do!"' The old courtesan walked her through a house whose magnificence served as another reminder of the overwhelming opulence of French taste, to the garden where a large black beetle settled on du Barry's stocking 'with the taste of a monarch'. She too would fall victim to the Revolution a few years later, struggling and weeping as she was dragged to the scaffold.[48]

But alongside frivolity, luxury and sensuality was another world; and though the Bastille might be almost empty of prisoners, the less notorious and now forgotten Bicetre jail contained more than 6,000 poor souls. Conditions here, moreover, were so atrocious that Anne was left unsure whether a capital sentence might not be more humane: prisoners were chained to a wheel, pumping up water for glass-making, and were flogged in order to sustain their efforts. 'They bawled loudly for charity; we gave them something, but not much.'

The cachots [dungeons] are more horrible places still; as we walked thro' the flagged courts, we heard a dreadful noise, and on enquiring what it was, were made to observe a number of holes in the pavement, about the size of a crown piece. This is the only light or air allowed to the very desperate villains who are fed on bread and water and enclosed here. Their state is so much worse than the others that I suppose a man escaping from one of the cachots would reckon himself in heaven when turning the wheel.

We next visited a few industrious rogues who in their cells earned something by making straw boxes, of which I bought a few very dear indeed. Had I bargained with them I suppose I should not have paid a quarter of the money, but I thought it would give them pleasure in their state to cheat an Englishwoman, so they had what they asked.[49]

In another section were confined lunatics, chained to beds by iron rings encircling the throat and legs. Anne was transfixed by the spiritual expression of one young man who, far from dangerous, to her resembled Jesus. 'Benignity, sweetness, oppression, woe and resignation were painted in his countenance.' He had been a priest and she wanted to stop to talk – at which he became excited and tried to rise from his bed, revealing himself to be quite naked, and hastily she moved on.

The Hôtel-Dieu offered further harrowing visions. At Paris's oldest sanctuary, the sick, the mad and the abandoned lived up to six in a bed, sleeping or playing cards on a table of another's back, scarcely aware when one of their number expired.

Men with unshaved beards, dirty and diseased, terrible looking creatures, some pale and haggard, others panting in fevers and half naked, each fixing his eye on us as we passed with looks of such dejection and misery as made me freeze . . .

Here too were some who had lost the power of reason.

'Tis surprising to observe after a human creature has fallen as low as it can fall, reduced by disease and poverty to reside in the Hotel-Dieu, how much it still has to lose, for the poorest creature in the other wards by the possession of reason seemed an emperor compared to the half-idiots ... They gazed on us, begging by signs and supplications for snuff, which I had unfortunately not provided myself with ... We had seen enough to know that there was such a place for misery to creep into, where no questions are asked, no disease objected to, where the poor of all parishes and descriptions are welcomed. It is the Hotel-Dieu, and He is no respecter [of personages][50]

Later Anne was questioned by a Frenchman, Baron de Stalis, who wondered how a woman of tender heart could bear such shocking sights. She was vexed for a moment, guilty at her *tour de voyeurisme*, before replying that it was important 'for careless beings such as we to be aware of how such people live'.[51]

France, indeed, had made a profound impression, as a lesson on life in the wider world. Anne found English aristocratic society limited in its horizons and interests, censorious in its judgements on the outlandish. She might have gained similar insights by entering parts of Hogarth's London, and the likelihood is that on occasion she did so. France did more than cast light on suffering humanity, however. The simple act of entering another landscape, another society, itself acted as a stimulant, and it gave her an appetite for repeating the experience.

Much about the French psyche and exploration of science intrigued her. As one with personal knowledge of 'the blews', as she and Margaret referred to the latter's bouts of depression, she heard about the study of magnetism, or hypnotism, as a way of 'awaking the mind to effect a cure'; and she attended a seance, although to no great effect.[52] The Hôtel-Dieu's remedy for lunatics, which was to pour water on their heads from a height, struck her as just another form of madness; but a Paris scientist's claim to have proof that the world was more than 4,000 years old struck her as quite plausible.[53]

France itself appeared 'a great theatre where everyone is acting a part and no-one is himself'. Yet for all the posturing, there was something deeply impressive about ordinary discourse. Even a French servant, Louis, she noted, 'astonishes me with his opinion on wise matters, which he has picked up behind my chair at dinner'.

> The quantum of talents is so much more equally spread over the French nation than over the English (where one man monopolises the portion of hundreds) that every man here, be his station ever so subordinate, possesses the power of talking well for half an hour on every subject.[54]

Among those she evidently had in mind was the Duc de Broglie, an army officer of far-sighted and liberal opinion who had served in the American War of Independence. Anne was flattered by his attention, while ascribing it to the fact that Margaret was married and Maria haughty, but in response she could only say 'that I had seven brothers and would never marry any man who was likely to carry arms against them'.[55] (Despite his support for the Jacobins during the Revolution, de Broglie was later guillotined.)

English society in Paris, on the other hand, appeared little more than an enclave of the louche pettiness familiar from home. The Duke of Dorset, the British ambassador and a man famed for indolence and philandering, snubbed the sisters at first because he was a favourite of George III – and hence a foe of the prince and anyone associated with Fitz – before being won over by their singing. Anne had never liked him, had cut him when he tried to debauch her in London, and found him vain about his skill as a violinist though he played 'very nearly as well as the worst fiddler at the Opera'. The duke had just begun a liaison with another visitor to Paris, Lady Elizabeth Foster, and went on to make her friend, the Duchess of Devonshire, his mistress a year later. Anne was no admirer of Elizabeth: not 'well-bred, engaging or sensible', but lavishly endowed with the talent of flattery.

Some of these episodes doubtless found their way into Anne's letters to Atkinson. His replies were generally reassuring: he seemed to be recovering and had returned to Brighton, 'abominably stupid this year – the Prince has destroyed it for the fine part of the season'.[56] His last letter brought the welcome news that her brother John had reached safety after four years a prisoner in India. At the end of the Paris winter, Anne and Margaret were planning an excursion with Fitz to Switzerland before a return to England.

Fitz had in the meantime been besieged by letters from the prince. His tactics had changed following legal advice, and in the spring of 1785 he proposed two options. If she would renounce Catholicism, he would wait two years until coming of age and laying her name before Parliament as his wife-to-be. Or – and he must have known by now she would not give up her faith – they could marry privately, in which case she would retain her name and her own home while he provided for her, making it understood she was his wife. On the king's death, she and their children would join him at the palace – the new royal family.[57]

Anne's advice on being shown this letter was as before. 'You have always said it was your duty to resist a union which, if repented of, could not bind him to anything,' she said, 'but which, if his mind was honourable, might harness him for life.' In the end Fitz prevailed on Anne to draft a reply which said, in effect, she was too much the prince's friend to accept either of his proposals.[58] It was the first of many letters she wrote on the widow's behalf.

Thus were matters poised when a thunderbolt landed from across the Channel.

How Anne heard of the death of Richard Atkinson, whether by letter or the newspapers, she did not say. 'Accounts had not of late been so favourable as we could have wished,' she wrote. 'Now all was closed! All was over! A paralytic stroke . . .' Otherwise, details of the event were submerged in a tide of guilt which she poured into her journal.

> Am I not a stone that I should have hesitated and postponed my return when his health became a question? Would he not have gone to the end of the world to do good to mine? Oh, my kind friend! Why had you not the shoulder of the person you loved to lay your poor head on? Why cannot I remember your saying, 'Here I resign my breath to her who came far, far to attend on me.' Alas, poor unfortunate Anne – unfortunate from being blameworthy, thou has no such consolation to revert to. Thy punishment is in thine own feelings.[59]

Atkinson had died aged forty-six at Brighton, where he had enjoyed some late happiness with Anne and Margaret. The cause of his death on 28 May was given as consumption, and his estate estimated at some £300,000. Even before the details of his will were clear, the press had identified Lady Anne Lindsay as the principal beneficiary.

She decided against an immediate return on the grounds that she could do Atkinson no good and that it would probably only give rise to further gossip about the curious spinster endowed with a superlative fortune. She had no very clear idea herself just how much she would get, though, when Fitz posed the question, she put it at about £30,000 with an annuity of £700. Nothing about the Atkinson estate would ever appear quite so clear again.

Anne's Continental adventure drew to a close. She and Fitz had been away together for ten months and the widow was to continue on her travels, delaying her return in the hope that the Prince of Wales's attentions might yet be diverted elsewhere. At their parting Anne was entrusted with his letters for safekeeping and promised to keep the fugitive informed of developments.

The packet carrying her and Margaret sailed from Dieppe for Shoreham but ran into a thunderous gale which brought waves foaming down into the passenger quarters and forcing a diversion to Dover. As it happened, Anne's stormiest passage was just beginning.

9

Royal Go-between

⟳ ⟲

1785–1787

Anne came home to find that a year's absence had added no end to her fascinations. Was this, she asked brightly, on account of her adventures on the Continent? Or might it have anything to do with the great wealth perceived to be her inheritance? Newspapers across the country had reported her legacy from Atkinson to be £35,000 and wherever she went she was met by eager-eyed well-wishers toasting her prospects.*

Wentworth returned with brazen effrontery. Still in her debt for the £3,000 handed over by Atkinson, he asked to see her and, when she did not respond, wrote: 'For heaven's sake my dearest friend, what can be the meaning of your persevering silence to me? ... Let me intreat you to relieve me of this torture and suspense.'[1] She replied with droll irony: 'I go into publick & see men who have pierced my heart watching for a look and trying to assure me that I have always been the secret object of their hearts! How I smile at the actors on this stage and know their value.'[2]

Wry cynicism was natural. She was, she told her former lover, 'an old bachelor ... no longer capable of marriage', and as such

---

* A legacy of £35,000 would have amounted to roughly £5.7 million in today's terms, but these figures do not accurately reflect their relative values: to take one example, the £2,600 paid by Anne for her house in Berkeley Square translates as about £420,000 now, scarcely enough for any London property.

now more interested in men as sources of patronage than as suitors. It evidently troubled her that in declining proposals as a young woman she had failed in her duty to family. Aged thirty-five, and having charmed her way to the heart of government and court, she could repair that by exerting influence with grandees like Henry Dundas. Lobbying powerful men had become an alternative to marrying one of them.

To start with, she stayed at Mrs Fitzherbert's house in Park Street. The family home was being rented and while the widow remained abroad she made hers available, though, she warned, 'I fear you must find my house very uncomfortable. There were bugs after I let it.'³ Bugs made for a brief residence and, in anticipation of the fortune to come her way, Anne bought a fine house in Manchester Square, along with a new coach, thereby attracting precisely the kind of attention she had hoped to avoid. 'Taste must approve,' the *Morning Herald* reported, 'the stile [*sic*] of Lady Anne Lindsay's new coach: it surely is a splendid compliment to Mr Atkinson's hearse!'⁴

Wealth notwithstanding, she was in a delicate position. With the royal family poised for a rift that might divide the nation, her desire to 'remain on good terms with the Prince, in friendship with Mrs Fitz, be respected by society and considered blameless of abetting the folly he was eager to commit' would require astute diplomacy.⁵ In their absence, the prince had appeared hopelessly drunk in public while consoling himself with a series of mistresses. As for the widow, a letter from Lausanne reflected her own contradictory emotions:

I die to know if you and St George have had a meeting . . . Pray good soul, tell me fairly your sentiments for you will be a better judge after you have seen and heard him . . . I suppose you know I have had another express [letter] and altho there is nothing essentially new yet it has cast me down and I feel ready to hang myself. I know your good heart feels for me and I know I can trust you. Do you think him sincere? Surely he cannot be if he will persist in persecuting me to consent to what must be so much to our mutual disadvantage.[6]

It appears from the prince's letters that Anne was trying to keep him at arm's length. She declined an invitation to join him with the Cumberlands, only for him to persist: 'Let me entreat you . . . otherwise the poor Duchess will not be able to go to the play . . . I hope you will receive the supplication of *yr SLAVE*.'[7]

When Anne did meet him again at Ranelagh, he was unable to conceal his misery even in public. 'His bright eyes filled with tears as he talked of the injustice that because he was Prince of Wales he should be debarred from the only state of happiness worth living for.' At the same time, he was baffled by the ambiguous tone of Fitz's letters, which he described as harsh yet always with 'some saving clause which shews me there is still hope'.[8]

Willingly or not, Anne now became drawn into his campaign – as a forty-two-page letter from the prince to Fitz shows.

I supped last night with your friend, Lady Anne, with whom I had already talked a great deal respecting you, and finding she knew everything respecting our situation I made no scruples of talking over our affairs very freely with her. It has been the whole delight of my life for above these three weeks past as she has been with her sister almost every day during that time at my house . . . and we have by that means had constant opportunities of talking the subject over with each other.[9]

Whether, as he claimed, Anne expressed support for a marriage, is extremely doubtful. Even now she was trying to avert what she saw as a calamity for the monarchy – and for George himself, were he to make this 'lovely but inconsequent and violent woman' his wife. The king wanted a match with Princess Louisa of Orange, whose portrait Anne had painted at The Hague, and when the prince asked her opinion, she declared Louisa pretty and pleasing, and sent him the painting. His reply was: 'I admired the artist more than I did the subject.'[10]

But his persistence had finally prevailed. In November Fitz wrote to Anne from Paris:

> I have told him I will be his. I know I injure him and perhaps destroy for ever my own tranquillity but I have nothing to reproach myself with.

This confusion and a tendency towards the melodramatic boded ill for what lay ahead.

> Could I banish from my idea the fatal consequences that may attend such a connexion I then might be happy in attaching myself for life to the man that has gone thro so much for my sake & to whom I feel myself very sincerely attached but also whenever I look upon it in a favourable light that idea vanishes in a moment & leaves such an oppression on my mind that I scarce know how to support myself. I shall make it the study of my life to make him happy.
>
> He in his letter desires me to come over immediately but that I cannot do. I purpose leaving this place the middle of next week but I have told him the moment I have fix'd the day I will write you word & you will have the goodness to tell him as I don't chuse writing by post to him.
>
> What will become of me my dear friend I have nothing to trust to but his honor. It is in his power by having a proper conduct in the beginning to establish my reputation in the eyes of the world and if he does not do I must sink under it. I wish you would prove to him how necessary it is, for we live in a malicious world. I am happy my Dr Lady Anne that he has told you everything. I have such an opinion of you that there is nothing I would not trust you with. Nobody loves you more sincerely than
>
> your affectionate Fitz.[11]

In the events leading to the secret royal marriage Anne acted as confidante to both parties and was in a unique position to add insight to the story – and to reveal one hidden scandal.

A widowed friend, Marianne Burton, possibly one of the prince's mistresses and plainly infatuated with him, was staying with Anne when she heard of Fitz's imminent return and started showing signs of mental instability. A letter to her from the prince was opened ('by mistake', Anne insisted) revealing that she had proposed a secret assignation, to which he had agreed. When Marianne prepared for their encounter by buying opium and a knife, Anne urged her to rest at home and wrote to the prince: 'Sir, If you are appointed to see anyone this morning, I *Entreat* you not to see the person alone.'[12] Later, on looking in on Marianne's room, Anne found she had stolen out. Down she raced, into a coach and to the meeting place, a cutler's in Park Street, where she was told a lady and two gentlemen were upstairs. Relieved that the prince had brought his aide-de-camp, and seeing it as a breach of decorum to go up herself, she returned home.

An hour later an agitated prince arrived, and tried to make conversation about Fitz.

> 'Is there nothing else, Sir, you have to say to me?' He was silent.
> 'Does she live?' said I gravely.
> 'Yes,' said he, 'and it is I who saved her.'

Marianne, as he explained it, had swallowed the opium and reached for the knife, saying she would 'give him a scene to last him for life'. He had saved her by wrenching the knife away. How a woman, he went on, to whom he had only ever paid a few compliments could have become so frenzied was beyond him.

Though deferential Anne felt the time had come to be firm:

'You know what you have to answer for. If you are without blame, so much the better. How this may strike an absent friend is to be considered.'

'She cannot hear of it,' said he. 'No-one would be so cruel as to tell her.'

'I trust you will tell her yourself, Sir. At any rate I must. The circumstance has happened in my house, and I should not act fairly if I concealed it from her.'[13]

Marianne was attended by a physician and an apothecary; but as Anne wrote in a hastily scratched note to the prince the following day.

Neither my sister nor I are known by her but are talked to as two gentlemen she saw yesterday. No liquid or food is taken. Forgive me Sir if I entreat you *not* to call – it might create speculation.[14]

The prince, meanwhile, was close to a breakdown over the lack of news from Fitz, writing to Anne: 'I am perfectly distracted – anxiety, fear torments me more than ever poor creature was tormented. MEN HAVE NERVES AS WELL AS WOMEN.'[15] When Fitz did land at Dover he was seized with panic and guilt at the prospect of a scandal over Marianne.

For God's sake my dearest Lady Anne let me hear something of your patient ... I suffer more for this poor woman than I can possibly express, being the unfortunate & I may almost say the innocent cause of her distress ... Pray tell me, can you see me anywhere today?[16]

Hours later, he took up his pen again. 'I have this instant a letter from my Maria. She may be in London tomorrow but begs it may not be known. If I could see you for one moment this evening I would show you her letter.'[17] It took a strong woman to repel a royal siege, and a stubborn one; Anne still declined.

*

Over the next two weeks events moved so fast that the most influential men and women in London could not keep up. As Fitz's closest friend, Anne became the focus of fresh rumours. Not for the first time, she was alarmed by gossip – only now it emanated from circles of power and held her to blame for a looming constitutional crisis: a hastily assembled meeting of leading men, politicians and eminences such as Lord Mansfield, the Chief Justice, had been told that Lady Anne Lindsay 'was the promoter of the step the Prince of Wales is supposed to be on the brink of taking' and that 'frequent meetings were being held between him and Mrs Fitzherbert' at Manchester Square.[18] Anne was grateful that Mansfield came directly to ask her if this was true but mortified to find herself 'torn in pieces [by] every statesman'. To distance herself, she resolved not to receive the prince and Fitz together.[19] It was only after a desperate plea from Maria – 'My Dear Friend, call upon me if it is but a moment. I must see you' – that she visited her.[20] Anne followed this by writing to them jointly:

> Dear Souls! I dare not even put up a prayer to God for you mutually, but if ever you are married (which it is my duty to wish you may never be) I'll make it up.[21]

Enclosed was a copy of another letter – to Mansfield. With conspiracy theories flying about, she was writing for posterity and evidently felt she must rise to the big statement.

> Allow me in the simplicity of fact to state that what is alleged is False. I give your Lordship my word of honour that I have not seen the Prince since Mrs Fitzherbert's return to England, nor have I had communication with him by letter on the subject. Mrs Fitzherbert has not yet been within these doors. I have called on her. As to my having been a promoter of his attachment and presupposed marriage

with her, the duty and respect I feel for my Sovereign I will not acknowledge to be inferior even to your Lordship's. I look up to His Majesty with gratitude for the favours I and my family owe to his goodness. As Lady Anne Lindsay, I am too independent to be tempted into building visions of future advantage to my fortunes out of such a measure. If I have any vanity I hope it will be better directed than to lead me to sacrifice my King, my Country, my Prince, my friend and myself to the pride of accomplishing an improper purpose.

She feared, she went on, that a marriage unsanctioned by the king and Parliament 'might one day prove the source of calamity to this country', and had said as much to the prince himself, 'supporting my ideas by the best arguments I could muster'. She concluded with an appeal: the king's ear had been poisoned against her; 'I trust it to the friendship with which you honour me to put it to rights.'[22]

Mansfield, a congenial soul who had entertained Anne and Margaret with Tokay and turtle, replied that night, 'with pleasure and admiration ... Your letter does honour to your head and your heart.'[23] The prince read the copy sent to him by Anne and replied: 'I have the strongest and firmest reliance on your honour ... all I can say is I had sooner perish than recede from what has passed.' A note added by Fitz read: 'A day or two at farthest will finish everything.'[24]

Two days did it. A curate just released from debtors' prison conducted the clandestine ceremony at Fitz's house with two of her relatives as witnesses on 15 December. Contrary to another spate of rumours, the Lindsay sisters were not there.

Even after the ceremony was over and the prince's passion finally consummated, many remained unaware of it. Pitt, the prime minister, only suspected what had happened; Fox, the prince's closest ally in politics, was deceived by him to the last, and another friend, the Duchess of Devonshire, could not be sure of the event either.* Anne called on Fitz soon afterwards and though 'a veil of mystery pervaded everything in the house and a direct reply to anything was not to be obtained', it was clear that fate had taken its course. Over a long conversation, during which she urged her friend to bear in mind how much the prince was potentially sacrificing, Anne may have delivered rather more advice than was welcome.[25] What is apparent is that her continuing refusal to receive them together led to a falling-out with Fitz.

Although the new royal couple continued to live in separate houses, and the king remained for the time being ignorant of the marriage, the prince made it clear that where he went Fitz was to accompany him. If she were not invited, he would not go. Anne and Margaret, partly out of what they saw as principle, but also with an eye to propriety, decided that 'the whispered command of the Prince should make no difference to us'.[26] Fitz was understandably put out that decorum should stand in the way of their friendship. When Anne invited her to dinner without the prince, saying 'certain folks would think we shew'd too much bravery in showing you off together', she received an icily imperious reply:

> Believe me my dear Lady Anne, I am the last person in the world to cause you the least uneasiness & for that reason, neither the Prince nor myself can avail ourselves of your invitation.[27]

Anne refused to see that she might have taken rectitude too far, passing over the quarrel by saying that 'from this time, our visits

---

* Anne suspected, mistakenly, that Fox and the Duchess of Devonshire had encouraged the marriage as part of a plot 'to manage the prince through Mrs Fitzherbert and in the event of the King's death to manage the country'. (Memoirs, vol. 4, p. 5) In fact, Fox himself and Georgiana pleaded with the prince not to marry Mrs Fitzherbert for fear that it would cost him the throne (Foreman, pp. 177–8).

to La Belle, tho' kind and cordially paid, were rather less frequent'. The prince was more forgiving than his wife, and on meeting Anne at the Duchess of Cumberland's told her that 'since his Maria had promised to be his, the tranquillity of his mind passed all description'.[28] From this oblique reference it may be inferred that the marriage was still not being explicitly acknowledged to even the couple's closest friends. As time passed, however, and rumours gave way to press reports and caricatures, the future king and the wife who was never going to be his queen became a new focus of London society. So too, with time, the rift between Anne and Fitz healed.

The acquisition of a large fortune and a close connection to the Prince of Wales helped to redefine Anne. So, too, did the year away in Europe, as it allowed the Hampden scandal to dim in memories. On starting a new page in a fine Manchester Square home, Anne avoided the racy set. Wentworth persisted for some time in his usual hapless way, encouraged by some of his family who now perceived virtue in 'the Scotch-woman whose fortune will pay his debts'.[29] Even his sister Judith's malice was subdued. 'I was much surprized at the immense legacy Atkinson has left Lady Anne,' she wrote. Anne, Atkinson and her brother had formed 'the most mysterious trio I ever heard of & I have ideas I do not chuse to commit to paper.'[30] Wentworth himself soon realised his was a lost cause. He had the decency on finding an heiress able to afford him to request Anne's release from debt – which she did graciously, wishing him happiness – and married early in 1788.*

What she hoped for now were simple pleasures: giving dinners and concerts at Manchester Square for witty old friends and

---

* Wentworth's wife, Mary, Countess Ligonier, thought Anne's action 'much to her honor' (Elwin, p. 328). But the marriage was not a success, his possessive sister Judith taking as strong an aversion to his wife as she had to his lovers Catherine Vanloo and Anne Lindsay.

important new ones, renewing family ties and enjoying diversions with her pen and brush. She had no further expectations of marriage, and thanks to her wealth had no need of it.

Instead she was soon desperately in love, and the fortune of Atkinson's legacy never materialised.

Two men dominated the years ahead. Henry Dundas was already a familiar. A more recent acquaintance, William Windham, had soared to prominence during her absence in France and started to pay personal calls. Both were influential political figures, both may have been seen as her lovers. Neither was after money and the agony Anne endured was of her own making. Yet her hesitancy about men gathered a further layer of wariness after her inheritance. Of a visit to court at this time she wrote: 'I heard my name echoed round in whispers and saw the eyes of half the bachelors in the room applying my fortune to their debts and myself to their ménage.'[31] Had they all but known it, the wealth was an illusion.*

The saga of Atkinson's will and the disputes it produced lurked in the background of the rest of Anne's life, but what started out as a fortune on paper of some £30,000 had already been challenged. Soon it started to evaporate and in a legal case that might have come from the pen of Dickens it would vanish entirely. She was in her grave before this episode of Jarndyce vs Jarndyce had been settled.

It began with objections by Atkinson's family. Whereas Anne had been left £30,000 and Margaret £5,000, plus annuities of £700

---

* As an example of the gossip surrounding Anne, James Boswell related the claim by Sir James Johnstone at a gentlemen's dinner almost three years later that Atkinson's will also included legacies 'to each of her three children and one of which she was then pregnant . . . she being then in France'. The implication was that Anne already had two children when she conceived a third by Atkinson and fled to Europe with Fitz to escape scandal. Johnstone was challenged by Anne's former suitor Sir Michael le Fleming, and a bet made that the loser would feed the entire company at the London Tavern. Boswell resolved the wager by inspecting the will and finding it made provision for any *future* children.

each, his nine nephews were to receive lump sums of £3,000 each and nine nieces annuities of £200 as they came of age. Among the nieces was Dorothy Atkinson, who had lived with Atkinson at the end of his life and looked after him during his final illness but received no special reward. Atkinson had told Anne that he thought modest incomes for life more likely to bring his nieces happiness than 'a sum which might be sacrificed to early ill-judged prosperity'. But his executor and brother, Matthew, felt 'mortification at the destination of his property'.

Deeper mires lurked within the sheer complexity of Atkinson's affairs. In addition to the £30,000 bequest, he had made large sums on Anne's behalf, based on her own initial investment. But because, as Anne said, 'it became a point alike of delicacy and prudence to remain poor in the eye of the world' and keep this knowledge from Margaret's husband Fordyce, a large amount – possibly a further £30,000 in bonds – was still in Atkinson's name at the time of his death.[32] In short, Anne had no proof that this was her money and had nothing to do with his will. Moreover, Atkinson's fortune was tied up – either in Jamaican sugar estates or in his partnership, Mures & Atkinson.

Anne was given a hint of what lay ahead by Atkinson's solicitor who warned her that what he called 'old debts' of the partnership might affect the estate. Next she called on the partners, to be told there were indeed debts and that before his death Atkinson had conducted a stock deal for which there was no sanction. As Anne related it, she knew enough to challenge this on the ground that Hutchison Mure, the senior partner, had given verbal approval. True, replied his son Robert, 'rubbing his hands with vulgar triumph', but the law required written agreement.[33] So she turned to Atkinson's closest political and business associate, John Robinson, who told her not to be intemperate. Anne was furious. 'Intemperance!' she fumed. ''Twas the speech of the Wolf to the Lamb.'[34]

We do well to bear in mind that Anne's account of the

Atkinson saga was highly subjective. Throughout these disputes, she felt subordinated – bullied or manipulated by those with some control over events, the lawyers and executors. Yet she had taken neither interest nor responsibility in how Atkinson had made her money, had deferred contentedly because her devoted guardian would only ever treat her gallantly. For all her defiance, her rebellious streak, she was still a lady of her time, submitting to male patronisation and playing the coquette to her advantage when necessary. The Atkinson case had nothing to do with gallantry. It arose by legal process from a flawed legacy. Anne saw only ruthless self-interest among men driven by greed and united by an intention 'to starve me into despair'.[35]

The conduct of Mures & Atkinson was especially cynical. Losing their ablest partner had left the firm with 'no head, no mind, to direct a set of stupid young men of pleasure who wished to spend without the trouble of gaining'.[36] Negotiations over the next five years only hardened this opinion. The assessment that Anne's legacy from Atkinson plus her bonds in the partnership's hands amounted to £60,000 was a figure that shrank as the troubles of Mures & Atkinson deepened. When it transpired that Atkinson's supposedly unsanctioned stock deal had done handsomely, his partners decided that they deserved a posthumous share of the profit. Years of legal bargaining and whittling led to a compromise when Anne, 'seeing only a life of war before me', accepted £10,000 and a £1,000 annuity.[37] That settlement too collapsed after the partnership was declared bankrupt in 1793.

Even then the wrangle with Atkinson's family had barely begun. In this instance, involving the Jamaica estates, Atkinson had named Anne's brothers Alexander and Robert as trustees with instructions to keep the plantations going 'with the slaves and appertenances [*sic*]' until 1803, when lump sums and annuities were to be paid to his nephews and nieces from the profits. However, the greater authority was vested in Matthew

Atkinson as his brother's executor. What amounted to a conflict of interests was thus not only left to fester for ten years but when it commenced was between members of the Lindsay and Atkinson families. In the ensuing legal squabbles Anne would engage briefly then withdraw, reasoning that she could manage perfectly quite well on what she had.

Whether Anne received any benefit at all from Atkinson's estate in the end is not clear. She stated that she received not a penny, and though there is no reason to disbelieve her, she may have overlooked a small annuity. Atkinson's previous efforts had, of course, transformed her affairs, turning a few hundred pounds into some £10,000 in capital and annuities of £200 and £150, which had been enough to keep her in comfort. But her anticipation of wealth led her into expenditure – maintaining the Manchester Square house and all that went with it, and buying another in Berkeley Square – that she could ill afford and obliged her to seek help from her brothers. She managed but was far less wealthy than the world supposed. The fabulous riches of Lady Anne Lindsay, it turned out, were a chimera.

A similar elusiveness characterised the love that overshadowed everything else in the years after Anne's return from France. She was unprepared, so it came with the shock of another windfall. Feeble wastrels like Wentworth and gamey pleasure-seekers like George Cholmondeley she knew of old. No such venality was evident in Cholmondeley's dashing friend William Windham – and for once her guard dropped.

Windham had become a public figure, as a pall-bearer at Dr Johnson's funeral, as a bright light in political life at Westminster and, dramatically, as an intrepid explorer of the latest science. After he took to a balloon over London in May 1785, his friend Burke wrote: 'Adieu star triumphant! And some pity show on us poor battlers militant below.'[38] Cholmondeley's response to the airborne phenomenon was to lay a bet at Brooks's: 'Ld Cholmondeley has given two guineas to Ld Derby to receive 500 guineas whenever his lordship fucks a woman in a Balloon one thousand yards from the Earth.'[39]

Anne had been intrigued by Windham from the start. Along with the cultured mind and learning admired by Johnson and Burke, he had features romantically scarred by the smallpox which almost killed him on a grand tour of Italy (when he was nursed devotedly by Cholmondeley). 'Apollo Belvedere bent by illness' she called him on meeting him again.[40] With it all he seemed without vanity, describing himself as 'a little of two characters and good in neither: a politician among scholars and a scholar among politicians'. It was as a politician that Anne observed him at the show trial of the day – the impeachment of Warren Hastings.

The return in disgrace of the Company's proconsul in India generated no end of hot air. After generations of ruthless plundering, Britain's rulers had discovered a conscience and resolved to settle their guilt on one man. This convenient tactic satisfied not only the righteous but those more corrupt and less able Company servants who had fallen out with Hastings and were delighted to see him shoulder a charge sheet of peculation and oppression. Among his trenchant critics was Anne's brother Robert Lindsay, who had profited handsomely in Dacca while excoriating 'so corrupt an administration . . . if another Hastings is let loose upon this country we must soon bid adieu to our empire.'[41] Hastings, who can still divide historians' opinions but was among the governors-general to assimilate most closely with India, was made a scapegoat as reformers at home rode a wave of sanctimony.

Hastings's impeachment opened in May 1787. Westminster was turned into a theatre for Windham, Burke, Fox, Sheridan and others to display their oratorical skills before an audience that included the queen, Sir Joshua Reynolds and Fanny Burney as well as Anne and Margaret. Windham, it was observed by Fanny, started out 'with the most palpable tremor and internal struggle', before finding his confidence and ending with the eloquence and fire for which he became renowned.

Anne, with ties on both sides of the debate (Dundas on one, Burke and Windham on the other) found herself uneasy at a spectacle of 'the stag pursued by hounds at Westminster Hall' and was disappointed by the speakers. Burke so roused himself that she was 'reminded of the account Dr Johnson gave me of him. "Burke, Madam, is a lion who lashes himself into fury with his own tail".'[42] Of Windham's speech she observed:

> His countenance shewed his whole soul to be up in arms on principles of offended humanity . . . the harmless old begums massacred for their treasures, their children thrown into dungeons, the harems violated, the poor starved to enrich the dependents of the Governor-General.[43]

Irony remained her first line of defence: but when Windham approached her in a black mask at a Soho masquerade, her resistance wavered; and once he came calling at Manchester Square it collapsed altogether. Here at last was her idea of a lover. Many years later, she could still write:

> Let those who know what elegance and intellect are, feeling and honour, ardour and eloquence . . . Let those who remember where they have seen them most united, and then think of Windham. His view of life, tho' shaded with melancholy, seemed to be so benevolent, his humility tho' undue yet so attaching and so unlike the presumption of others who had less reason to be vain, that there was a serenity conveyed to my heart in having found what it had scarce ventured to hope for, that becalmed every agitated feeling, and made me see happiness in prospect at last.[44]

With happiness in prospect at last, she plainly felt able to contemplate marriage as well.

10

The Weathercock

1787–1791

The mistress of Manchester Square was transported by Windham's visits. She would await his knock in the evening and go down to find him in the drawing room, arms folded and imposing, whereupon conversation would open with the persona who happened to be calling that night – the man of letters, the man of the world, or the man of dreams. And she surrendered. Whoever the individual of the moment might be, here at last was a suitor who seemed 'more formed for domestic love, and all the calm enjoyments of intellectual and happy existence, than any person I had met'.[1]

The world at large thought them suited as well. Both were thirty-seven, Windham the older by just a few months and plainly destined for high office in government, both brilliant in their own ways, a couple with liberal ideals and high expectations. Even some who did not understand or necessarily approve of them thought it a good match. 'I hear Lady Anne Lindsay is going to be married to the eccentric Mr Wyndham [sic],' wrote Fanny Burney to a friend. 'His choice suits that character.'[2]

In tête-a-têtes 'over Newton or Politics or Euclid' – or Windham's ancestral home of Felbrigg Hall, which inspired him to poetical descriptions of nature and the birdlife of Norfolk – Anne grew blithe. Months 'flew by on downy pinions and the great question Will You? and the next great question When? were according to my procrastinating genius felt as matters of no consequence while I saw him contented and living for me only'.[3] So the months turned into a year, and though Anne remained confident, sure it could only be a matter of time, she must have noted how Windham's oratorical brilliance at Westminster was qualified by his reputation for prevarication. Not for nothing was he known as 'Weathercock' Windham.

The first flush of her exhilaration is visible in the revitalised figure she presented in public, a lady defined less by her quirky dress sense and humour than assurance and a mature bloom that attracted men younger as well as older than she. 'Handsomer than ever,' Alison Cockburn, her old Edinburgh tutor, thought. A new acquaintance did not stop there, and he was to have a critical influence on the next stage of her life.

Thomas Barnard, the Bishop of Limerick, made an unlikely Cupid. He was devout, hearty, plump, a lover of art and books, member of the Literary Club and one of Dr Johnson's supper coterie at the Turks Head where he entertained the table with his rendition of 'I rage, I melt, I burn' from Handel's *Acis and Galatea*. Anne was introduced to Dr Barnard at the Tunbridge Wells home of Lord North, the former prime minister, who 'put my hand into the bishop's, saying "Love each other, for my sake".'[4] Both were pleased – she to know another of Johnson's celebrated fellowship, he to meet the woman whom her fellow Scot, Lord Mansfield, had called 'the best specimen Scotland ever sent to London'. The sixty-three-year-old bishop joined Anne's circle of older devotees. 'A rose in full blow, in all its glowing brilliancy,' he called her, 'a flower in full perfection.'[5] Early on, it seems, Thomas Barnard identified her as in need of a husband and to consider possible candidates.

Edmund Burke, already a friend, had also become fond. 'You show that good nature is not always at variance with wit,' he wrote after a dinner. 'You make yours the attendant and handmaiden of your kindness. In that place wit will not always be terrible and good nature will never pass for weakness.'[6] Burke was delighted that his friend Windham seemed to have found a suitable mate. Entering a party at Lord North's a few nights later and seeing Anne wearing her favourite star diamond, he came over as Windham joined them. 'Ah,' said Burke, 'I saw the star and was certain the wise men were near.'[7]

But an early sign of Anne's concern that Windham was not moving more decisively can be detected in a letter from the bishop attempting to reassure her. 'I do not say that he will make you happy; but I know of no other man so likely to do it, and I am persuaded he will try. Upon the whole I think he is good enough for any *Other* woman in England.'[8]

Windham's attention tended to wander. His interest in foreign places took him to Europe with a fellow Whig, Sylvester Douglas (better remembered as the gossipy diarist Lord Glenbervie) and he was often away in Norfolk. Returning with 'all the gay spirits of gratitude and love', he would call, describing with renewed ardour 'the scenes of delight Felbrigg would afford, when [our] rambles over the fair face of nature in the morning were crowned by the sweetness of the evening – by music, painting and books'.[9] Still no proposal came, and when Anne took up his allusions to their future 'the rainbow seemed to vanish'.

> He would start from my side to walk hastily thro' the room, sit down and look at me with a sort of pity, calling me by every endearing name, but reproving me for wasting my regards on one in every respect so undeserving of me. 'Oh, say no more of this,' I replied, 'my best esteemed, my gentle Windham. Who can be more deserving than the man I love?'[10]

Vacillation was the hallmark of Windham's political life. After one of his elegant circumlocutions Sheridan called him 'an irresolute arguer to whom it is a great misfortune that there are not three sides to any question'.[11] His indecisiveness was not confined to politics, and in his private life it became symptomatic of a more troubled state. Sheridan touched on the root of the problem: 'Conviction, like enjoyment, palls him.' Windham's reaction against a dissolute age was to distrust pleasure. The exuberant young sportsman had become a hypochondriac who considered abandoning politics because late nights in warm Westminster chambers might damage his health. But it was his soul that suffered most. His friend Sir Gilbert Elliot said: 'He carried hell about with him in his mind.'[12]

Anne's first real intimation of his ills came when Windham broke down and confessed that he had decided to remain single. Smallpox, he said, had left him susceptible to palsy or loss of intellect, conditions so degrading that he would take his own life rather than submit to either. Professing to be full of remorse at having inspired her love, he said he was more in need of a nurse than a wife, warning: 'Cold would be the winter which must succeed to the summer of my Anne with me.'[13] This explanation for his moodiness rendered her euphoric.

> O Windham! Windham! You say you love me ... Lean on me through life. You will find me a faithful friend, a tender wife, anxious to be your solace and comfort through calamity or good.[14]

Such diagnosis was typical. Once again, she had identified and romanticised the figure of a man in need of rescue; in this instance, however, the subject was even more indecisive than she, and possessed of further symptoms to darken the prognosis, for Windham's condition had less to do with his physical than his mental state. He had still revealed enough of himself for Anne to have read the signs. Moreover, he had told her he would not marry, so there was no ground for misunderstanding. She might have accepted what amounted to a rejection, as Atkinson had done. Instead she plunged deeper into a misery which she remained oblivious of having brought upon herself.

Windham's changes of mood were mercurial, one minute 'imploring my pity' as he put his head on her shoulder, the next turning darkly resentful. It took time for the reasons to emerge, but at bottom this was a man who shrank from love and commitment of any kind. His relationships with women in general were troubled. At the hint of an attachment he became unsettled and recoiled. The clearest evidence for this is contained in abusive notes from the later years of their mutual torment when he wrote to Anne of what he saw as the 'unmerciful tyranny' she had once exercised over him. He spoke bitterly of being 'subject to your dominion', and likened her to bird-lime, an adhesive used by sportsmen to trap birds.[15] His petulance would have been ludicrous had it not been so hurtful. 'That a statesman and a patriot should be such a very, very woman!' she wrote in exasperation later.[16]

For the time being she was bewildered but still in thrall. Nearing forty, still desperate to believe she had found the love of her life, she clung to hope.

The political aspect of this attachment placed her on awkward ground. Through her alliance with Dundas, she had associated herself with the rise of Pitt's administration. Windham was still in opposition, a follower of Fox. It did not help that women attached to a politician usually took their creed from him, and because Anne did not make her position clear with a strong opinion on party lines she was, if anything, more open to suggestions of personal disloyalty. Her position seemed more awkward still when Dundas and Windham became not just political foes but love rivals.

Late in 1788 the king went mad for the first time, triggering the Regency crisis. Initially a change of government appeared inevitable as the prince was set to assume the mantle of regent, empowering him in effect to bring down Pitt and install his

favourite Fox as prime minister. Anne tried to bring the prince
and Pitt together, with Dundas acting as an intermediary, and
the basis was laid for a pact.* It did not last. In the ensuing riot of
acrimony, pamphleteering and intrigue, Pitt retained power. Fox
never came as close to it again. The king recovered but the prince
was publicly discredited and had begun his transformation from
beautiful young man to the grotesque of Gillray caricatures.

Anne's lack of guile made her ill-suited for such intrigues.
Real female politicians like the Duchess of Devonshire, Fox's
hostess, and the Duchess of Gordon, entered the fray with relish.
'The ladies are as usual at the head of the animosity,' wrote Lord
Sydney at the height of the crisis. Anne had a rueful admiration
for the Duchess of Gordon, who was not only Pitt's hostess but
reputedly Dundas's mistress, writing: 'She ruled them [both] with
an iron sceptre tipped with beauty and wit sharp as a lancet.'[17]

A second drama opened the following summer and this one
would engage the entire nation for a generation. Four years after
Anne's impish frolic with the governor of the Bastille, a Paris
mob stormed the prison and cut off his head.

The French Revolution was welcomed by many in Britain,
notably Whigs. Fox called it 'the greatest event that ever happened
in the world' and Burke wrote of 'the wonderful spectacle'
across the Channel.[18] Burke soon changed his mind, publishing
Reflections on the Revolution the following year, but Tom Paine's
riposte in *Rights of Man* was the more influential. Anne did not
leave a record of her views at this stage, possibly because they
were nearer those of Fox than Pitt, who was ultimately vindicated.

---

* After a dinner at Carlton House she wrote to Dundas: 'What course would
you counsel me to recommend the Prince to take? He wishes to act dutifully
by his father and to maintain good faith to his political friends. He talks
confidentially to me and not everyone is as disinterestedly his well-wisher as
I am.' Dundas followed up this letter by meeting the prince. (27/2/59, Henry
Dundas to Anne Lindsay, undated [1788].)

Her observations in France five years earlier inclined her to the Whig side and an interest in the Revolution would take her there again with Whig observers. In the meantime, while Pitt adopted a wait-and-see approach and Dundas went off to Scotland for eight months, Windham told Anne he was bound for Paris himself. Four weeks after the Bastille's fall he departed, reassuring her that the dangers to English visitors were much exaggerated. 'I cannot conceive any more is to be apprehended from visiting France than at any other time,' he wrote.[19] Here at least her lover was engaging in a bold quest she could admire.

It seems to have been during Windham's absence that a younger man first appeared on her doorstep.[20] Andrew Barnard arrived with a letter of introduction from his father Thomas, the Bishop of Limerick, and enthusiasm for meeting Anne's well-placed friends. He was an army captain on half pay, just back from Constantinople and Egypt, and called on her often to give accounts 'of pyramids, temples and tombs'. (The bishop's son attended a dinner given by Anne at Manchester Square when other guests included Burke and Sir Joshua Reynolds. The artist had recently painted the Duchess of Rutland and the Duchess of Devonshire, equally renowned as beauties, and Burke was curious to know which he thought the more handsome. 'Do you ask me,' said Sir Joshua 'as a man or as a painter?' 'Reply in both characters, if you please,' said Burke. 'Then as a painter I say the Duchess of Rutland, and as a man I say Devonshire.')[21]

In the weeks Barnard spent in town Anne noted his charm and unworldliness. He had served with an Irish infantry regiment in America and the West Indies where he contracted a fever, forcing him to retire on half pay. The bishop's letter asked her to make the introductions his son needed for a new career and she discerned a potential to work in the diplomatic line. 'If he was not absolutely handsome he was so near to it that to be more was unnecessary. His countenance & his smile had a bond of good fellowship, which attracted the stranger to hook him under the arm and make a property of him.'[22] But there, on his departure to rejoin the bishop in Ireland, it was sure to end. He was, after all, twenty-six and she thirty-eight.

The fact that she was spoken of as a wife for Windham did not deter other men from expressing their interest. Admittedly there was nothing very uncommon in being invited into the bed of Nathaniel Parker Forth, a louche neighbour whom Anne thought both fascinatingly eloquent and 'the most artful, malignant, unsafe person it was possible to conceive', and who had recently departed for France to continue his career as a secret agent.* A marriage proposal from the prince's friend Tom Onslow was as easily dismissed: 'Incomparably dull and very dissipated,' she thought him, 'what was called "a man of honour" but what should be called "a fish".'[23]

Dundas was another matter. The self-serving aspect of Anne's relationship with Pitt's partner has been noted, but it was durable and fond. They exchanged confidences and trust, and Dundas had come to see her as a companion with the grace to polish his own rough, clumsy manners in public. Although he had been in no hurry to remarry after divorcing almost ten years earlier, Anne realised he was showing signs of an increasing attachment which, obsessed as she was with Windham, 'it gave me no pleasure to perceive'.[24]

Windham spent a month in Paris – though to judge from the

---

* Anne also became convinced that Forth was the real Junius, the pseudonymous author of letters published in the *Public Advertiser* between 1769 and 1772 consisting of vituperative, some said treasonable, polemics against the king and government. Anne believed she had extracted a confession from Forth that he was indeed Junius, but he may have been toying with her. About sixty candidates for the authorship have been suggested, including Horace Walpole and Edmund Burke. Anne's claims are made in her Memoirs, vol. 4, pp. 24–8.

single entry to his diary on the eve of returning home he had not explored the revolutionary *événements* in any depth. Nor had he ventured to the darker corners visited by Anne. He wrote:

> All the time I had for employment at Paris was occupied in reading and writing French for study. Was unwell for much of the time – the food or the water. My mornings were principally spent with my French master & my evenings at the different theatres.[25]

On his return in September, the old pattern resumed. He embraced her, saying: 'How generously you have acted by me, my sweet Anne.' Visits commenced, endearments and ideas were exchanged. Then, one evening when dinner was set, she dressed, 'tried my new fortepiano, sang my new song . . . Six o'clock struck. No Windham. Then one of his terrible notes arrived. He would not be tyrannised over. "Engagements formed under compulsion ought to be considered of no force."'[26]

The question that arises is perhaps less why Anne submitted for some five years to this manipulative relationship for, like most such victims, she was in thrall to her captor when he wished to be charming, and appeared to have run out of options. Rather it may be asked what provoked Windham to the cruelty of which, in his better moments, he was ashamed. 'Oh Anne,' he would say, 'if you should ever cease to love me, how you will hate me.'[27]

An explanation for this enigma appears to lie in Windham's past, and Margaret may have sensed the root of the trouble. 'Windham is very pleasing,' she once said. 'My only fear is he is a friend of Cholmondeley's.'[28]

The two men had known one another since university, had been love rivals. Yet while Windham was inspired by noble ideals even when he could not sustain them, Cholmondeley was drawn to the dark side of human nature. In their early twenties they mixed with the daughters of a wealthy naval widow,

Juliana Forrest, who hosted parties at her Birdcage Walk house. Windham fell in love with the eldest, Bridget Byng, though she was married, and seems to have seduced her. Another daughter, Cecilia, became besotted with Cholmondeley, a man incapable of love. Windham, frustrated in his love for Bridget, turned his attentions to Cecilia while rebuking his friend for the 'life of vanity and voluptuousness' that caused 'the utter ruin and extinction of her peace of mind'.[29] A conflict between good and evil was intrinsic to their bond, and may even have had the perverse effect of bringing them closer.

Only competitiveness can explain the preposterous proposal of marriage made to Anne out of the blue by Cholmondeley one night in a tone combining threat and bluster: 'Your confiding, unsuspecting mind attaches my malignant nature to it ... You must love me Anne. If you don't it shall be the worse for you.' She gladly accepted the alternative and he stormed from the house.[30]

She came to the conclusion that Windham and his friend were part of a 'school of male coquets'. An anonymous letter had warned her against 'the bad pointers who rush in before the steady dogs and spring the game then turn aside'.[31] But in this case she was mistaken. Whatever Windham's flaws, he was more than a common flirt.

The bond with Cholmondeley may have had a homoerotic aspect to it. Windham had been nursed by his friend with uncharacteristic selflessness during a near-fatal illness in Italy, a complex experience in itself. A portrait of Cholmondeley by Reynolds was placed by Windham in the drawing room at Felbrigg, where it hangs to this day. No such portrait is known of Cecilia Forrest, whom Windham eventually married when they were in their forties, and there were no children.* Whereas

---

* Windham also had difficulties with a doting, manipulative mother. When the elderly Sarah Windham was on her deathbed, she wrote imploring her only

Cholmondeley bedded women wherever he found them, leaving natural children scattered in his wake, Windham had anxieties about his sexuality. Of the surviving entries in his diaries, one scrap is revealing:

> I felt the strong sense of the unhappiness of my own celibacy; that lively conception of the pleasures I had lost . . . Unless I [can] resolve manfully to fight against such images & force my mind from the contemplation of evils admitting no remedy, the most fatal mischief must ensue, both to my happiness and my powers . . .[32]

This entry – made roughly midway through what Anne called 'the period I was held in bondage by [Windham's] pleasing manners, love of power and hesitations' – seems to clarify one aspect of their relationship.[33] Up to this point at least, it remained chaste. Other than this one tortured reflection there is no indication of what made him celibate. A venereal disease such as syphilis might explain it. So might guilt over homosexual longings.

Whatever turned Windham from sex, frustration would help to account for the puerile conduct in private of a man celebrated in public as a righteous campaigner. Anne saw to the heart of the paradox. 'How pleased I feel,' she wrote grimly after a rousing speech he gave to Parliament on the persecution of street traders. 'I hope he will not treat me worse than the hawkers and pedlars.'[34]

Obsession with Windham did bring one accidental benefit. In the summer of 1790, while attending a furniture auction in Berkeley Square, Anne noticed that the upstairs drawing room looked across to the door of Windham's house in Hill Street. As the Berkeley

---

son to visit her. He resisted until being persuaded by Anne, then declined to attend the funeral, saying he had been an unkind son and to pretend otherwise 'would look like ostentation'. The press reported him to have been 'too much affected by grief' (27/4/22, vol. I, p. 129).

Square house was also being auctioned she raised her hand on impulse, and when the price reached £2,600 heard the hammer's knock, followed by the cry: 'Madam, I wish you joy.' Windham wrote a snidely knowing letter of congratulation: 'It is unnecessary to ask whether you like the situation for you would not otherwise have taken it . . . Before long I shall probably be better acquainted with it.' Despite this inauspicious beginning, 21 Berkeley Square was Anne's home in London for the rest of her life.[35]

At the start finances were tight. Expectations of what she and Margaret might receive from Atkinson's will had already been drastically pared down and the unashamedly self-pitying tone of a letter to Windham after she decided not to pursue Mures & Atkinson through the courts is a mark of her wretchedness:

> My hopes of ease are at an end, my prospects closed. I look to the time before me with sorrow and despondency . . . A mind a good deal broken down by disappointment is not the mind fitted for those active exertions so necessary on such an occasion.[36]

Once the sisters pooled resources they were still able to summon something above £1,600 per annum which, as Anne said, was a comfortable independence, even if it left them far shy of their reported wealth. Berkeley Square was among London's grandest addresses, placing Anne on the fashionable side – that is to say the south – of Oxford Street for the first time, with neighbours including her old acquaintance, the ageing Horace Walpole, and the man-eating Lady Jersey, who was about to embark on her most famous affair, with the Prince of Wales. While Anne kept up appearances with servants and a coach, habitual thriftiness drove her to buy furniture at auction and sew her own curtains. One lady was heard to say with exasperation that 'she wished to God those two very agreeable women would leave off being upholsterers and begin to be women of fashion'.[37]

Margaret had always been more the woman of fashion and, after years without male affection, was in a position to remarry. Following their final separation, Fordyce had retired to Feltham where he survived thanks to an allowance from her and mellowed, acknowledging before his death late in 1789 that Margaret was 'a noble creature sacrificed to chagrin'.[38] Among her qualities he cited a refusal

> to take to your bed a younger and more agreeable husband – an event which a woman less virtuous would long ago have anticipated the advantage of and which must have procured the man more envy than all the good fortune in ye world.[39]

Aged thirty-six when Fordyce died, Margaret remained beautiful and esteemed. The last thing she needed was another bad man, but one soon presented himself in the form of Cholmondeley; and because an alarmed Anne felt bound to warn her against him they quarrelled when Margaret shot back that she was in no position to lecture about painful love: it was time Anne shook off Windham's witchcraft.[40] Both were right, but for the first time a distance opened up as Margaret became estranged 'from habitual reference to my counsel'.[41] Margaret's pain at least was not prolonged. Her hopes, such as they were, closed a few months later with Cholmondeley's marriage to Marcia Pitt, who became the first of his three wives.[42]

Word of Anne's misery had meanwhile reached Dr Barnard, the Bishop of Limerick, and it could hardly have been coincidental that his son Andrew Barnard returned to London at the same time as another letter from the bishop reached her:

> May I presume to recommend him to your protection. I know your goodness sufficiently to think you will not be angry, and I am assured at the same time you will not find him an unworthy object of it . . .

Though he has seen a much greater proportion of the world than you have done, I am sure he does not know it half so well.[43]

Andrew became a regular caller, and she promised to mention his name in the right quarters. From her account, she saw herself as an aunt-like figure to a protégé twelve years her junior. As it transpired, the bishop and his son had discussed more than Anne's connections. When she asked Andrew what would make him happy, he said he wanted to marry. Indeed, she replied, did he have someone in mind?

'My object,' said Barnard, 'is yourself.'

Dumbfounded, her first response was anger. 'This is a bad jest,' she said, 'and unlike your usual good breeding and good sense. Let us forget it.' On realising he was serious, she pointed out the obstacles: 'the disparity of years, prospects so fair as his, mine so clouded ... He must allow me to talk as an aunt to him ... Our conference was short and clear.'[44]

Misgivings were natural, for were she to marry Andrew Barnard it must give rise to hilarity. Apart from their age difference, he was an outsider, a junior army officer without distinction or connections. Whatever her eccentricities, she was a high-born woman known at the heart of power, and still widely thought to have inherited a fortune. The fact that Barnard was not only much younger but handsome and charming would add a whiff of salaciousness to the gossip.

Anne perceived the bishop's matchmaking designs and wrote to him, 'For a moment I felt rather a little angry.'[45] Dr Barnard owned up, saying that although he had warned his son against any expectations, 'He knew we [his parents] should be delighted above measure if he succeeded.' At this point the old gallant was roused to his metaphor for her beauty:

You are not a fading rose but a rose in full blow, in all its glowing brilliancy; a flower in full perfection . . . Nor will I grant you the other part of your simile, that you must expect to drop a leaf every day. For the leaves that are the highest ornament of my sweet rose are of the pure amaranthus species that never can decay but remain fixed to the stem till at last the flower itself must drop.[46]

A general perception that the connection with Windham was leading nowhere stimulated another proposal, in the autumn of 1791. She had been invited to join the Glenbervies in Paris, where the National Assembly's constitution was to be presented to the deposed king, and plans for their departure were advanced when she received a visit from Henry Dundas.[47]

Anne knew Dundas wanted to marry again and expected him to approach Margaret. Instead, when she mentioned her intention to visit Paris, Dundas opened his heart – about family, his hopes for ennoblement, and plans to retire in peace and love to the Highlands – before dropping to his knees and declaring that all this could be hers.

Anne's account of the courtship by Dundas bears scrutiny, and some scepticism.* His political power being what it was, she felt able to patronise him without the searing guilt she felt for another man whose love she had turned to her advantage, Richard Atkinson, even though, in Dundas's case, the opportunism was explicit. In acknowledging that Dundas had become 'a hearty patron' for her brothers after Atkinson's death, she wrote, with startling cynicism: 'To lose such a friend in the mischance of becoming a suitor was studiously to be avoided.'[48] If she is to

---

* There are no other sources. While a considerable volume of Anne's correspondence with Dundas survives, it all dates from after her rejection of him. The first of his letters to be found in her papers dates from 1788, so everything prior to that would appear to have been burnt by her. Her letters to him, mainly from the Cape, date from 1793.

be believed (and here she should be) she had had no hesitation in rejecting his physical advances in her drawing room.[49] Yet her claim to have been aghast at his proposal has a thoroughly disingenuous ring:

He petrified me! I had seen vanity in men before and had even observed it in Dundas; but for him to have found anything in my poor manner to build on! With a heart devoted to another! And no sway of partiality to himself except as a friend had I been free, was to me extraordinary![50]

She was unkind too, suggesting that no explicit proposal had taken place, though it is hard to untangle the elements of seduction and courtship from her description of his impassioned plea:

'O, my angel, daut me [fondle me] and tell me you like me as well as I like you, and make me forget every promise and everybody in the world but yourself.' I burst into tears . . . 'O, precious draups,' said he, 'precious draups! If you kent what baum they are to me heart, you would na gae to Fraunce, you would gang to Crieff with me. You will not give up your journey to Fraunce for me, Annie?'[51]

Her reply was that she could not do so. She had promised to accompany Glenbervie's wife, Catherine. Her reply to the proposal was that she needed time to consider. An inner voice was less equivocal: 'Dundas's partiality was of no value from the situation of my heart.'[52]

Her family's reaction was dismay – and not only because of Dundas's influence. Her brother Hugh, who was especially indebted to him, said: 'Windham uses you like a dog, and you use Dundas like one.'[53] Margaret was inclined to agree. 'You are the waxen image which Windham sticks pins in before a slow fire. If you could put him out of your thoughts and be candid about Dundas, you might be very happy with him.'[54]

Before departing, Anne learnt that Lady Glenbervie had decided Paris would be too dangerous for her. Dundas called again, this time with a green box full of despatches about the latest disturbances, urging Anne to stay at home as well. 'France does not know from one day to another what it will be at,' he said. 'A lawless banditti is getting possession of the country.' Anne said she was not afraid. She was to meet friends at a hotel in Paris and would be back within three months. Dundas looked hurt but kissed her hand and said, 'God bless you.'[55]

What she did not tell Dundas was that another traveller was sailing to Calais and would be in Paris as well. Anne had known for weeks that she was to be joined by Windham.

II

A Captive in Paris

1791–1792

Anne left Berkeley Square early on 7 September with Dundas's warning in her ears of the lawless mobs roaming France, accompanied only by her maid Lucy and a manservant. Rather than anxiety, however, she felt free. Partly, she told herself, this was due to relief at having evaded Dundas. It was also the scent of adventure. She was going where the world order hung in the balance, where seven years earlier she 'had seen the fallen Louis and Antoinette in a situation so different', to discover for herself what had become of 'that once polished, pompous, superficial, ferocious country'.[1]

The first phase of the Revolution had brought little radical change to French life. For almost two years, social conservatism prevailed against the transfer of power implicit in the National Assembly's Declaration of the Rights of Man. Louis, although reduced to being 'King of a Free People' and living with Marie-Antoinette at the Tuileries, where they were subject to public scrutiny and abuse, could still command some support. But rage was simmering, notably among impatient artisans and intellectuals who had begun to shout '*Les aristocrates on les pendra*' (the aristocrats will hang). In a panic the royal couple fled for the Austrian border disguised as servants, were discovered and taken back to captivity in Paris.[2]

By the time of Anne's landing at Calais, real change was at hand. The assembly had drafted a new constitution, abolishing titles and hereditary rights, paving the way for a constitutional monarchy. The event that had drawn Anne and other British observers was the presentation of this landmark document to the king for signature. Yet as her coach covered eighty miles in a day to Abbeville without incident, much seemed as it had been. That night she wrote to Fitz from the hotel where they had stayed in 1784: 'If there is private turbulence and evil disposition in the lower classes, it does not appear here.' What struck her about the intervening years was how she had wasted them on Windham.[3]

As they neared Paris the mood changed. Money was extorted by an unruly postilion and a landlady. Sternly Anne reminded herself of a friend's advice, that though she might be in no danger in travelling, there was a danger in being frightened; and she made light of abusive shouts of *'Aristocrate'* on passing through Montreuil. The closer they came to the centre, however, the more hostile were the faces turned to the passing coach. Her irony in describing these events in a letter to Fitz may not have matched her feelings at the time.

> As we drove thro' the Rue St Honore to our hotel, our carriage was so loaded with *Poissardes* who clustered like bees on it that I thought we must have broke down, and it being their practice to extort money from *les gens nouvellement arrives* in whatever manner they think will terrify them most, no sooner did we stop at the hotel than two viragoes got into the carriage, horrible young women with faces of scarlet, their dress indecent and their countenances so masculine that it did not require their beards to render their sex very equivocal.*
>
> They kissed us so immoderately that you (who know what a refractory subject they would have in me) will easily believe me when I tell you that I promised them all the money in my purse if

---

* *Poissardes* were the women fish sellers and market vendors of Paris. It was of one of their protests that Marie-Antoinette was supposed to have said: 'Let them eat cake.'

they would let me out of the carriage and dance for it, an offer they gladly accepted. So throwing the silver and copper I had all over the pavement, I left them fighting for the spoils and taking to my heels ran up the staircase into the hotel.[4]

Aristocrats trembled, naturally, at the spectre of mobs running amok. Yet in this early age of class struggle Anne apparently felt no hostility. Like others of her kind, she treated servants as social and intellectual inferiors. She spoke of her maid Lucy as a child, fearful and confused by what was going on around them, unable to answer her mistress's question whether she felt herself to be an *aristocrate* or a *démocrate*. Anne nevertheless took an interest in her servants, wrote about them fondly and felt a maternal instinct for them, even the miscreants. Lucy's predecessor had been Betty, who 'took to gin and naughty ways' and stole from her employer. Rather than turn her over to the law, Anne dismissed her. Margaret thought this indulgent. When another maid was found to have stolen from them, Margaret insisted that this time prosecution must follow or there would be no end to it. Sarah Gower was duly tried and sentenced to seven years' transportation to New South Wales. Anne wrote directly to Evan Nepean, the Home Secretary, reminding him of a promise given to her that Sarah should be pardoned.[5] In the end Margaret may have been right. While Anne was still in Paris a male servant was found to have pawned some of her diamonds and Margaret wrote: 'He will see Botany Bay. We are grown common hacks of mercy to be ridden to death. The man's life is in no danger.'[6]

Anne had been invited by Glenbervie to join a party of Whig politicians and opinion-formers. The Palmerstons had yet to arrive but on fleeing into the hotel from the *poissardes* she encountered an elderly man and a beautiful younger woman. 'Good God,' she said, 'Sir William Hamilton.'

'Lady Anne Lindsay ... What a *rencontre*. Permit me to present

Lady Hamilton to you. We were married a few days ago.' The former Emma Hart, according to the ambassador to the court of Naples, was not only the loveliest woman in the universe, but an artist capable of bringing alive the statues of antiquity 'without any drapery but a white shawl'.

> 'Without any drapery,' said I mournfully.
> 'I mean Madam, without any unnecessary drapery, but you will see perfection when you see her'[7]

Anne's memoir of Paris in the autumn of 1791 records a world on the brink of momentous change: of English lords, ladies and intellectuals clustered for a moment like an audience at the theatre, mesmerised by events being played out in the National Assembly, on the streets outside their hotels and in their midst. Windham and the Spencers were staying on the other side of the street; the Palmerstons were with the Hamiltons and Anne, and they were to be joined by her sister, Elizabeth, and her husband, Philip Yorke, who had recently inherited the title of Lord Hardwicke. The men had one thing in common, as Whig politicians initially supportive of democratic reform in France but now profoundly alarmed over the course it was taking: Windham, still ostensibly a Fox loyalist, was the most prominent; Anne's brother-in-law, Lord Hardwicke, had already crossed the floor to Pitt. Lord Spencer had embarked on a similar passage and would be made First Lord at the Admiralty; Viscount Palmerston was also to join Pitt. Two sons of the former prime minister, Lord North, were of the party as well.

Emma Hamilton was a spectacle in herself. A former artists' model and plaything of prominent men, she was beamed at and fussed over by a husband thirty-four years her senior who appeared more like a fond uncle than a lover, and whose real passion, for art and Classical antiquities, was reflected in his choice of bride.

Emma gave a performance at the hotel of her 'Attitudes', inspired by Hamilton's collection of Greek vases, that Anne found transporting as she 'animated out of their cold marble most of the distinguished females of antiquity':

> All that a form can combine of beauty, grace, dignity and virtue was united in her, as she passed from innocence to meekness to sorrow, from sorrow to devotion, from devotion to frenzy, to passion, to courage, to envy, hatred &c.

Among the dramas played out in Paris, Anne's as a captive of love might as well have been conducted in public as well. It certainly attracted an audience.

Windham, dapper with a hat and cane, called as soon as she arrived. Anne knew she was already compromised by reports circulating at home 'that Mr W has carried a Mistress abroad'.[8] She no longer cared. From the complete collapse of her sense of propriety, as she allowed Windham access to her hotel apartment at all hours, and her inability to control her emotions, it is clear she was desperate. Among the letters which she preserved as testimony to this fact is her response to one of his frequent bouts of hypochondria.

> O, Windham, why, why most particularly with such a state of health as yours, don't you marry? I know it will be to me like the stroke of death & that by saying what I have said I am doing myself harm; but everything I foresee for you is so full of conviction that you should do so that I must, must preach, altho I should have my hand cut off for it.[9]

She told him of Dundas's proposal. 'I felt it right, I knew it was necessary, and my agitated heart determined to be governed in some measure by Windham's conduct when the chance of losing me came to a point.'[10] Whatever Windham's conduct, her agitated heart was beyond being governed by herself. Over agonising weeks in Paris, his treatment turned from unkindness to a domineering cruelty. She who once had borne the reputation of a heartless flirt had become a victim of emotional manipulation at its worst.

She had, moreover, been deceitful to Dundas in a way that would have shocked her younger self. She was blinded, justifying herself on the revealing ground that 'to tell Dundas that I was attached to another, to his political enemy Windham, would have chilled him not only to me but to every branch of my family'.[11] In fact, almost all London knew of the affair, as Margaret and their sister Elizabeth had pointed out. Even in this state of self-deception, though, she was capable of a certain honesty. 'I have been studying my behaviour,' she wrote to Margaret, 'and frankly I do not admire myself.'[12]

The National Assembly gathered on September 14 for the formal transfer of power from the throne to the people. Observing proceedings from a gallery was the party of British *aristocrates* who gazed down through opera glasses and occasionally turned to Anne Lindsay as one of their number for a translation. An opening motion on whether the assembly should rise for the king produced a vote in favour, though on entering Louis was placed on the same level as the president and presented with the constitution. His own contribution was a brief speech, anticipating a restoration of peace and unity. The assembly resounded to acclamations of '*Vive le Roi!*', a hot-air balloon decorated with tricolour ribbons was released over the Champs Élysées and Paris celebrated with fireworks and public dances.[13]

A few days later Anne saw the royal couple for the last time, at the theatre, and noted Marie-Antoinette's quiet dignity, 'so much to her honour'.[14] Anne never had personal contact with the French royal family and the only time she saw them in their pomp, seven years earlier, had been at a celebration of excess. (Of her visit to Versailles with Margaret she wrote: 'We were obliged to fib and say it was charming or we should have been reckoned Goths.'[15]) She remained nevertheless a thorough monarchist, mortified by the humiliation of the 'prisoner-king' and his wife. Looking down from the assembly gallery, she shuddered: 'Nothing could be more vulgar, ill-looking, mean and worthless than the appearance of the body that governed all.'[16] A few days later she was similarly repelled on meeting that most agile of revolutionary puppeteers, Maurice de Talleyrand: 'His eye was malignant, his smile supercilious, his manners disdainful of pleasing unless he had a purpose to serve by it, and then I was told his powers were infinite.'[17]

These observations were enclosed with letters home. Anne had realised by now that Dundas's feathers were likely to have been ruffled – not least by her open association with his Whig opponents – and, perhaps as a kind of palliative, sent him accounts of all she had seen. His replies were reassuring: 'Never apologise for your billets doux,' he wrote. 'They are always a repast, and particularly so when I am immersed in business.'[18]

On the night of the king's speech, Anne retired to her hotel at the rue Sainte-Honoré. All excitement at the adventure had evaporated, her spirits were low and she went back to Margaret's last letter, urging her to abandon Windham: 'Dearest Anne, be not the Dupe.' Across the top in large letters was written: 'DEMOLISH CARTHAGE!' Anne stoked the fire, slipped into her *peignoir* and had begun a reply when Windham entered unannounced.

Windham spotted Margaret's letter, and recognised the hand.

'Demolish Carthage. I know whose counsel this is. Perhaps 'tis a wise one.'

'Perhaps?' said I faintly, 'are you not sure of it Windham?'

'It takes much to make me sure of what is problematical.'

The tears stood in my eyes.

'Why is this,' said he angrily. 'When people come to Paris it is to be gay and happy.'

'But why people come to Paris at all is a point necessary to be explained ... Be but good-humoured to me while I stay and you will find me as gay and as happy as anybody.'

'Ah! But when there is not a little *salutary pain* inflicted now and then, you forget that everything is not to be your own way.'[19]

Windham faced his own demons. He had recently confided to his diary: 'I tremble lest my powers of thought are not what they ought to be. I certainly have continually most alarming instances to confirm the fears first conceived last summer.'[20] Whatever the causes, he had spells when his perceptions sound unbalanced. A letter to Anne from this time reads:

> My sweet A, you shall be punished, so far as I can pretend to the power, for the unmerciful tyranny exercised over me the last time I was subject to your dominion. Though I am come back from the country I will neither dine with you nor come in the evening.[21]

Later that night Anne resumed her letter to Margaret: 'He has just left me ... He now says I am as unsuited to him as he is to me, and that he would hang himself in a month if he were married to me, such is my anxiety and *exigeante* [demanding] character of mind.'[22]

Windham seems to have taken malicious pleasure in his power. A few days later the third Lindsay sister, Elizabeth, arrived in Paris with her husband Lord Hardwicke, prompting Windham to observe how much she resembled Anne. 'But do not expect,' he added in a whisper, 'that I shall let you make a Lord Hardwicke of me.'[23]

Among a party of about twenty set up in two hotels, they became objects of attention: while Anne's wretchedness was obvious, Windham affected nonchalance, lolling and dozing by the drawing-room fire, reading newspapers. One evening, Glenbervie walked in on them during an intense exchange, embarrassing Windham.[24] When an outing was arranged to Saint-Cloud, he 'said cutting things to me under the mask of raillery to make me cry, then grew angry and hoped I would stay away from the party unless I could behave myself better'. As they walked in the Sèvres factory he whispered in her ear that she was like bird's lime.

> When young Lord Holland good-naturedly came up to say 'What is the matter, have you been frightened?' I hardly dared trust my voice to reply ... Windham seeing I lagged behind came up, 'For God's sake join the herd. You expose yourself.' ... He feared to be suspected as the cause, so he began in a boyish manner to pelt the skirt of my riding habit.
>   'Let her alone,' said one of the young Mr Norths, 'she seems to be in a bad humour.'
>   'Is she apt to be so often?' replied Windham in a careless manner, as if he knew little of me or my humours.[25]

A new pattern emerged. In mixed company Windham 'took the opportunity to whisper in my ear whatever disappointments he meant to inflict, darting away to avoid any explanation, leaving me in a state of despair at the shock and attracting the eyes of the company to her who had received it and to him who had given it'.[26]

In trying to account for Windham's cruelty, Anne told herself it was down to his belief that she had once exerted control over him. Even now she could not accept that what he really wanted was to be free of her and, deterrence having failed, was trying to drive her away. Sex had become another factor. The intimacy of

Despite her social prominence, Lady Anne Barnard shrank from self-display
of any kind and no full portrait of her is known to exist. This miniature
from about 1780, the earliest of the young Lady Anne Lindsay,
is believed to be by Richard Cosway.

Anne's primordial bond with her younger sister Margaret endured through similarly turbulent lives. Margaret was one of the beauties of the age and this painting by Gainsborough was commissioned soon after her marriage to the tycoon, Alexander Fordyce.

Alexander Fordyce by Gainsborough, shortly before wild investments brought ruin upon him and Margaret.

Henry Dundas, 'the uncrowned king of Scotland', saw Anne as a partner in his endeavours long before rising to political eminence beside Pitt the Younger.

The young Anne Lindsay was noted for animation rather than beauty but bloomed in maturity when she had disastrous love affairs with an aristocratic wastrel and a fickle politician, before being courted in her forties by an unknown young army officer, Andrew Barnard.

Maria Fitzherbert was trying to escape an infatuated Prince of Wales when she turned to Anne for help. They travelled together in Europe for almost a year before Maria's return and secret marriage to the prince.

William Windham, eloquent, cultured – and deeply flawed. Anne's misery in loving a politician known as 'the Weathercock' came to a head during their visit to witness the Revolution in Paris.

'The Morning After Marriage' by James Gillray. Anne was accused of fostering the Prince of Wales's illegal marriage to Mrs Fitzherbert.

Andrew Barnard, aged about 44. He and Anne had enjoyed the happiest years of their lives at the Cape when she commissioned this portrait to keep her company at Berkeley Square, shortly before he returned to Africa in 1807.

Sisters at heart: Margaret and Anne had miniatures painted of one another by Anne Mee to wear during the years of their separation while the Barnards were at the Cape.

George Macartney. The first British governor at the Cape supported the Barnards' efforts to conciliate Dutch settlers and preserve peace with the indigenous inhabitants.

Anne was exhilarated by the Cape, her artistic and literary talents stimulated. Within weeks of landing she climbed Table Mountain and drew the descending route of Platteklip Gorge (top). The lovely village of Stellenbosch (bottom) opened the way to the interior.

Mountains drew Anne's eye wherever she travelled at the Cape, as here in the Breede River valley of the Overberg region.

Legend had it that Anne used to enjoy bathing nude at Paradise, the Barnards' cottage below Table Mountain. The artist of this mysterious painting 'Lady Anne Barnard's Pool' is unknown. An inscription on the back reads 'My own bathing place'.

The young Anne Lindsay was noted for animation rather than beauty but bloomed in maturity when she had disastrous love affairs with an aristocratic wastrel and a fickle politician, before being courted in her forties by an unknown young army officer, Andrew Barnard.

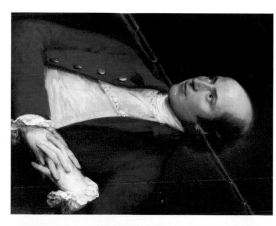

Alexander Fordyce by Gainsborough, shortly before wild investments brought ruin upon him and Margaret.

Henry Dundas, 'the uncrowned king of Scotland', saw Anne as a partner in his endeavours long before rising to political eminence beside Pitt the Younger.

Anne's primordial bond with her younger sister Margaret endured through similarly turbulent lives. Margaret was one of the beauties of the age and this painting by Gainsborough was commissioned soon after her marriage to the tycoon, Alexander Fordyce.

Despite her social prominence, Lady Anne Barnard shrank from self-display of any kind and no full portrait of her is known to exist. This miniature from about 1780, the earliest of the young Lady Anne Lindsay, is believed to be by Richard Cosway.

Maria Fitzherbert was trying to escape an infatuated Prince of Wales when she turned to Anne for help. They travelled together in Europe for almost a year before Maria's return and secret marriage to the prince.

William Windham, eloquent, cultured – and deeply flawed. Anne's misery in loving a politician known as 'the Weathercock' came to a head during their visit to witness the Revolution in Paris.

'The Morning After Marriage' by James Gillray. Anne was accused of fostering the Prince of Wales's illegal marriage to Mrs Fitzherbert.

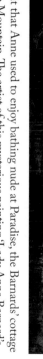

Legend had it that Anne used to enjoy bathing nude at Paradise, the Barnards' cottage below Table Mountain. The artist of this mysterious painting 'Lady Anne Barnard's Pool' is unknown. An inscription on the back reads 'My own bathing place.'

Mountains drew Anne's eye wherever she travelled at the Cape, as here in the Breede River valley of the Overberg region.

Andrew Barnard, aged about 44. He and Anne had enjoyed the happiest years of their lives at the Cape when she commissioned this portrait to keep her company at Berkeley Square, shortly before he returned to Africa in 1807.

George Macartney, The first British governor at the Cape supported the Barnards' efforts to conciliate Dutch settlers and preserve peace with the indigenous inhabitants.

Sisters at heart: Margaret and Anne had miniatures painted of one another by Anne Mee to wear during the years of their separation while the Barnards were at the Cape.

Anne was exhilarated by the Cape, her artistic and literary talents stimulated. Within weeks of landing she climbed Table Mountain and drew the descending route of Platteklip Gorge (top). The lovely village of Stellenbosch (bottom) opened the way to the interior.

the detail Anne gave of meetings in her apartment when she was wearing only a nightdress showed that if they did not have sex it was not for lack of willingness on her part. Such is the point, she appeared to be saying, to which I was reduced. Given Windham's anxiety about sexuality, however, this opportunity represented a challenge. It would seem to have been declined; having suffered for his celibacy, Windham's only satisfaction was a perverse demonstration of his power.

Now Anne 'mixed a little in public but not so much'. At a party given by the British ambassador she revised her opinion of Emma Hamilton's talents when instead of performing her 'Attitudes' she made a stridently discordant attempt to sing.[27] After another gathering the amorous American ambassador, Gouverneur Morris, recalled 'a curious conversation with Lady Anne Lindsay, who is desperately in love with Mr Windham and tortured by jealousy'. He wrote in his diary: 'I tell her that if she wishes to bring back a lover she must alarm his fears and if she chuses to make use of me I am at her orders . . . She says that if it becomes necessary she will apply to me.'[28]

Another of those to witness her humiliation was Glenbervie, looking on 'with silent sorrow'.[29] The youngest Lindsay sister was also present, though Anne rarely wrote about Elizabeth and a thirteen-year difference in age never really dissolved into intimacy. When Elizabeth looked at her older sisters, one a spinster, the other a childless widow, she could only have blessed her own fortune in marrying a provident man by whom she had six children; and Anne felt too proud to confide in her.

Instead she poured out her heart in letters to Berkeley Square. The Hardwickes, she wrote, were about to leave, but she was staying to resolve matters with Windham once and for all. Margaret, who was so alarmed that she 'wept in bed over the state of your mind and your sufferings', had become the one to dispense wise counsel:

Paris is a devilishly bad place for you but if you come home without seeing this matter [through] I know what TRICKS your mind will be at. Besides D[undas] goes to Scotland and will not return till the first week in Novr. You must stay if you do stay with as much propriety as you can. Can't you be ostensibly with the Gibbs? . . . Try not to expose yourself by *manner* to observing eyes.[30]

The climax came when Anne finally posed the questions that she must have known should have been asked and answered years before. Why, she asked Windham, did he continue to see her if he no longer loved her? Did he not realise this was duplicity? Did he not regret the pain he had caused?

'God of Heaven!' cried he frantic with rage, 'are *you* to make a stricture on *me*?'

'I know, I know that you detest me, but why those hard words? It is not manly!'

'No, I do not always detest you, but I sometimes feel sentiments which I should be sorry you knew the extent of.'

'O, for mercy's sake spare me,' said I, and I believe I fell on my knees before him. He moved to a distance and I drew myself to a sofa and sobbed so loud that those in the antechamber must have heard, had not my maid sent [them] away.

'And what is this,' said he, 'but the *hackneyed trick* practised by women who have failed in their aims and resort to this stratagem with their lovers and husbands to carry their point.'

I looked at him. 'The hackneyed trick?'

'Yes,' said he, 'the hackneyed trick.'

'Go!' replied I. 'This is not the language for you to utter or for me to hear.'

'There now,' cried he gaily, 'this is the right way to treat me. Keep to this.'

'Go!' said I looking at the door. 'It is time.' Already he had returned thrice.

[184]

'Yes, Madam, with all my heart (taking his hat) but remember this must be *final*.'

I saw he expected to be called back, but he was not, and he took his departure after lingering a long time in the antechamber . . .

A different set of impressions at last forced their way to my heart. Grief was over; a deep and calm resentment took its place. I determined that the rupture which he bade me was to be final should be so.[31]

On her announcing that she was leaving as soon as horses could be arranged for her post-chaise, Windham tried to dissuade her. For the first time she rejected him. 'I have been here much too long, and I am sensible of it.'[32] He insisted. He would join her the following evening for dinner. She told him to do as he pleased.

Four days brought her to Calais where she was pursued by a letter that casts further light into the corners of their mutual torment. Offering compliments upon what he called the 'performance' of her departure, he wrote:

> So brilliant an achievement atones for a multitude of sins. I cannot say that it atones for them altogether. It is not my way to give you unmixed praise; but it atones for a good many . . . Nothing ever succeeded more effectually. I called faithful to my promise on Saturday evening and when the answer was given of your being gone, understood it so little that I concluded you would return.

Instead, he went on, he had spent an evening with one of Paris's most exotic mistresses, Madame de Souza, 'the pleasantest I have had here', and that very night was to join another flamboyant creature, Madame Gilbert.

> Such is the gay life we lead here! How could you be so cruel as to leave it? I am afraid however that I must do so too ere long, and then the return of Lady Anne Lindsay about a week or so before that of Mr

Windham will with some degree of ease be construed into coming together. It has been said in London that we have been at the same hotel . . .[33]

Taunts so mocking to the remnants of her dignity steeled her. Advice from Glenbervie added to her resolve. 'Who marries the person beloved?' he asked. 'None. We marry virtues, qualities, affections, duties. Close the connection with Windham. It will be a fruitless one.'

Some years later she wrote bitterly: 'I look back with astonishment, I could almost say with contempt, at my own patience.'[34]

A week after leaving Paris, and in the gloom of a November evening, Anne's chaise pulled up in Berkeley Square. Margaret was away, their friends were out of town, and pain returned in force. She was resolved, but found it hard to go out among mutual acquaintances without meeting Windham. She may have submitted to the compulsion, noted in some dependents, to cast herself in the path of her obsession. One evening she called on the now-exiled Madame de Souza at her lodging in Half Moon Street, and tapped at the bedchamber door – to have it opened by Windham. While madame was in bed with a headache, he offered a hasty explanation that he was there as an apothecary administering bark.* Anne claimed to have left 'with a portion of disdain more calculated to brace the resolutions of my heart'.[35]

For much of 1792 her spirits were as bleak as the news from

---

* Madame de Souza, also known as Madame de Flahaut, went on to make a name for herself as an author, her first novel, *Adèle de Sénange*, being published in London a few years later. Anne did not mention this success, perhaps affected by the combination of disapproval and envy she felt for women novelists, preferring to recall the service she had rendered in comforting '*la petite et charmante comtesse*'.

France, where the mob was closing in on the prisoner-king. Windham continued to vacillate over his political loyalties, prompting the Duke of Portland to declare that he 'should be glad to hear Windham argue the points of every question, but when an opinion was to be given, he should wish him to go downstairs'. Finally, after the massacre of the king's guards in August, Windham turned his back on the Whigs and crossed the floor to Pitt. In the war cabinet he would join Dundas, an instinctive enemy. The only thing the two men had in common was Anne.

Dundas, despite what would have been seen as his own public humiliation, gave no sign of offence at the reports from Paris and, without making mention of Windham, resumed his courtship. Sitting on her sofa, he admitted having considered a proposal to Margaret, but went on, 'I always loved you Anne, and admired you.' When he was called away by the mounting demands of state affairs, he left with declarations of love: 'Adieu my Angel, adieu my bonnie, bonnie laumb! Till the day after tomorrow . . . I canna do without a sight of you longer than that.'[36]

Theirs would never have been a love match. Dundas wooed her because he needed a refined wife who would move naturally in the circles where he was still liable to appear something of a misfit. But with Windham gone, she had to consider her position. 'One great perfection [Dundas] had which everyone allowed him,' she noted, 'he was constant in friendship if not in love.'[37] What further recommended him, of course, was his power to confer favour on the Lindsay family.

For once she turned to one of her brothers for advice. Charles Lindsay was alone in having opted for the Church over the army, navy or East India Company, and his detachment from worldly ways qualified him as a disinterested counsel: Dundas, he said, was an 'honest Jupiter' and in their divorce had treated his adulterous wife with uncommon kindness. But as for marriage, Charles went on, 'I can see no reason why you should sacrifice your comfort for a good to be purchased for your family.'

> What! Are we then to receive a benefit wrung from your heart? No, my dear friend, we must not give you up so easily. You have already done more for your family than any Honest, Single Woman ever did before.[38]

What Dundas called Anne's 'inflexible reserve' kept him at the other end of her sofa until his patience ran out. While electioneering in Scotland late in 1792, he drank a third bottle of claret at a country ball and proposed to, and was accepted by, Lady Jane Hope, a sister of the immensely wealthy Earl of Hopetoun. 'My heart suffers nothing,' Anne wrote to Margaret.[39] Perversely, Dundas's engagement may even have given her a stronger claim on his loyalties. Although far too proud to admit regret, he later told Anne his impulsive proposal to Lady Jane had been 'mad'. They remained friends and allies. Of all the men in her life, Dundas stands out for his unruly maleness, a figure to be respected and, because of his authority, sometimes feared. 'There is nothing so whimsical as the masculine heart,' she wrote of him, 'except the feminine one.'[40]

Her candour in setting down these reflections bears re-examining. By then Anne was an elderly widow, thought by family to have married beneath her. The purpose of revealing her obsession with Windham and rejection of Dundas was to justify the mystery of her life: what had possessed this woman of title and talent to prefer a nonentity to two of the leading men of the day? Decades on, she wanted to show what she had been saved from. Yet the details she gave of the climax to her torment with Windham, the account of her degradation 'over the years I was held in bondage by his pleasing manners, love of power and hesitations', is still an extraordinary outpouring. At a time when literary legacies were almost invariably pruned of anything too close to the bone, hers could be utterly raw.

Of Windham she wrote: 'What were we? Two persons carried on by our foibles, one to be ungenerous, the other to be unhappy.'[41] To this she appended 'The Rose and the Thorn', a poem with echoes of her best-known work. But whereas the subject of 'Auld Robin Grey' was Margaret's doomed marriage, this thirty-six-verse lament points to her own suffering and ends with the death of the subject, a country lass named Annette. It concludes:

> Hard by the Rose there grows a Thorn
> The last blooms sweet, but fruits – oh never!
> The other buds each May's first morn
> Then withers, droops, for ever, ever.

Anne was a product of the Romantic age, in literature, philosophy and art, and her writing may have brought some painful release. If she had suffered, she had known the exhilaration as well as the agony of love. There, however, it was bound to end. Marking her forty-second birthday that December, she would have expected to spend her remaining years in solitary reflection, writing by the fire when she was not painting or sketching.

Six weeks later Louis went to the guillotine and the world was transformed.

12

'A Blackguard Lover'

1793–1796

The thud of the guillotine in Paris on 21 January precipitated what has been called the first total war. For Britain, consequences ranged from the threat of invasion to financial turmoil, from the introduction of income tax to the militarisation of citizens' lives. Radical libertarianism was stopped in its tracks, as was the brand of feminism espoused by Mary Wollstonecraft in her 1792 book, *Rights of Woman*. At the same time Britain's empire advanced to a new corner of the globe, carrying with it a middle-aged woman on an adventure. If few at the time grasped the scale of this revolution, fewer still looked on 1793 in a positive light. For Lady Anne Lindsay, however, it counted as 'the year of my escape from captivity to a land flowing with milk and honey'.[1]

The onset of the Revolutionary Wars brought political foes in Britain together. While the Francophile Fox blamed Britain rather than France for the failure of peace – as he continued to do even after Bonaparte's rise – his failure as a leader was manifest and his influence declined. On the heels of an agonising rupture with Burke, he was deserted also by Windham and another of Anne's companions in Paris, the Duke of Portland.

Windham persisted in calling at Berkeley Square despite being refused entry several times. When he wrote in aggrieved tones Anne agreed to see him, more out of *politesse* than anything else, but made sure she had other visitors as well. The visits soon ceased.

The exit of one lover from her drawing room was followed by

the wedding of another. When Dundas married Lady Jane Hope in April it appeared that Anne had lost the last two men in her life almost simultaneously. In fact, their departures cleared the way for a third who had been biding his time, and now saw his opportunity.

Soon after Dundas's wedding, a letter reached Berkeley Square:

> I was in the hope this morning My Dearest Friend that I should have had the good fortune to have found you at home and alone ... but Alas! on coming to your door a frightful Chariot stopped the way. It was Sir William Fordyce who I concluded would be a long visitor.

Andrew Barnard had returned from Ireland some months earlier. Anne's efforts to find him a position had been unsuccessful and while thankful 'for the many & repeated acts of kindness I have received from you', he told her the war had resolved him to rejoin the army. First, however, he alluded to his proposal two years earlier when:

> I found a person possessing of every Charm, both of Person and Mind. To her my heart fell a Willing Sacrifice and I disclosed my sentiments, *but Alas!* hers did not coincide with mine and my suit was rejected, but in such a manner that so far from cooling the affection I felt for her it was redoubled and her Kind and Endearing conduct to me since has augmented to such a degree that I now feel the Cruel Necessity of Banishing myself (as much as possible) from her presence lest I should at some unguarded moment be guilty of a Second Breach and lose her Friendship for ever. This is the true reason why I wish to go abroad.
>
> On my knees I entreat you to forgive me writing you this letter ... I do not ask you to commit your sentiments on this subject to Paper, but I request five minutes Conversation with you.[2]

Whether this letter came out of the blue is not known, but the intent was clear. Anne's reply brought Barnard back that same evening. As he explained it, he was in debt and his only alternative to military service was marriage to a fortune: a widow with £3,000 a year, Mrs Orby-Hunter, had hinted to his father she would be happy to accept him; he preferred the army, despite the prospect that poor health would kill him before the enemy. Unless – and he dropped to his knees – 'there is a chance for me still'. Again, Anne faced a choice:

> When I reflected on the suffering of my past life, and the little probability there was of my future one being happier, every feeling in my nature cried, 'Pause on the awful question which must decide your fate.' That moment's pause decided it.
>
> 'Do not go abroad,' said I, 'do not marry Mrs Orby-Hunter. I will stand the world's smile, and if a very inferior fortune to what she offers will make you happy, I am yours.'[3]

In that moment, after twenty-six years of prevarication since receiving her first proposal at sixteen, having attracted innumerable admirers, more than twenty serious suitors and at least eleven more proposals – twelve if the first by Barnard is included – Anne finally cast hesitation aside and in an act of pure spontaneity ended her single state.

Or so she wished to portray it. Clearly, though, Barnard had never disappeared from the scene. Anne would still have had his first proposal in mind when she was trying to help his career, and the letter cited above – the earliest of his to survive – plainly heralded a second. Having dwelt in her memoirs on Windham's cruelty, she passed swiftly over her acceptance of Barnard, then went on to emphasise how she had been vindicated. Both treatments were to explain what had puzzled her relatives – why she had rejected (as they believed) two of the most eminent men of their day for an unknown junior army officer burdened with debt. And being inhibited by decorum, she could not spell out exactly what it was that made Barnard so attractive – his youth and handsomeness.

Barely had she reflected on her rashness than she saw how it would strike others. She spent the next few days dashing off letters to forestall the shock that must follow. As she anticipated: 'The world will probably think me absurd.'

To the Prince of Wales her tone was light-hearted: 'I am about to resign a liberty which I have hitherto most cautiously guarded.' A previous proposal, she went on, had been declined as 'Mr Barnard happens to be considerably my junior'; but, referring to a mythical source of rejuvenation, 'no Medea's Kettle being at hand to boil me younger' she had accepted a 'man of worth and principle'.[4]

When it came to Windham, she could not refrain from a last tirade. She was, she said, 'sheltering myself in a port secure from misery, where no kindness or coolness of yours will reach … But away with reproach. *I have found my reward!*' In fact, she was not done with reproach, and had to go back to what she saw as Cholmondeley's toxic influence.

> I think you have lost as much thro' him who perverted your mind first as I have done … But of this no more. Pardon me for having said so much … It wrings itself from me and is *the last triumph you will ever receive* … Adieu! While you continue the favourite of the public I shall wish you well without vivacity.[5]

Altogether more simple and collected was her response when Windham asked to see her. She refused.[6]

The family's reaction seems, on the whole, to have been less critical than she feared. Her sister Elizabeth actually sounded a note of enthusiasm. 'I have seen goodness and steadiness in none of your lovers but in Barnard,' she wrote. 'Barnard loves you. He knows his own mind.'[7] On the other hand, Alexander, the head of the family, would have nothing to do with Barnard and remained unreconciled years later when, as governor of Jamaica, he refused to help him find a post.[8] Otherwise, there may have been a general sense of the relief expressed by Anne Keith, who wrote: 'You had been so hard to please that I grew frightened.'[9] Her mother's crisp opinion was that the match was 'not brilliant' and Barnard was too young. 'But one cannot get everything ... I had too many superfluous years in my husband [and] that did better than expected.'[10]

Of most importance, naturally, was Margaret's response, and from her few surviving words on the subject she was cool to start with. 'He has seemed much more amiable to me during the past four letters than before,' she wrote cautiously.[11] Barnard reached out with heartfelt condolence on the death of Margaret's favourite brother, Colin. 'My dearest sister,' he wrote, 'altho' you have lost one brother dear to you, let me be your brother in Love and not in Law only.'[12] Although Margaret warmed gradually, she mourned the loss of her lifetime soulmate and, behind a flippant reference to what she called 'my widowhood', some of their friends thought her envious of Anne's happiness.[13]

Lady Anne Lindsay and Andrew Barnard were married at St George's, Hanover Square, on 30 October 1793. She was just short of her forty-third birthday, he was thirty. It was a simple affair for a few family members, the ceremony performed by her brother Charles and with Anne being given away by Hugh, youngest of the Lindsay boys. The couple left London afterwards for a few days with the Hardwickes at Wimpole Hall.[14]

They did not linger. Anne anticipated that society's verdict would be damning and the Barnards were to withdraw to Ireland for the winter. They had barely departed when her critics in London alighted with relish on the morsels served by a sensational new book.

*

Lady Anne Barnard never had any doubts about what she called 'the saddest and apparently the silliest, but in reality *the wisest act of my life'*. Reflecting on the husband who brought her adventure and fulfilment, she went on: 'Sweet, Amiable Man! His peculiarities were almost invisible to the eye of an attentive wife. Yet he had some!' And so it proved.

Along with charm, the virtue that best summed up Andrew Barnard was warmth of heart. That was the opinion of many, including Margaret Coghlan, his mistress and mother of his first child. 'From him,' she wrote, 'I have uniformly experienced every kindness that the tenderest affection could bestow.'[15] A courtesan who had been used and abused by lovers from New York to Dublin and London, Margaret knew something of men and – in her racy memoir – owned up to having taken advantage of the one she called 'Captain B******'.

> His fortune could not keep pace with my former extravagance . . . I should have been spared the suffering I have undergone if he had possessed the power . . . [but] his finances could by no means keep pace with the liberality of his mind.[16]

Mrs Coghlan, as she was better known, had reason to extol her former lover's virtues (and exploited his generosity even more than she admitted) but her words chime with what others had to say of him. Anne recalled of their first meeting: 'His countenance & his smile had a bond of good fellowship, which attracted the stranger to hook him under the arm and make a property of him.'[17] Further evidence of Barnard's winning ways comes in a rare burst of affection from Anne's mother after the wedding, addressed to 'My Son, my dear son Barnard – and it gives me much pleasure to call you so.'[18] (The chilly old dowager came over quite giddy about the Barnards, father and son, referring to the bishop as 'my Lover'.)

For Anne he reserved a loving eloquence she had never heard from a man before. Shortly before the wedding he wrote:

You can neither expect Rank or Riches with your husband but a Heart you shall have, and I will say a Heart that Shall Study Night and Day to Please and Make You Happy. I write this in strong characters that what I now say may be imprinted on your memory and may appear in Black and White against me should the smallest change arise in my conduct towards you ...

It is you alone I want to possess and not a Fortune ... All I ask of you, and which I trust you'll grant to no other man breathing is your Heart. Such a one as yours would be a Fortune for an Emperor ... My letter will be too late for tonight's post if I don't conclude. My Diamond, my Pearl, then be a Good Girl until I come to you again.[19]

How much they confided in one another before the marriage about the darker aspects of their respective pasts is unclear. It is unlikely Anne was a virgin. Despite Windham's battles with celibacy, he may have been a sometime physical lover, as was Wentworth. 'I had two lovers,' she wrote later. 'The name of each began with W. Indecision governed both, the one allowing others to argue him out of his happiness, the second reasoning himself out of it.'[20] She fretted over whether she ought to tell Barnard about Windham's power over her, and was encouraged by her brother Charles.[21] When she raised the subject of previous lovers, however, Barnard said: 'It would hurt me if you were to ask me anything of the past.'[22]

Concerns vanished in the consummation that followed in Ireland. Anne's introduction to what she called 'that land of social hilarity' passed in disordered dinners and carefree dancing, with companions less correct than agreeable, and always hospitable. From Dublin the Barnards moved to St Wolstan's, a former priory ten miles away owned by the bishop, where Anne wrote: 'I found myself welcomed as the Queen of Sheba might have expected, all the inhabitants opening their arms to receive me, the old servants grinning with satisfaction and every dog wagging his tail.'[23] It was a blissful spot for a honeymoon, a large house and well-kept grounds on the banks of the Liffey. She wrote to a friend:

> I have the bank, the river, the cascades, the summerhouses all before me, not the sleepy, dull old river called Father Thames, not the drunken, boisterous, galloping rivers of our Scottish mountains, but a pretty sort of cantering river which sports without roaring & contains plenty of good Salmon & other fish.[24]

Andrew was 'gay as a lark' during the day and, although Anne did not exactly say so, warmly physical at night. They were – he said in a typically disarming letter to a friend – among those 'married people unfashionable enough to sleep in the same bed', and made this clear when asked for their preference as guests.[25] Also revealing are his surviving letters to Anne. (For while naturally inclined to purge the record of their intimacy, she was constrained by devotion to his memory and wrote on a folder of his letters: 'I have burnt many but I *cannot* burn all.'[26]) Andrew would talk of 'when the Pot Boils' as an indication of passion: money did not matter so long as the pot boiled when they were together; Anne adopted the term, remarking of an amorous young couple: 'I fancy there is enough to make the pot boil together.'[27] The Barnards' physical relationship is directly addressed in Andrew's letters during separations, when he spoke of home as 'that beautiful and enchanting retreat called Cuddle Hall'. In another, he wrote while off on a hunting trip:

> How do you sleep? I wanted a Certain Something which I cannot now do without. My case here is desperate. Poor Bonny [a dog] is my only bedfellow and she is a bad substitute.[28]

They also shared an earthy sense of humour. Enclosed with the letter was a surprisingly funny drawing of a hunter firing a gun and farting simultaneously; a bird lies expiring beneath the fart with a caption: 'An improved method of shooting game with a Double Barrel.'

It had taken forty-three years, but somehow – after the grim adolescence at Balcarres, the rebellion against a loveless marriage, after the frivolity and loneliness when no man seemed trustworthy and only Margaret returned her love, after torment with Windham and resigning herself to spinsterhood – she had found desire and affection, amusement and a human touch. Andrew shared her joy. 'Anne,' he said to her one day, 'am I married? They tell me I am, but I fear you are only my mistress.'[29]

'How easy it was to render such a man happy, and how sweet was the task of doing so,' she reflected. Blitheness accounts for her reluctance to disturb sleeping dogs. 'I never once asked the question of where he was going, or where he had been. If he told me, I went on with the subject. If he did not, I checked the wish to learn, whatever it cost me.'[30] Even so, some secrets were always going to come out. A return to England was in hand when word reached them of a book entitled *Memoirs of Mrs Coghlan*, just published in London and relating the writer's escapades 'with a series of lovers'.

Mrs Coghlan had met Andrew Barnard about ten years earlier, at some point between her liaisons with Charles Fox and an assortment of titled libertines. As she explained it, after a spell of the high life with a house in Grosvenor Square, she had been passed around the friends of Thomas Pelham-Clinton, the Earl of Lincoln and, on being cast aside, was left with serious debts. Naturally she was delighted when, after she fell pregnant, her new lover, Captain Barnard, accepted the child as his. Curiously, though, when the boy was baptised on 31 December 1786, it was as Henry Augustus Hervey. The surname belonged to another of her lovers.

To do her justice, Mrs Coghlan was exceedingly grateful to Barnard, who 'at once administered to my wants and cheered my sorrows', and who dismissed the advice of those who said she was misusing him.

> The excellence of Mr B******'s heart was my security against those frivolous and ungenerous excuses which, in the hour of adversity it has been my lot to receive from so many others ... He would not consent to abandon me so these cruel efforts of my enemies ended in disappointment.[31]

But, as she also acknowledged, the unworldly Barnard's pocket was far from adequate to her needs; her debts mounted and she moved on to other lovers. While he had met Lady Anne Lindsay, Mrs Coghlan by her own distinctly chaotic account of events had been in flight from creditors, had given birth to their child during a two-year spell in debtors' prison and had written her story in the hope of raising £400 through 'the Gallantry and Liberality of the British Nation.' The two-volume *Memoirs of Mrs Coghlan* were published in 1794, and won instant popularity as a picaresque romp, the adventures of a real-life Moll Flanders.*

---

* Margaret Coghlan, the daughter of an army officer, Major Moncrieff, was a child of the world, born in America where he was on service in 1763, but educated in Ireland. On returning to America she came to know leaders of the War of Independence, notably George Washington. She was forced into marriage at the age of fourteen with John Coghlan, another army officer who was a midshipman on the *Resolution* during Captain Cook's second voyage to the Pacific, and whom she described as a 'brutish, unfeeling tyrant'. She blamed Coghlan for introducing her to 'libertines and women of doubtful character' in New York, where her career as a courtesan began. Her book won a large American readership and she was cast as a beautiful revolutionary spy in an early American novel.

One upshot was that while the Barnards were off enjoying love in the country, London was reading Mrs Coghlan's account of the kindly Mr B******'s recent union 'with a lady who, I am told, possesses every virtue & every accomplishment to secure his happiness'. The narrative proceeded with just a hint of threat:

> Let me, however, indulge the hope, without wishing to strew the thorns of jealousy or discontent on her bridal pillow, that he will never *utterly* neglect his *former* friend – the *mother* of his *children*! If I am rightly informed of Lady A***'s character, she is not the woman to encourage a dereliction of those duties.[32]

It is by no means certain that Barnard was, in fact, the father of either of Mrs Coghlan's two children, the second of whom was seemingly conceived while she was living in France. This would not be the only point on which the memoir plays fast and loose with fact. Even her authorship of parts is open to question. The racy if haphazard narrative is interspersed with articulate polemics against overbearing aristocrats and in favour of revolutionary change, and given the author's self-proclaimed intimacy with Fox, 'an ardent lover and liberal benefactor', and Richard Sheridan, these radical hands may have been at work. In any event, Barnard accepted paternity of two boys. What became of Margaret Coghlan thereafter is unknown.

Anne's feelings about her husband's indiscretions are not recorded. But there was nothing rare about those termed natural children other than their fathers' willingness to accept responsibility for them: it was said every fifth child among the London gentry was illegitimate; and Anne was too forgiving and too much in love to resent imprudence in Andrew's former life.

What they had intended as a few months in Ireland turned into a year. The publication of Mrs Coghlan's memoir may have played a part in this extension, although Andrew also used the time to test whether he could turn the bishop's gift of the £1,000 living from St Wolstan's into a livelihood. It was not a success. Between Andrew's large debts and extravagance – which kept his thrifty wife on edge while he was busy 'planting and building new barns and cottages for his labourers till he had not a guinea left' – it became apparent they could not manage in Ireland.[33]

Anne returned to London to hear she had degraded herself by marrying a man whose youth and want of position defined him as an adventurer. Andrew, who had stayed to settle his affairs, soothed her: 'Never mind them Love. Our meeting again will give the Lie to anything they may say.' Her 'despotic husband', would soon return to 'Cuddle Hall . . . where he has passed the happiest hours of his life'.[34] But the sneering did not pass. Anne wrote to Margaret: 'A band of people [have] cruelly treated Barnard as a blackguard.'[35]

Andrew wanted employment. 'Your fortune, my Love, shall be all your own,' he said. 'What I can muster shall be yours also.'[36] The fact was, however, that without her fortune he was lost; and without her influence he would not find a post. Meanwhile his debts had grown, obliging him to sell his captain's commission. Fortunately, her house so rashly bought in Berkeley Square turned to their advantage – and made a property developer of Anne when she had a second built on the same land: 'The one to inhabit, the other to sell.'[37] Such practical economics did her no good with the likes of Lord Glenbervie, whose opinion was always coloured by disapproval of her needs-must ways, and who threw up his hands at the 'buying and renting of houses', which made an 'inveterate jobber' of her.[38]

Who among her former friends treated Barnard as a blackguard she did not say, but from the silence that falls on her memoirs as to social activity it seems Lady Anne Barnard was not as welcome a guest as Lady Anne Lindsay had been. A cheerful exception was Sir Horatio Mann, who combined love of cricket with an egalitarian spirit and welcomed the Barnards to Linton House, his country home, where Andrew could indulge his passion for hunting and shooting. Anne's long friendship with Edmund Burke found a late if melancholy expression in letters after his son's death left him bereft. Otherwise, gaps in correspondence are further suggestive of a degree of social isolation in the years after her marriage.

Another old friend was heedless of niceties, and despite a distance from Henry Dundas since rejecting his proposal, Anne had been assiduous in sustaining that connection. This proved prudent, for Dundas now held in his hands the destinies of not only her brothers, but her husband.*

That genuine fondness endured between Anne Barnard and Henry Dundas is a tribute to her charm and his gallantry. For one so powerful and masculine, he showed generosity remarkable in a rejected lover. She was duly grateful and in years ahead served him dutifully, not least as a source of intelligence. But she could be tiresome and demanding as well.

In petitioning for Barnard she demonstrated both vulnerability and cunning. At first she professed to harbour no great expectations of what they might expect: 'Place him in *Any* office, no matter

---

* Dundas was closely involved in the fortunes of clan Lindsay at this time. He appointed Alexander as governor of Jamaica, where resistance to slavery was on the rise. Rarely was Anne's judgement – 'I think he will make a wise and temperate governor'– wider of the mark. A protest by freed former slaves known as Maroons was badly handled, leading to a rebellion, brutally put down using hunting dogs. Alexander justified himself on the grounds that French agents on nearby Saint-Domingue would exploit the unrest but he then outraged his own military commander by reneging on a promise not to punish the rebels with deportation. In one of his rare letters to Anne, at the end of the campaign in April 1796, he adopted a tone both crowing and defensive. 'My success has been compleat, not a rebel is left in the country, they have to a man surrendered and the value of property is at least 20 per cent enhanced in consequence of an internal tranquillity being fixed which never heretofore was the case.'

how *little salary*, in which he may have something to do & prove himself useful,' she wrote to Dundas. 'He wishes to attach *himself* to *yourself*.'[39] From that point she veered from chatty to cheeky, from humble to insistent. One appeal, soon after her marriage, was nothing short of presumptuous:

> You owe me some Happiness – in Truth you do – pay me by making me the means of serving a man who has rebuilt in a considerable degree what tumbled to its foundation.[40]

The trouble was that in the secretive and underhand world of Georgian power play, Barnard had little to offer. He was, it happened, loyal, honest and capable as a diplomat, but had no real accomplishment and was every bit as artless as his country pursuits and affectionate nature (which embraced horses and dogs) would suggest. Dundas, shifting with an iron fist the pieces of a global struggle in which he perceived rightly that Britain's colonies, trade and sea power would be critical, had little time to bother himself with the fate of a former infantry captain. For more than two years after their marriage he was impervious to Anne's pleas.

Even after British ships carrying troops appeared off the Cape of Good Hope, in June 1795, the Barnards had no immediate anticipation of change. An expedition to secure the sea route to India by seizing this Dutch settlement had long been contemplated but launching an invasion across the world was a protracted exercise. It took five months for its success to be confirmed and another year passed before a civilian administration was appointed.

The first hint of a Cape posting was made by Dundas to Anne in the spring of 1796 and, reading between the lines, she was petrified. Three of her eight brothers had perished in the imperial adventure: since James's death at Cuddalore, Colin had succumbed to injuries on military service and William had drowned at St Helena. A fourth, John, freed from years in a Mysore dungeon, still languished among lower-ranking officers in India. Barnard had never fully recovered from his West Indies illness and what his post would be was not spelt out, other than some role in a colonial regime of indeterminate longevity. Anne's tone turned to caution but she was anxious not to offend their benefactor: 'While I see [Barnard] delighted by the idea of this new Territory, I cannot help saying that *I* should be much better contented with a very inferior employment at home ... Much is not necessary to content me with respect to emolument.'[41]

No new offer had been forthcoming when she called on Dundas a few weeks later. His home in rural Wimbledon was an unofficial war office where William Pitt was a regular guest – the prime minister had his own bedroom – and coaches streamed in procession up the drive to conferences which proceeded for days on end. Anne, in hope of seeing Dundas 'at leisure, to ask more questions', managed only to corner him briefly and was told Barnard's position would be as secretary to the governor. She confirmed that if this were the only post on offer, she would go with him.

> Though sick at sea, cowardly, and not quite young enough to think a new climate very safe, I am ready to put on my cork jacket for his advantage.[42]

'Good God!' cried Dundas. 'You go to live with the Hottentots?'[43]

It did not quite end there. Anne wrote another long and, to Dundas's eyes, exasperating letter, raising questions over Barnard's status. How would the secretary stand in terms of patronage? Was it true, as she had heard, that he would be no more than a clerk? His salary of £3,000 per annum was doubtless a handsome one, but Margaret had told her it was inferior by £1,000 to similar positions in India. So she went on, suggesting 'we talk the secretaryship a little more fully over', then retreating: 'You have but to send Mr Barnard & me *Where* you please, *Whatever* situation you offer & in whatever line, we shall accept & *follow up your views* to the best of our powers.'[44]

Dundas's patience had run out. If Anne was indeed willing to 'live with the Hottentots', well and good; but, he added in a curt note, there would be no negotiation over rank or patronage: 'If you put these questions to me with the knowledge of Mr Barnard, you had better advise him to resign the situation.'[45]

Anne was hardly contrite. If she had used the term patronage, she wrote, it was out of carelessness. Such power would obviously be superfluous at a place like the Cape 'unless we were to patronize the Ostriches and Elephants'. Why could Dundas not just have 'scolded me kindly, telling me how abominably in the wrong I was, without writing me this cruel letter?'

Repairs were made at what Glenbervie called 'a sort of Cape Dinner' given by the Barnards for Dundas a few weeks later. Glenbervie was a candidate for the governorship, as was another guest, George Macartney, the frail but doughty veteran of various colonial expeditions, notably a trade embassy to Peking and a four-year spell as governor of Madras. Happily for the Barnards, the choice fell on Lord Macartney. A member of the Literary Club, he was also an indefatigable traveller, entirely without airs, fair-minded and unusually honest for an East India Company man. He liked Barnard; and he was half in love with Anne.

Her own willingness to go to the Cape was exceptional, and it placed her among the ranks of those intrepid Scots who joined the global diaspora – and, moreover, as a woman of rank. A new age was dawning that ushered in aristocratic proconsuls, such as Lord Wellesley at Calcutta; but their ladies avoided sailing across the world in dangerous and insupportable conditions in order to live in sweltering hellholes. Lady Macartney would no more go to the Cape than she had gone to Madras; but in Lady Anne Barnard the governor would have a titled and witty lady to act as his hostess.

Anne would also have a maternal role. In three years of marriage she had failed to produce a child and, at the age of forty-six, she was unlikely to do so now. All the while Andrew had been providing for his son Henry, or Fitzroy as he was known. Here, it seemed, was an opportunity to bring them all together as a family:

> I felt it a duty I owed to my kind husband, who forgave me for having brought him nothing of our own, to propose to let me carry the boy along with me. The offer was accepted with gratitude.[46]

The year of 1796 closed in a flurry of preparations. The Barnards were leaving behind debts, disapproval and the Berkeley Square houses – which had been rented by an Ottoman bey – and were doing so in some style. Having been warned that luxuries were not to be had at the Cape, Andrew stocked up on English beer and porter, good claret, madeira and port. As well as the post-chaise Anne had acquired from the Duke of Queensberry (or 'Old Q' as he was known), Andrew took 'a good collection of saddles' along with dogs and guns. Anne had her own priorities: 'Sauces, liqueurs, sweetmeats, pickles, stationery, botanical apparatus for preservation of flowers … six dozen Windsor Chairs, without cushions, their legs made to screw off … a large collection of Staffordshire ware … a noble collection of glasses, lamps, shades, bedsteads.' Equally indispensable were her *portable library* and the plants and fruit trees given to her by the royal botanist, Francis Masson, including new varieties of strawberries and gooseberries.[47]

How much space the Barnard's baggage left in the hold of the Indiaman *Sir Edward Hughes* for anything else is not explained, though it may be added that at the last minute Andrew was told

Start of the journey – Anne's drawing of the coach setting out for Portsmouth

his favourite horse could not accompany them.

Bad weather at Portsmouth delayed departure by a week – long enough to bring a laughing Andrew to their lodgings under the cover of darkness one night after evading arrest over a £75 debt. Fortunately, a good wind was sweeping down the Solent and on the morning of 4 February, Captain James Urmiston called, requesting them to board in time for dinner. The *Sir Edward Hughes* would sail at dawn with the *Britannia*, the *Chichester* and the *Trusty*, a fifty-gun man of war taking Lord Macartney.

Anne was hoisted over the side in a ship's chair and entered the tiny wooden space that passed for luxury in an Indiaman's passenger quarters, wearing a miniature portrait of Margaret around her neck. Separation this time would be across hemispheres, and whatever else fate held in store they would not see one another for years. Both had had miniatures painted by an emergent young woman artist, Anne Mee, to keep close by their hearts.

Anne kept also a farewell letter from Margaret as a benediction, an avowal to pray constantly rather than just when she was unhappy.

God bless you, my dearest and best friend that I ever had, or ever can have ... To Him, my beloved Anne, I recommend you all with the most pious wishes of my mind. The day is calm enough to make me feel you may sail tomorrow. Once more, May God Almighty Bless You![48]

PART THREE

13

A Cape of Hope

Life at sea was no cruise for passengers in the eighteenth century. A voyage to the southern tip of Africa took around three months, India twice as long, and both involved conditions no civilian embraced without close reflection. Apart from the dangers of shipwreck and capture, sailing on an Indiaman meant confinement for a hundred and fifty individuals in a wooden shell fifty paces in length. Lord Macaulay thought it unmatched for creating close friendships or deadly enmities. In so limited a space there was no escaping one's fellow humans, with the consequence that, 'the great devices for killing time are quarrelling and flirting'.[1]

Andrew and Lady Anne Barnard occupied one of the half-dozen or so cabins in the stern, looking out from a gallery on the sea, high enough to stay dry in rough weather. But the *Sir Edward Hughes* had twelve other passengers sharing these quarters and an area on the quarterdeck above – a dining saloon known as the cuddy, and a common room across the stern, the roundhouse. The Barnards' retreat measured about ten feet by twelve, with room for a table, sofa and two separately slung cots of green canvas, from which Anne looked across to Andrew, 'a young Neptune hung round with seaweed'. She liked also to stand with him at the quarter gallery of their cabin, gazing out to sea, 'which seemed to be full of fiery sparkles as we went through the water, like those which issue from a smith's forge, or what we see in a sheet of paper after it ceases to flame'.[2]

*Moonlight on the Atlantic. After her initial dread, Anne found sea life
'full of interest and amusement'*

Harmony was less easily maintained in the roundhouse where
idleness and gossip, gambling and heavy drinking could give rise
to the kind of disputes that led to duels. The *Sir Edward Hughes*'s
passengers were a relatively composed company, not least thanks
to the diplomatic talents of Lady Anne Barnard, first lady at
the captain's table. Among the rest were General James Hartley
and Colonel James Lloyd, and though army officers often made
difficult companions at sea, this pair were forbearing and hearty.
Five other women included Elizabeth Barnard, a young cousin
of Andrew's who was joining them in the hope of finding a
husband at the Cape. All might have gone along smoothly
enough but for Captain Donald Campbell and Mrs Campbell,
his status as port captain of Table Bay being sufficient to make
her in particular inclined to impose her contrary opinions and
company on others.

Anne made it quite clear she was a coward, moving Captain Urmiston to reassure her that whatever the dangers of storms, their speed would enable them to outsail any enemy. By the time they entered the notorious Bay of Biscay, she had sufficiently found her sea legs to watch the men dance and run out the guns. Just as she was noting in her diary 'the Bay has behaved civilly to us and shall never be abused in my company', the wind came on to blow.

After the first night of being cast about, the furniture flying and the dogs howling, she confessed her dread to Barnard who for once told her sternly not to be a fool, the wind was merely fresh. Six days later, he admitted it was 'hard weather, my Anne'. She had not stirred from her cot. Beyond the quarter gallery, seas rose in mountains, burying behind them the ships in their wake. All four vessels had lost rigging, the *Chichester* masts as well. Anne reflected: 'To undress was impossible. I cannot help feeling a greater honour in the idea of being drowned totally undressed than in being drowned decently clothed.' When she did undress it was to note that she had been left 'pyebald with bruises'.[3]

With a fair following wind, passengers could venture out again on the quarterdeck in the evening, and now with a sense of awe.

> The Firmament full of stars . . . the Stupendous Ship with all her sails up, raising her proud head to the God under whose care she moves . . . Stupendous to my eye, but what an atom to his![4]

A ball was staged under an awning on the quarterdeck with music from a hand organ and a fiddler. Anne and Captain Urmiston set the pace, and at the end Andrew pronounced it a fine amusement, with pretty women, good music, plenty of spectators 'and instead of having 20 weary miles to go home after it, we were advancing in our journey all the time'. Food was another unexpected pleasure.* The Barnards had excellent appetites and the dining was of rare quality for an Indiaman. Geese and turkey as well as pork were still being served weeks into the voyage, though Anne was not taken with shark, which she thought 'an oily, hard fish' and ate merely to say that she had done so, rather than being eaten *by* one. General Hartley astonished the table with intelligence that the creature's fin was thought a delicacy by the Chinese when 'stewed in strong gravy till quite glutinous and transparent'.[5]

Anne and the general established a warm friendship. A veteran of India and voyaging to the Eastern Seas, Hartley was a modest, informed companion who answered her keen questioning about culture and faith in the land where he had spent most of his life. Already she was responding to the exotic world that awaited. She cheerfully warned Andrew that if he left her a widow, 'I mean to accept of the General – perhaps to propose to him myself.'[6] For his part, Hartley wrote to her just before his death in the storming of Seringapatam two years later that, after their months at sea, he could happily say there was not a woman 'who unites with so much good sense those accomplishments & sweetness of disposition which Your Ladyship so eminently possesses'. No one was 'better qualified to enliven [the Cape] and make it pleasing to its inhabitants and visitors'.[7]

As weeks passed, life at sea took on its own rhythm. Anne never quite got her bearings as to navigation but was intrigued enough by the ship's progress to make her own copy of the logbook, illustrated with sketches of their shipmates. Onboard society, the seamen's world, intrigued her. One day, observing a

---

* Anne described the inaugural dinner for fifteen on the *Sir Edward Hughes* as follows: 'Pease Soup; Roast Leg of Mutton; Hog pudding; Two Fowl; Pork Pye; Stewed Cabbage; A Ham; Potatoes; Mutton Pyes; Two Ducks; Mutton chops; Corned Round of Beef; and an enormous Plumb Pudding'.

lascar in obvious misery, she asked the surgeon what ailed him. Lascars were Bengali Muslim seamen and it transpired that after being mocked by other hands for eating pork in his soup, the man had tried to hang himself. Anne offered him gingerbread and two oranges, and was relieved when he ate them, peel and all. So remote did her fears of seafaring now seem, she pooh-poohed the opinion of Dr Johnson, that a ship was 'a prison with a reasonable chance of being drowned'; in fact, she went on in anthropological vein, 'I should not care how long my voyage was to last, there is so much interest and amusement in the novelty of a sea life.'[8]

When discord arose it concerned the Campbells. He bristled with everyone besides his wife, before whom he quailed. She carped and sniped, and from her cabin was heard to abuse and beat her maid 'with such a volley of oaths as petrified the quiet men of the cuddy'. All the while 'the General smiled slyly, and locked himself in his own arms, as old bachelors do when they hear things going forward that lead them to congratulate themselves on being out of the scrape'.[9] As the voyage went on, however, Anne's concern became the boy she had accepted as her own, Andrew's son.

To another age, Henry's turbulence seems natural. He had been given up by his mother, passed from hand to hand (quite where his childhood was spent is not known) and was now quartered with other boys sailing across the world. Aged just ten, he was bound to feel bewildered. At the start Anne had been full of optimism, but she was ever too inclined to blitheness; and she had taken on the role of surrogate mother aged forty-seven without experience as a parent. Her charge turned boisterous, then surly. He spat in the face of a black lad, whose dignified response impressed Anne as 'an instance of pride founded on the *Rights of Man*'. He climbed over the side and, when Andrew remonstrated, lost his temper. He wished, he said, to fall into the sea and drown. Challenged to repeat this unutterable sentiment, he was beaten – father and son both being left in tears. Anne insisted there was nothing dishonest about him and thought 'tenderness and reasoning' the way to redemption. Barely had he put his arms round her neck, kissed her cheek and raced off than he was brought back, having become violent again. Opinion in the cuddy was that unless sent home to school he would be ruined. Anne's response reflected her own experience of childhood. No faith was to be put in reformation 'worked by flogging, hypocrisy and fear.'[10]

They had run far south down the Atlantic – one day covering just fifty miles from noon to noon, another 230 miles with white foam churning at the bow – when, at dawn on 3 May, a servant called urgently at the door. 'The land, my Lady. The land appears at 14 leagues distance.'

Precisely three months after the Barnards came on board, the *Sir Edward Hughes* anchored in Table Bay. Among the casualties of the voyage was one of Andrew's dogs which had gone overboard, and the last of Anne's strawberry plants had expired, 'a great mortification, as I know not anything after men, women and children I love so much as a large fine strawberry'. But here and now . . .

> What do I see? . . . is it the vision of a painter's fancy? . . . or a poet's dream? The sun is conquering the mist and the Lion's Head appears . . . The Table Mountain, its neighbour, flat as a board, is covered with some of its purest damask . . . The New World opens itself to my view.[11]

A few weeks after coming ashore, Anne stood on a plateau 3,500 feet above the sea gazing out from one of Africa's wonders, across Table Bay and down the Cape Peninsula to where the Atlantic and Indian oceans meet. Having just clambered up a ravine to reach the top of Table Mountain, she was warmly complimented by her companion, the geographer John Barrow, on her traversal of an especially daunting spot, 'across which a deep rugged stratum stretches'. Surely, Barrow said, Lady Anne

Barnard was the first of her sex to climb the mountain. It was a pleasing notion, but one she properly refuted.[12]

'I must tell you a little about this expedition of mine,' she wrote home. Having been unable to obtain any information about the mountain from the inhabitants – who 'consider it as next to impossible to get to the top *as an excuse for their own want of curiosity*' – she had spoken to Barrow, who was 'just one of the pleasantest & best informed & eager minded young men in the world about everything', and they had set out on a morning in June with two other companions and bearers carrying cold meat and wine. In this, the earliest of her despatches, she invites her readers to observe her there at the top, still red-faced and perspiring, her bodice set off with a pair of Andrew's trousers belted with cord and rolled up to her ankles, then wandering off on her own, gripped by the spectacle and the mountain itself, 'this immense mass of stone rising perpendicular on poor Mother Earth who groans, but bears it without floundering'.[13] From a case she took her pencils and paper and began to sketch the panorama below, the lower mass of Lion's Head which, from up here, she thought resembled little more than a molehill. She dug up bulbs and plants, and popped them in a jar slung around her shoulders. Finally, she handed out bumpers of madeira to Barrow and their companions, an army colonel and a surgeon, and urged them to a rousing chorus of *God Save the King*, before beginning the descent down Platteklip Gorge by sliding from rock to rock on her bottom.[14]

The Cape of Good Hope brought Anne the happiest years of her life. She never ceased to say as much, and her letters, her diaries and journals – even her drawings – sing it. She fell in love with what she saw as a new America, and if that was part of the love she enjoyed with Andrew it is still clear that their happiness flourished in this bizarre, magnificent space because it offered freedom of a kind unavailable at home. Africa took Anne back to the innocence of childhood, wandering in an elemental place almost like the girl who once rode a pig at Balcarres. More significantly for historians, it renewed her creativity and curiosity, stimulating her to anthropological, botanical and zoological observations in much the same way that the wider world did the scientific recordings of male travellers. Andrew won respect as an honest, conscientious colonial official. Each found the roles, the activities, for which they might have been formed.

Anne's first despatch to Dundas set the tone. The Barnards' social circle consisted of army and navy men who, having seized the colony two years earlier, sneered and sniped incessantly at the Cape and its Dutch inhabitants. True, she observed, the price of food was high and there was a lack of entertainment. So she set out to impress Dundas with the prospects for improvement. More than two centuries on, her words have the resonance of prophecy.

I like the Cape & see much of the disgust with which it is talked of by others as arising out of their own acid humours . . . I know that I have a natural disposition to pick out flowers amongst weeds if I can, but independent of this being the turn of my mind, let us look at the facts.

Here is *a divine climate*, at least I have found it so . . . . a clear pure, yet not sharp air, full of health and exhilaration to the spirits. Here *is* scarcity, but here *will be plenty*, I am convinced when the harvest comes round – which quickly follows the sowing here, at least a 3rd quicker than in England . . . The features upon nature's face [are] magnificently strong – I love these bold strokes with which the Almighty has separated the dry land from the sea in his chaos. The Bay opens beautifully at the foot of the mountains, while the Hottentot hills [Hottentots Holland Mountains] at 20 miles distance rise in forms so stupendously eccentric that I look at them with admiration every time I see them.

It is in the power of activity & taste to make this the finest scene in the world by planting. I have but little of either but if I was only sure of living a couple of hundred years to see the effect of my labour I would begin to plant tomorrow with alacrity . . .

> I will do as much as my *private* purse can fairly do for *publick* spirit, but a great deal I can't, unless I can persuade others to do so too.[15]

Twenty years earlier the economic sage of the Enlightenment, Adam Smith, had described the discoveries of the Cape passage to the East Indies and of America as 'the two greatest events recorded in the history of mankind'. Trade from India and China had been the making of British prosperity and – as Dundas perceived – the consequences of the Cape falling to French hands would have been calamitous. The Dutch had used these sheltered bays as a refreshment station for their own Indies trade for 150 years, but in the words of a perceptive navy officer, Captain John Blankett: 'What was a feather in the hands of Holland will become a sword in the hands of France.'[16]

At this point the Cape was seen purely as a stepping stone to Eastern riches. That it could have potential for settlement, or that southern Africa itself might yield riches, were not even contemplated in London. Among those to make such suggestions, however, was Dundas's lady informant. She told him that Barrow was off to explore whether the interior might contain 'a good silver or gold mine'.

> Of the first there is no doubt of there being several & containing a much greater quantity of silver than there is to be found in any of the mines we have in England. I hear also there is gold. If we could pay off our paper debt with some of this & hand you over some to pay off your national [debt] it would be pretty.[17]

Over the next five years, Anne wrote regularly to inform Dundas of what she termed 'every point however minute which regards a publick concern'.[18] She was as good as her word. Of these letters, nineteen fall into the category of what could be called despatches, and even that does not adequately describe the length and detail of the most extensive: four are of between 4,000 and 6,500 words, one is 9,000 words, and two of her expositions run to more than 10,000 words each. How closely they were read by Dundas who, with Pitt, was in effect running the war against France, is unknown. He rarely replied and when rebuked by her for his silence responded that 'to write on Publick subjects you know is out of the question'. Only after the peace did he write: 'Your letters were real and original sources of information to me.'[19] At the time, validation came from his wife who told Anne: 'Mr Dundas says he has more knowledge of the Cape from them than anything else.'[20] Influencing government policy was, perhaps, beyond her capacity. But while her letters kept the Secretary of State for War informed (and amused Jane Dundas 'more than any book I have read on the subject') they stand the test of time mainly for the perceptiveness and vividness of the writer.*

Two weeks after landing, the Barnards moved to the Castle of Good Hope with Macartney. Here, in the seventeenth-century Dutch fortress serving as the governor's residence, Anne commenced the activity for which she became celebrated – as the hostess who kept guests charmed, amused and informed, and challenged those who ascribed to the view that the Cape was 'the cussedest place ever found, nothing good in it and even the hens [do] not lay fresh eggs'.[21] And because the Cape was now a port of call for officials and merchants, soldiers and nabobs, sailing to and from Calcutta and Canton, Bombay and Madras, there were a good number of visitors to be entertained.

---

* A detailed résumé of the contents is beyond the scope of the present volume but *The Letters of Lady Anne Barnard to Henry Dundas 1793–1803*, acquired at auction on behalf of the South African Library and published in Cape Town in 1973, established Anne as a figure in South African history in a way that continued to elude her in her native land and gave rise to further publications there of special interest to historians, *The Cape Journals of Lady Anne Barnard, 1797–1798* and the two-volume *Cape Diaries of Lady Anne Barnard, 1799–1800*.

Possibly more important, Anne believed, was making herself agreeable to the original colonists. The Dutch naturally saw the British as invaders and with few exceptions adopted a 'sulky and ill-affected attitude'. Setting out the stand she and Andrew would adopt, Anne wrote: 'We never despise anybody, which I perceive has been one great error in some of the English.'[22] Their initial line of contact with the Dutch was Willem van Rijneveld, the fiscal or treasurer of the old colony, who retained his role under Macartney and became a good friend to the Barnards. Their success, however, and that of the first phase of British rule at the Cape in general, was attributable to the governor himself.

George Macartney's experience of foreign lands, from Russia to China, the West Indies to India, made him sensitive to established customs even as he was setting in place reforms consistent with British rule and necessary for prosperity.[23] His approachability surprised the colonists who – in line with their experience of the military – had expected him to be severe and withdrawn. There were those among a conservative population who objected to the relatively liberal regime imposed on them. There were also those who were glad of progress, and individuals who had cause for gratitude, such as one petitioner, William Palm, who was allowed to have his child by a slave woman baptised after being refused by the Dutch.[24] Of all the issues facing the new administration, none was more challenging than slavery.

Race was as inescapable a feature of the Cape as the landscape. The pastoralist Khoikhoi – the 'Hottentots' seen by early European visitors as irredeemable savages – had in large part retreated with their cattle to the interior, although some racial mixing had taken place with Dutch settlers. Other indigenous inhabitants, the Bantu-speaking Xhosa, remained by and large hundreds of miles up the south-eastern seaboard. A census conducted in 1798 put the colony's white population at around 21,000 with some 26,000 black slaves, many imported from Mozambique and Madagascar.

Cape Town itself was estimated to have a population of about 6,000 settlers and 12,000 slaves. [25]

Anne's first glimpse of slaves had been on their arrival, walking from the quay as a group 'returned from 7 or 8 miles distance, loaded each with two bundles of sticks slung across his bare shoulders'.

> It made one sigh at first. The only comfort in looking at the weight of the bundles was that one of them only was for the master, the other was for the private benefit of the slave. [26]

Some reforms were in hand, notably abolition of the Dutch East India Company's methods of torture and execution, which included breaking on the wheel. But Anne lamented that under the terms agreed at the surrender there would be 'no change in the Slave laws tho' they were eminently necessary, & no rules to defend the Hottentots from the oppression of the boors [i.e. Boers, a reference to the frontier Dutch]'. [27] At the same time, she accepted the status quo in so far as slavery was concerned. The Barnards' apartment at the Castle hosted 'a great many people who eat and drink with us in a family way', and on finding that if she wanted a cook she would have to buy one, did so – then felt revolted at having 'bid for a fellow creature'. [28] She hastened to assure Margaret that, in Cape Town at least, slaves were comparatively well treated, like servants in Britain but without freedom of movement or pay.

It was also the case that the colony was dependent on slaves for cultivation, especially after the army and navy added some 10,000 to the number of mouths to be fed. Against a background of rising parliamentary support at home for abolition, Macartney wrote to Dundas that he had allowed the sale of 200 slaves, with an assurance that, 'as [they] are brought from the short distance of Mozambique and Madagascar, they have to encounter neither the hobgoblins of the Middle Passage nor the scramble of a West

India market'.[29] This number was still far too few for the Burgher Senate, which represented the colonists' views and protested when Macartney banned further human imports. More strenuous objections to reform came from the tough frontiersmen who farmed outlying districts. They had rebelled once before against their Dutch East India Company rulers, and the prospect of another insurrection became clear when a ship was intercepted in August with arms for a troublesome cabal in the most distant station of Graaff-Reinet, some 420 miles to the north-east. Food remained scarce and Macartney trod a fine line between 'the subsistence of the people committed to my care' and what he termed 'modern philosophy'.[30]

Macartney, unfortunately, was never going to be an enduring presence at the Cape. Infirm and subject to crippling gout attacks, he had made it clear he would stay only until the structures of government were firmly in place; and he had Dundas's agreement that if his health deteriorated he could return home. Part of the success of his eighteen-month administration is attributable to his fostering of the talents accompanying him, among them his personal secretary, John Barrow, a self-educated man of humble background whom he had taken to China. Barrow was despatched to explore the interior and report back with intelligence from Graaff-Reinet. He would go on to fame as a travel writer, an ardent promoter of exploration and co-founder of the Royal Geographical Society.

The governor's official secretary and more recent protégé also flourished under his avuncular patronage. Encouraged to express himself, which he did with growing confidence, Andrew Barnard started to show abilities that cast the image of a sensitive but rather ineffectual man in a new light. His papers suggest a tireless appetite for work, a willingness to accept responsibilities beyond the usual office of secretary and utter contempt for corruption.[31] His bond with Macartney was exceptionally warm and it endured.

A few months after their arrival Anne remarked that it appeared Andrew loved the governor as well as he did his father. 'I wish he *were* my son!' Macartney burst out.[32] For the time being, and as a little company, they enjoyed a harmony found in few colonial administrations.

The Castle's bastions enclosed the sole preserve of luxury at the Cape. Here stood the governor's residence, entered from a raised balcony set off with columns and classical embellishments like icing, which led into a grand hall sixty feet in length and a forty-foot drawing room. Luxury was still a relative term in the formidable pentangular fortress which Jan van Riebeeck had started to build in 1653. The striped yellow wallpaper was dirty and peeling, the damask curtains were faded, the furniture and chandeliers chipped. On climbing to the apartments above real grandeur emerged – not of a man-made kind, because diminutive, whitewashed Cape Town resembled 'an encampment rather than a town ... [it had] no edifices, no squares, no publick buildings and the roofs of all the houses [were] flat'. Majesty at the Cape was only ever to be found in the landscape, and here the observer looked out on Table Bay and back to the immensity of Table Mountain, Lion's Head and Devil's Peak; and because the sun blazed out of a clear sky more often than not, the entire panorama was lit up, presenting itself boldly in blue and granite.[33]

To start with the Dutch were suspicious of the hostess who represented a hostile nation and was not even the wife of the governor. Little other diversion was to hand, however, and once the first lady had recruited regimental carpenters to knock up sofas to loll on, and half a dozen black fiddlers to dance to, colonists flocked to the Castle where they joined 'poor ensigns and cornets as well as the generals'; and because the Dutch ladies were known to 'love dancing or *flirting* still more', Lady Anne Barnard's monthly balls and parties led to a palpable improvement in bilateral relations, in the form of marriages between eager-eyed young British officers and local Dutch girls. When curmudgeonly colonists objected to fraternisation, their wives were able to reply that because Anne was so attentive 'they could not be other [than] civil to me in return'.[34] Reports of her success elicited letters from friends at home: 'Every account confirms what we who know you foretold – that you are the Support and Life and Spirit of the whole Colony,' wrote Jane Parker.[35]

The vividness Anne brought to the Cape is apparent too from the impression she made on visitors. She had shown winning ways at home, but London was full of hostesses and the most influential were not always the warmest human beings. Here, when fleets came to anchor bearing distinguished guests, they landed to be met by a shining face and an unexpected wave of kindness, humour and intelligence. Visitors would be invited to share the Barnards' apartments in the Castle, despite Macartney's advice that they were under no obligation and might be making a rod for their own backs. Among her earliest and most appreciative guests was Lord Mornington.

Mornington – Richard Wellesley, older brother of Arthur, the future Duke of Wellington – was the Governor-General designate of India, bound for Bengal, a figure of pomp and circumstance who appeared with his brother Henry, pleading for rescue from the bugs infesting his ship. 'I will be docile and grateful, and will not tease you with the wife and children I have left behind me,' he insisted.[36] They ended up staying for two months.

Wellesley was a rake who flirted when unable to philander. One of his disingenuous notes home to a jealous wife reads: 'I am staying with Mr Barnard whose wife, Lady Anne (who is very plain and 45 years old) is one of my oldest friends.'[37] To Anne he wrote: 'I continue to be ready to fall at your feet whenever you chuse to shew me their beauty.'[38]

There was purpose to her hospitality. Supplementing a network of powerful or useful friends had become second nature. But Anne could not have been half so well liked had she been a straightforward opportunist. Richard and Henry Wellesley were seated at feasts that became as renowned as her dances, though with up to 150 guests they severely stretched the Barnards' pockets. She had always been fond of food, a pleasure she shared with Andrew, and believed if she had a lasting reputation at the Cape it would be as 'a prodigious great Gourmand'.[39] She liked her wine too and became an ardent advocate for the local grape, despite the disdain of grandees like Wellesley. 'I never saw the force of prejudice more apparent than in the way our countrymen turn up their foolish noses at the Cape wines,' she wrote home. 'Mr B drinks nothing else himself, tho' we have every other good wine at table.'[40]

The connection with the Wellesley brothers was sustained. Richard became an informative correspondent, keeping her abreast of events in India and, therefore, as a link in lines of communication connecting Calcutta with London. He gave her news of his younger brother Arthur's early battles with the Marathas before it reached Henry Dundas and did so, moreover, in gossipy letters full of bawdy and vulgar jokes.[41] Anne tailored her style accordingly. As has been pointed out by Antony Robinson, who edited her letters to Dundas, she adopted different personas for her correspondents: to Dundas she was a familiar as well as an informant; with Macartney she was witty but respectful; with Wellesley she would indulge her mischievous side while flattering his surprisingly fragile ego.

They continued to exchange confidences after a scandal over his mistress in Calcutta, which led ultimately to the breakdown of his marriage.[42] His wife Hyacinthe was one of those aristocratic women who had chosen to remain securely at home, with the consequent infidelity that Anne saw as almost inevitable. Had she 'shewn that *lovely daring* which would have transported my Lord', all might have been well.[43]

*

Between parties and playing hostess, Anne filled the hours when Andrew was working with what she called 'my occupations'. Pen, pencil and brush were, as ever, her mediums, so initially her explorations of botany, zoology and anthropology were conducted on paper. The African wilderness engaged her like no other place, however, and because living specimens were at hand, she started collecting insects and cultivating plants, especially those with flavour, like a pineapple from Batavia. And as she became more familiar with the environs, she started to venture further from Cape Town.

Her attempts 'to draw and describe everything I see in the best manner I can' were ostensibly to illuminate life at the Cape for those at home.[44] Draw and describe she certainly did. Her voice has been heard throughout this narrative. Now her eye also started to produce striking results. She sketched people, animals and plants with a precision that marks her as one of the traveller artists of her time, for although she had dabbled at drawing since childhood, it was finding herself in an outlandish place with curious humans and creatures as subjects that moved her to set these down as best she could for others – the Khoikhoi inhabitants, slaves, animals, plants and landscapes.*

Her most ambitious work dates from this time – a watercolour panorama roughly sixteen feet in length, executed from the roof of the Castle apartments, encompassing a full 360 degrees and presenting in detail the town, mountains and bay. She intended it as a farewell gift for Macartney though the complexity and difficulty meant it was not completed for three years. 'I wish I had not undertaken this Panorama,' she wrote halfway through, 'I

---

* Some of her African sketches have been reproduced in volumes published in South Africa, mainly by the Van Riebeeck Society. A more ambitious work on her watercolours, *Lady Anne Barnard's Watercolours and Sketches: Glimpses of the Cape of Good Hope*, was published in a limited edition in Cape Town in 2009.

The 'Black Madonna' moved Anne to one of her most intimate drawings

am really very bad at it & yet having undertaken it I do not like to give up.'[45] It hangs to this day at Balcarres, the closest we can come to a vision of Cape Town in the eighteenth century.

One of her more personal and affecting images, 'A Hottentot suckling her child' was drawn after Anne observed the subject, a teenage maid, run from a house where she worked in order to nurse her baby.

> While she sat like a black madonna, her method of kissing it from time to time had a softness in it which I think had I been a man would have inchanted me, as it pleased and surprised me as a woman.[46]

A year into their African adventure the Barnards had only one cause for regret, yet for Anne it was especially painful because it amounted to failure on the most profound human level. Her attempt to show the boy Henry that she could be 'as fond of him as if he were my own son' came too late for an angry, neglected lad and Andrew decided that he must be sent home. Why they had been unable to pacify him, enfold him into a family, is a matter for speculation: Henry had been passed from a courtesan mother through unknown hands to his often absent father; and despite Anne's avowals of affection, she had come late to her maternal role. 'The education of children makes no part of my habits,' she once said. (As much may have been inferred from her surprise at the 'black madonna's' tenderness in kissing her infant.) It happened that one of her brothers, Captain Hugh Lindsay, arriving with a fleet of homeward-bound Indiamen, offered to take Henry under his wing and arrange his schooling in England. Such improvisations were common in distant colonies, and Anne bade 'adieu to the pleasing vision of breeding up this child to love and respect us both'.[47]

A sense of failure went deeper – to an inability to conceive children herself; Andrew was as affectionate as ever and she would indicate discreetly that 'those ties I had not been so lucky as to give him' were not for want of trying.[48] Seeing a new-born child, she wrote

> I wishd it had been my own, but one must not wish for anything now so improbable. Fortunately for my happiness, tho my B would have much rejoyced in having two or three, he is too reasonable to permit himself to be unhappy about what can't be helpd – it is no fault of his, poor fellow![49]

Although dreams of a family of her own were gone, a sense of maternal duty to her husband's children would endure.

14

A While in Paradise

1797–1798

The Barnards had their first glimpse of Paradise a few months after landing at the Cape. A year then passed before they could enter it, but the sight had been enough. Although this particular heaven lay no more than a few miles from the Castle, it opened a door to the African wilderness. It could be said to have made an adventurous traveller of Anne.

Paradise was the name of a dilapidated cottage, amid a forest some way up the side of Table Mountain, set about with blossoming orange trees, aromatic bushes, wildflowers and a stream running by. At the time that Macartney invited the Barnards to inspect it as one of three country houses within his gift, suggesting it might suit them as a weekend retreat, it was reachable only by horse or on foot. It was also far more run down than the other two houses and in need of repairs including a new thatch roof. But once Anne had inspected it and found it the ideal spot for 'Adam and Eve to raise chickens and potatoes', she would have no other.[1] Andrew, who had seen a house by the sea 'with a coast well calculated for bathing', had to agree that 'all things considered, we shall feel more snug in Paradise'.[2]

John Barrow's letters lured the Barnards further inland. Since their clamber up Table Mountain, the indefatigable Barrow had wandered hundreds of miles up the eastern seaboard, reaching the most powerful Xhosa clan and inspiring him to descriptions that embody the ideal of the Noble Savage: 'The Kaffirs I admire exceedingly,' Barrow wrote to Anne. 'They lead a true pastoral life, united in clans like those of the Highlands of Scotland. They live chiefly on milk and the spoils of the chase... Their persons are finely formed, their deportment bold and their countenance cheerful.' As for their chief Ngqika, he was 'one of the most prepossessing men I ever saw, black or white'.[3]

So distant an objective lay beyond the Barnards' reach, but Barrow's suggestion of a visit to Paarl – a settlement only forty miles distant albeit over rugged terrain – was attainable, and rendered exceptionally alluring:

> Your route would be through Stellenbosch, Drakenstein, France-hoek, Little Drakenstein and Paarl, and I venture to say you would be highly gratified. Nowhere have I seen the sublime and the beautiful, the tame and the terrible, so well arranged as in the valley on which the places above are situated. The enclosing mountains are immensely grand ... the sight is worth a journey of 1,000 miles ... It would make a fine subject for the pencil.[4]

The opportunity for rural escape was provided by a crisis. In September news reached the Cape of the naval mutinies five months earlier that crippled Britain's first line of resistance to an apparently imminent French invasion. The grievances of seamen at home over pay and conditions were felt at the Cape too, and on 2 October nine ships mutinied in Simon's Bay. Anne sympathised, to the extent of telling Rear-Admiral Thomas Pringle it was only fair that the hands should receive the same concessions granted at Spithead.* But after more ships arrived in a state of mutiny three

---

* Anne wrote two despatches to Dundas devoted to the Cape mutinies. They would have had no influence on events and so are omitted here. Typically, however, she singled out for praise one captain, Andrew Todd of the *Trusty*, 'a man who has risen from a very low class of life by undisputed merit in his profession', and who, alone among the commanding officers 'remained on board

A coach journey to Stellenbosch gave the Barnards their first view of the Cape hinterland and stimulated more adventurous travels

weeks later, unrest spread to the Castle gates. Soldiers were being won over by the mutineers when she wrote to Dundas:

> The sailors come ashore in numbers, partys of 12 at a time, they pillage the markets, get drunk, riot & endeavour by every means to corrupt the army ... We are solitary enough but have no fears and the sentinels have orders to permit no sailor to pass into the Castle.[5]

While this confrontation was still unfolding, Barnard was ordered to Stellenbosch to deal with dissident Boers who had refused to take an oath of allegiance to the king. The official reason was that if anything could win them over it would be Andrew's diplomatic skills. The unofficial reason was that a revolutionary spirit appeared

---

his ship, watching [for] the moment when lassitude should render it possible to make a few of his men listen to reason'. (Robinson, 1973, p. 67).

to be abroad and with the crisis finely poised Macartney had decided that ladies should be moved from the Castle.

When Andrew left Cape Town on 9 November, Anne and his cousin, Elizabeth, were with him, anticipating a little adventure upcountry, oblivious to the showdown Macartney had delayed to this point. Two hours later, as the carriage crossed Salt River and started up the pass to Stellenbosch, a cannon thundered out from the Castle. Only then did Barnard explain that it marked an ultimatum for the mutineers to surrender or be bombarded to pieces. News reached them that night. The ringleaders had been handed over, the mutiny had ended.[6]

Serenity returned in the lovely, fertile valley that Anne always called 'Stillingbosch'. The first inland village founded by the Dutch was hardly a wilderness, being a single-day journey from Cape Town and much favoured by French refugee Huguenots who planted the seeds of Cape vines and libertarianism. There was still a pleasing oddity to travelling in the chaise bought by Anne from the Duke of Queensberry (which retained 'Old Q's' faded coat of arms on the side) as it wound up to Stellenbosch, and they congratulated themselves on 'how out of all calculation it seemed that we should be driving together amongst the hills of Africa' in it.[7]

Unlike Barrow, whose aversion to the Boers was intractable (and arguably influential in shaping a British colonial attitude that gave rise to mutual antagonism and future strife) the Barnards were impressed by the men of the interior.[8] 'Their height is enormous, most of them six feet high and upwards, and I do not know how many feet across,' Anne wrote. 'I hear that five hundred miles distant they even reach seven feet.'[9] More to the point, they established a rapport. The Barnards admired the Boers' spirit, identifying it as a desire for independence from the exploitation they had known under the Dutch East India Company, rather than Jacobin subversion. Andrew went a good way to placating the dissidents at Stellenbosch.*

While he was off negotiating, Anne wandered along oak-lined lanes to the little church and the Drostdy, headquarters of the magistrate, among the Dutch *vrouws* and their children, slaves with fruit baskets balanced on their heads, and the whitewashed cottages. This rustic place and its surrounding district had a settler population, the so-called free burghers, of some 200 families living in farmhouses with characteristic Cape Dutch gables, dotted around a countryside producing grape and corn.

Her first experience of travel in an ox-wagon was a trundle with Elizabeth to the Hottentots Holland Mountains in hope of seeing the San, or Bushmen. In this she was disappointed, 'they poor things having been driven up the country'.[10] Although denied sight of these famously wild humans, her pencil was as invigorated as Barrow had foreseen. Just as the landscape around Cape Town was dominated by mountains, so was the interior of the Western Cape, and the majestic trajectories on every horizon mesmerised her. 'They rise above our heads in all sorts of extraordinary shapes,' she marvelled. The mountains, along with the natives, are a constant feature of her drawings. In Stellenbosch she produced half a dozen portraits, and idyllic watercolours of the Drostdy and an oak-lined Church Street.

A week later the Duke of Queensbury's carriage was on a trail heading north-east, further into the interior over the Groot Drakenstein Mountains towards another village, Paarl. The surroundings, as Barrow had said, were nature's arrangement of the sublime and the beautiful, the tame and the terrible. Having

---

* Ultimatums were issued to a dozen Boer dissidents to swear allegiance to the Crown. Eight complied. The other four resisted Barnard's imprecations, and then surrendered to face deportation to Batavia. After their wives wrote to Anne and were allowed to visit them, they submitted and were freed.

no knowledge of their whereabouts the Barnards surrendered 'with the confidence of honest people who suppose no harm is to be done to them, tho' in Africa and under the guidance of a black stranger'.[11] They stayed with families, getting by on a blend of Andrew's willing but execrable Dutch and Anne's exhilaration, sharing bedrooms and tucking in with a will to anything on the table, especially when it came to a feast on the hind quarters of an antelope. They were invited to a dance where mothers breast-fed their babies openly, with 'no false delicacys to prevent the little ones from having their repast as well as we'.[12] And they joined a peasant family in their living room with 'ducks and chickens walking about as if part of the company'.[13] London society and its sensibilities were more than merely thousands of miles away. Anne felt she had entered a world where 'we might have venerated the simplicity of the golden age'.

These were among the reflections in one of her lengthy despatches to Dundas, along with – should he be left in any doubt – her opinion as to the land's suitability for colonisation:

> Barren & ill-cultivated as it now is, it strikes both Mr B and me to have great powers in itself to become one of the finest countrys in the world. How far it will be the wisdom of England to encourage it to become so is for England's Sovereign and his ministers to determine, or whether it will be judged most for the advantage for our possessions in India to keep it subordinate . . . is for you to determine and you only.[14]

The voice of an imperialist was tempered with belief that for a British colony to succeed, trust must be invested in new settlers. It seemed to her that the Boers' endeavours had been repressed rather than encouraged.

> They tell me there is nothing this place is not equal to, particularly if we can suppose the intercourse between the inner part of the country

and Cape Town to be rendered more easy. It is certainly a healthy spot. We have lost but one officer here.[15]

All this went off to Dundas with half a dozen ostrich eggs, plus cooking instructions, and an admission that although her opinions might be flawed, she felt bound to express them – not to him as a minister, she added hastily, but as a friend.

The future of the Cape was, in fact, already being intensely debated. French victories in Europe had left Britain isolated. Worse, the mutinies had exposed vulnerability in the navy, the nation's sole source of strength. Anne's friend Jane Parker wrote to her from Tunbridge Wells full of fear about 'the total Overturn & Destruction of Everything by those Scourges of Europe'. The war was going so badly that an invasion of England was not only feasible, it seemed probable; and while the likely consequences were anyone's guess, a peace would almost certainly spell a surrender of the Cape.

In the meantime theirs was a blessed place. The Barnards moved to Paradise in April. A road had been built, repairs to the cottage completed and Andrew suggested that they make it not just a weekend retreat, but a home. Such it became. He would ride into town every morning, returning in the evening to their haven in the shade of the mountain. The house was too small for servants, so Anne rose at six, went for a ride herself, cooked breakfast, then set about feeding the chickens. A little menagerie of wildlife required attention too.

Late in the Cape summer, with just a hint of cool coming off the mountain, Andrew sat out on the veranda writing 'a letter from Paradise' to Margaret. It was novel, he agreed, that it should be coming from him, but Anne had gone off 'to play with a young buck and now she is dancing it about like a young child. Did you ever hear of such a sister, so fond of bucks?'[16]

Anne picked up the thread. She had, she told Margaret,

collected other pets beside the buck, including a seal: 'His method of walking has too much of the waddle in it to be *graceful*,' she wrote, 'but when laughed at, he plunges into the water and is in his kingdom.' There was also a penguin – which spent 'half the day in the pond with the sea-calf and half of it in the drawing room with me' – and a pair of secretary birds:

> majestic creatures with long legs, black velvet breeches and large wings who strut about with an air much resembling that of some of our fine Gentlemen.[17]

Dark came quickly, as the sun was lost behind Table Mountain two hours earlier than on the Table Bay side. Mosquitoes (muskatos, Anne called them) would start their vexatious whine, and gangs of baboons came down to plunder the fruit trees. Andrew blasted away with his rifle until he scored a hit, then was mortified at his victim's shrieks of agony. One evening, with a fire in the grate, he said: 'How happy are the days we spend here, love . . . How much better is our own company to each other than company who speak without conversing, and are noisy without enjoyment.'[18]

This natural Elysium is captured in a painting which still hangs at the Castle, showing a naked woman stepping gingerly into a stream. It is entitled *Lady Anne Barnard's Pool* and it reflects local legend that the first lady of the Cape enjoyed bathing in the nude. Much about this mysterious work is unknown, including the artist, but an old inventory turned up in a recent search at the Castle describes it as a 'small oil of Lady Anne Barnard bathing at a pool at Platteklip Gorge on Table Mountain'. On the back is inscribed, 'My own bathing place'. The artist and the voluptuous bather may have been one and the same, the location a stream known as Capel Sluyt that gurgled down to Paradise from the mountain.[19] Anne's dreams of an Eden, for 'Adam and Eve . . . to raise chickens and potatoes', sometimes prompted her to slip out of her shift and into the water.[20]

A verse inspired by the painting by the South African poet Anthony Delius imagines the governor's hostess caught between her official duties at the Castle and the call of the wilderness:

> . . . until I flee
> The twinkling clavichord and wine to show
> My nakedness in hostage to a tree.[21]

Like all perfect moments, it could not last. Macartney's deteriorating health often confined him to his quarters and he had written to Dundas, requesting that he be relieved.[22] Finding a successor would take months of wrangling, and months more for him to make his way to the Cape, but Barnard was not going to find another superior so congenial. Already he was at odds with an overweening military establishment.

The British soldiers who regarded the inhabitants with contempt were little better disposed to those who treated them as friends. At dinners given by the Barnards, officers' behaviour towards the other guests verged on the boorish unless the governor was present, and since the arrival of General Francis Dundas as commander-in-chief matters had got worse. The general thought Barnard a parvenu and made clear to Anne 'that he conceived I had married a man beneath myself'.[23] General Dundas's attitude was no doubt coloured by the fact that he was a nephew of Henry Dundas, the Secretary of State for War, and as mystified as everyone else that she had rejected his uncle in favour of a nobody.

It may not have been coincidental that around this time the Barnards went through an upheaval of their own. Just what it was Anne did not explain, though she was candid enough to place it on record as 'the only moment in my married life during which my happy heart knew a pain, something accidental having occurred to pain it'.[24] That was all; but she may have learnt of an infidelity. As we have seen, she asked few questions of Andrew and her use of the term 'accidental' has a sense of unexpected as well as unwanted disclosure. Five years of marriage, her childlessness and their age difference may already have introduced a maternal aspect to the relationship. She was not far from the matronly age of fifty and, perhaps only half in jest, Andrew had started to address her as 'Dearest Nanny'.

Whatever caused her pain, she did not permit it to last. Of her 'sweet, amiable man', it may be recalled, she wrote: 'His peculiarities were almost invisible to the eye of an attentive wife. Yet he had some!' Having accepted Andrew's foibles, she set the subject aside and turned back to the sunlight of a time 'so dear to my heart ... a Character so near to perfection', while thanking God 'for having allowed me a portion of Existence innocently happy, so soothing to me on reflection'.[25] There is a characteristic that had come to define her as a woman of mature years and many sorrows, and to which we will return: Anne Barnard shared with Jane Austen what a biographer of the author called an unwillingness to lead a disappointed life.[26]

A second journey provided the opportunity for reconciliation. In anticipation of his early departure, Macartney gave Barnard leave to take Anne on a real journey: a trek. A full month away would give them time to follow in the wagon tracks of John Barrow, who had thrilled her with a gift from his travels, the bulb of a strelitzia, 'a curious plant which will be a very acceptable thing in England', and had sent her accounts of 'more kinds of beasts than ever entered Noah's Ark, scampering around the plains of Africa ... ten thousand Springboks ... Elephants, Buffalos, the Gnoo, a most extraordinary animal, Zebras, Quachas'.[27] The season was not ideal, for the Barnards would be travelling at the start of the Cape winter, which brought downpours that could make routes impassable. However, time being short and with no other opportunity in prospect, they departed the Castle in a wagon on 5 May.

Anne's venture to the interior in 1798 was no pioneering epic. Wandering Dutch pastoralists known as trekboers had been drifting eastwards for decades, living at the pace of the ox on the sunny uplands with a fierce determination to escape the interference of administrators. Wagon travel was nevertheless an adventure. As the historian Noel Mostert has pointed out, partly because of the mountains which encircle the Cape Peninsula and isolated it from the interior, and partly because the trekkers left nothing behind them, barely any network of posts or communication existed by which authority could pursue and control. Once the traveller passed beyond the handful of houses at Swellendam, almost 200 miles to the east, no European settlement was to be found until Graaff-Reinet, which lay more than 400 miles off and had been founded only ten years earlier in a late and hopelessly misdirected effort by the Dutch to impose law on the trekboers.[28] In short, while the Barnards were not exploring virgin terrain, they were entering unmapped space, and doing so for the pleasure and novelty of it. Anne was the first British woman to make such an African journey and friends at home were naturally anxious. 'I only tremble for your activity going beyond your strength,' wrote Jane Parker. 'Remember how many as well as Mr B are interested in your life.'[29]

They were not alone. Elizabeth Barnard again joined them, along with an army officer cousin of Anne's named John Dalrymple, and a Khoikhoi driver and guide, Gaspar. Communication would be helped by having on hand Andrew's servant Pauwel, a Flemish-speaker whose tongue was close to the language already evolving into Afrikaans. The wagon was drawn by eight horses on the first stage as they left Cape Town by the road for Stellenbosch, but within a few miles the trail turned south-east and by the second day they had begun a steep ascent to the Hottentots Holland

Mountains, across passes that could be negotiated only by a team of twelve oxen.

The modern traveller ascends to Hottentots Kloof by car over Sir Lowry's Pass at a rate that leaves scarce opportunity to pause and digest the epic scale of the Cape Peninsula – 'Africa's appendix' one writer has called it – as False Bay is left in a great sweep below.* The Barnards' movement by wagon was agonisingly slow, each turn of a wheel a little progress. Grinding their way up to the kloof under Gaspar's lash, the oxen seemed to Anne 'sensible creatures, for much did they appear to dislike the business they were going on'.

> As we ascended it grew worse and worse & sometimes the path was so perpendicular and the jutting rocks over which the wagon was to be pulled so large we were astonished how it could be accomplished at all . . . At length we reached the summit and the new Canaan opened on my view. 'The World was all before me where to choose my place of rest, and Providence my guide.'[30]

The quotation, from Milton's *Paradise Lost*, was apt. The region to which they had come is known as the Overberg, and it is arguably the loveliest part of a Western Cape landscape renowned for craggy grandeur and bountiful harvests. Anne had been right: 'Here *is* scarcity but here *will be* plenty.' The rich tableland of the Overberg has since been transformed into an African food basket, a source of grains and fruit, bound by mountains in the west and north, the Breede River in the east and the Indian Ocean in the south.

Here the travelling became easier on a trail following the south-eastern seaboard while the mountains, always the mountains,

---

* The opening of Sir Lowry's Pass from Cape Town to the Overberg in 1830 reshaped travel even by wagon.

shadowed them to the north. Anne had no names by which to identify the Riviersonderend and Langeberg ranges, and there were no more passes quite so hair-raising as Hottentots Kloof, yet her eye was drawn to the horizon continually and she sketched away busily, even from the back of a lumbering wagon. Cattle were seen grazing on treeless plains of *fynbos*, the indigenous shrubland. Again she was reminded of Barrow's contrasting of the tame and the terrible, the beautiful and the sublime.

Towards evening a stop might be made at the farmhouse of a Boer family, the Brands say, or the Cloetes or the Morkels. Here ethnic distinctions became blurred, for slaves lived in close proximity to their owners. In contrast to the Cape, racial mixing and intermarriage was quite acceptable to the frontier folk. Anne referred to the 'blue friends' she met along the way, meaning people of mixed blood, usually women with Boer husbands. At the Jouberts' one night, near what is now Grabouw, their hosts welcomed a neighbouring farmer and his mixed-race wife of 'a most pleasing countenance and fine teeth', and although they were unable to converse, when Anne asked her what the farm produced, 'she begun crowing like a cock, quacking like a duck, wabbling like a turkey, [going] thro' the articles of her trade by sound or gesture'.[31] The evening ended in hilarity with Anne declaring the woman so much better company than most of those they met that she invited her – rather to Andrew's concern – to visit them at the Castle.

The farms scattered along the easterly trail were hospitable, but with rough beds and discomforts came the odd night in the open and the occasional danger. Rivers became a more regular obstacle than mountains and while the travellers often had reason to praise Gaspar's skills, during one fording the wagon pitched over, trapping the occupants until they managed to crawl out, bruised but unbroken. After that they would get out at points of awkward traversal and walk.

Of real peril, however, they saw nothing. One evening Anne declined Andrew's offer of a walk – 'I am bad company when drawing' – and went off alone to sketch 'while the setting Sun fell behind the Stupendous Mountains', and though eventually her thoughts turned to the carnivorous animal that might leap out and devour her, or the renegade native possibly in search of plunder, she was no more at risk than at Paradise.[32]

As the wagon trundled on towards Swellendam, the frontier beckoned. Anne longed 'to see a little of the *real natives*'. The Xhosa described by Barrow were always going to be beyond range, but she did get some insight into tribal life at Genadendal, a mission where three Moravians ministered to the local Khoikhoi. Curious as ever, she could not restrain herself from entering their mud huts, marvelling at the sparse rigour of the contents – a few skins, some firewood to boil water, calabashes, wooden spoons, an iron pot. Addressing a common belief that 'the Hottentot' epitomised primitive barbarism, she noted: 'On the contrary [he] is so cleanly that he is washing himself all day long . . . As to horns, I believe they have not more than other Country Gentlemen.'[33]

Observing the Khoikhoi women interacting with their men brought her to the heart of the matter. Ultimately, she cast aside fashionable notions about the Noble Savage, just as she shunned views of racial inferiority, and came down on the side of a universal humanity:

> Real & true love, such as he who made the sexes meant them to feel for each other, when it takes place in good hearts, whether clothed in a dark skin or a fair, whether in man or woman, will always be ready to sacrifice every thing for its object.[34]

It took eight days to cover about 180 miles to Swellendam. The sole disappointment was that they had not encountered more wildlife. Bontebok and springbok were abundant, along with zebra and ostrich – an animal 'wildly, madly and beautifully angry' – but of carnivores such as leopards and hyenas nothing was to be seen.

At this point they diverted from the eastern trail, starting south across rollicking hills that run beside the Breede River towards the Indian Ocean. Their host here was Jacob van Reenen, who offered Andrew some hunting. Anne was more interested in information. Eight years earlier van Reenen had joined a mission to answer a great mystery: what had become of the *Grosvenor* castaways? For a woman who had sailed on an Indiaman and was now visiting the shores where the *Grosvenor* had been lost, this was an enthralling subject.

In 1782 six emaciated English seamen appeared on the Cape frontier, survivors of a homeward-bound Indiaman wrecked far up the coast. At home the news created a sensation, for the 141 souls on the *Grosvenor* had included some of the elite of Bengal society and their families, all of whom had escaped the wreck only to be attacked as they came ashore. As the London papers reported it, the men had been killed by 'savages' while three women had been carried off to 'the vilest brutish prostitution'. A rescue party sent out by the Dutch found a few seamen, but no trace of the women and six children. Ten years passed before more searchers set off up the coast. Jacob van Reenen was among them.

Van Reenen spoke English and over dinner at his farmhouse he related how the trek had proceeded almost 600 miles up the eastern seaboard, to a region where 'the natives were fierce and poor and no civilized person before had ever dared to visit'. What they discovered was shocking. The castaways had lacked leadership and broken up into smaller parties. All appeared to have died, leaving only skeletons and traces of clothing. The sole castaway to be found was an elderly white woman who had become the wife of a chief by whom she had sons. As van Reenen related, he suggested she join them in returning to the Cape, but although she 'seemed intoxicated with pleasure' at the idea, she said she could not leave before the harvest.[35] Anne was gripped. 'I wish she would make her words good while I am here,' she wrote to Margaret. 'I should be very glad to give old Caffraria an apartment in the Castle.'*

The next day they went down to the Breede mouth, a broad sandy lagoon where one of the great rivers that carve up the Indian Ocean coast debouches into the sea, and while the men fished, Anne wrote and sketched, marvelling again at this Africa, so dangerous, so forbidding as it seemed to the world, yet so tranquil and grand.

Another paradox to emerge from the self-declared gourmand's pen is how, amid the discomforts of the trail, the travellers enjoyed better fare than was to be had at the Cape – or London for that matter: Anne savoured 'dried buck . . . very good indeed', possibly the first mention in English of the South African titbit known as biltong, along with pickled fish, wild honey and mutton chops. One dinner of broiled fowls with plenty of potatoes and good butter she declared 'a repast fit for an emperor'. Even that was surpassed by a supper at the van Reenens, 'the best I ever eat [*sic*] in my life', of roast veal, stewed bontebok, partridges and curry. Here at the Breede mouth a cloth was laid out for a picnic of grilled fish washed down by madeira.

After warm farewells, the Barnards' wagon turned inland again on 17 May, back towards Swellendam. Anne hoped they

---

* The account given by van Reenen to Anne does not match his narrative of the expedition, which states that three white women had been found who, on sighting their would-be rescuers, set up a cry: 'Our fathers are come!' However, they declined to leave their new tribes and their children, and appear to have been survivors of an earlier wreck, probably Portuguese. The fate of the *Grosvenor* castaways is the subject of *The Caliban Shore* by the present author. It concludes that one of the women castaways and two children were taken in and assimilated with local tribes. At least two seamen are also known to have made new lives among the natives.

might proceed to Graaff-Reinet, from where the trek could have extended further, 'to parts of Africa where nature becomes wilder and there is less affinity to what has been seen before'. Her imagination had been fired: 'Nations are to be found in the Interior by those who have courage to look for them, whose names we only know on the Map and some who are not *even there*.'[36] In truth, covering such a distance was never feasible in the month available. She insisted, however, that if they could not go east a route should be navigated across the colony to Saldanha Bay on the west coast. Feathers of the flamingo might be had there, and she wanted some for Margaret.

A guide was found at Swellendam to navigate a route to Saldanha and the wagon started west towards the Atlantic, still with the mountains haunting the northern horizon. Soon they were back amid immense gnarled ridges of stone. The trek's longest leg took them across the Langeberg range and another rocky, dangerous pass at Cogmans Kloof where the women alighted and walked while the men pulled on ropes to hold the wagon upright and prevent it toppling down into the Kingna River. More passes took the wagon through what is now the Boland and the towns of Worcester and Tulbagh. With the horses able to cover forty miles a day, the wagon reached Saldanha Bay in a week.

On 28 May Anne stood at the lookout point called Uitkyk, around 600 feet up on a peninsula above the Atlantic, drawing a panorama of the bay below where, in 1620, two captains of the East India Company landed and claimed possession in the name of King James. No further action was taken before the Dutch settled in Table Bay thirty-two years later, but Saldanha's excellence as a natural harbour was recognised by this first British female visitor who thought, 'It appeared to my Ignoramus eye as a place where ships may ride most *securely sheltered*.' Such, indeed, was attested by its subsequent use.

The journey was nearing its end. Anne had recorded it in a diary

– one, like her journal of the voyage, in the form of an extended letter to Margaret, complete with knowing asides and *entre nous* references. The 'Tour into the Interior of Africa', as she styled it, reflected a bashful desire that her creative side might receive some recognition. She was too self-effacing to seek publication. Instead, an elaborate hand-produced volume was compiled, incorporating 'sketches and figures taken on the spot', in what amounts to a travel narrative.

It was consistent with Anne's social position and her time that the work should have been designed solely for family. She shrank from exposing her talents as a writer and artist because of the modesty expected of a lady. But self-effacement also played a part in concealing these gifts. In the end Anne Barnard, like Anne Lindsay, simply lacked the assertiveness that would have claimed attention. Admittedly, the 'Tour into the Interior of Africa' is too wordy even by the standards of the day to count among her best writings. The illustrations, however, foreshadow the aquatints of Samuel Daniell, an artist who visited Africa a year later and produced beguiling yet romanticised versions of similar subjects. A better comparison may be made with another woman traveller, writer and illustrator who journalised her adventures in India a generation later. Fanny Parkes has been described as 'an enthusiast and an eccentric with a love of India that is imprinted on almost every page'.[37] Apart from their other similarities, Fanny's exhilarated cry, 'Oh the pleasure of vagabondising in India!' has a clear echo of Anne in Africa.

Three more days brought the party from Saldanha to Blaauberg, where the Barnards looked once more across Table Bay to Cape Town and its unmistakable mountain skyline. If not exactly home, it was still so for the time being, and all the more appealing for offering comforts absent over the past month and some 700 miles in the back of a wagon.[38]

15

Paradise Lost

The departing governor did his best to protect Barnard. Before sailing home, Macartney wrote to Henry Dundas suggesting that until his successor arrived, authority at the Cape should be vested in a council of three that would include Andrew. The aim was to save him from bullying by a military regime. The flaw in the strategy was that General Francis Dundas had been sent out by his uncle to seize this opportunity for advancement. Word duly came from London that the choleric general was appointed acting governor, pending the arrival of Macartney's replacement. Life at the Cape was never the same again.

Outsiders like Barnard were naturally vulnerable in distant stations and, being familiar with male circles of power, he knew what to expect. For Anne rudeness from social inferiors was novel as well as discomforting. At home she could summon allies with a letter. At the Cape she was 6,000 miles from support; and when Macartney sailed home at the end of 1798, she and Andrew were abruptly isolated. The whole tenor of colonial life altered: the hand of reconciliation extended to the inhabitants by a civilian ruler was withdrawn; under the army, bridge-building collapsed. The Dutch and their friends were confronted by red-coated blockheads who held them in contempt. For the only time in her life, Anne found herself excluded and disregarded.

She did not, it should be said, best serve her own or Andrew's interests. In the years that followed, those in charge of Britain's destiny, from Westminster to the Cape and Bengal, had their plates full dealing with the war as Bonaparte's spectacular trajectories kept Britain poised for invasion – at home, and in Egypt and India. In her isolation Anne failed to see how trivial her concerns might appear, particularly to the man in overall charge of the war effort, Henry Dundas. She thought General Dundas a hot and haughty oaf, had told Margaret as much, and while taking a more oblique line with his uncle still went further than she might.

> I tell you in the *perfect confidence* of friendship that he [Barnard] is a *little* afraid from the General's manner that he is not disposed to like him . . . The General is Hasty & he has not learnt that charming page in Lord Macartney's book, to respect others in order to have it from them . . . Mr Barnard would not be pleased with me if he knew I had said this much, *therefore I shall not tell him I have* – but I do not think I am wrong.[1]

Her frankness has been noted before. So has her wordiness. Neither was suited to a time of acute crisis. When she wrote to Dundas of her embarrassment about the 'thoughtless John Bulls' who went about abusing the Dutch as if 'forgetting that some of them understand English enough to comprehend an insult', she perfectly summarised the state of relations between the military and the colonists.[2] But a feminine voice needed to be clear if it was to be heard over a hot-tempered military leader – one who also happened to be the minister's nephew – and too often her most pithy observations were buried amid pages of detail

Disquiet was still natural. It was not only General Dundas who treated Andrew with disdain but his deputy, General John Fraser. The ostensible reason was that, although he was the colony's senior civilian, Barnard had been disproportionately favoured in salary and choice of Castle apartment, which he retained along with

Paradise. More to the point was the fact that Andrew – a mere captain in his army days – had benefited thanks to his aristocratic wife. It followed that, having married the fellow, the lady had sacrificed her own station.

Petty feuding at remote stations was intrinsic to the imperial saga. Through it all Anne continued to exchange outwardly cheerful, gossipy letters with Wellesley in India, Frederick North, the governor of Ceylon, and other friends at home. 'You are a Divine Correspondent,' enthused Macartney, now back in London. 'You paint everything in so quick and lively a manner that I am on the spot to see it with my own eyes as if it were immediately passing before them.'[3] And she still played hostess to grandees – the Earl of Powys and Lord Teignmouth, sailing to and from India; and Philip King on his way to take over the administration of New South Wales. 'Never saw I such a succession of governors,' she marvelled, 'the sea has been quite covered with them.'[4] There was no shortage of lesser personages either, and one batch sent her way by Lady Elizabeth Foster, mistress of the Duke of Devonshire and a woman she had never liked, elicited a grumble about those who

> anxious to pay off some debt . . . take the load off their own back & lay it on their friends, recommending to every civility and attention persons who they would not put down at their own table or go half an inch out of their way [for].[5]

Some of the guests brought to Paradise were 'astonished at our farm house – at the stile [*sic*] so unlike the magnificence and luxurys of India'.[6] They were doubtless taken aback too by their hostess's style of home management. Although slaves and servants had become part of the household, Anne believed these should 'be made friends of as well as servants; the one is never compleat without a little mixture of the other', and because she knew her staff 'feel harried when we have company', she joined in the preparation and cooking.[7]

A letter to Elizabeth Harcourt ('Doodle Doo' from Anne's racy London set) captures the quirky pleasures of life under Table Mountain. In it she describes herself as 'a sort of Ladyship Jack of all Trades, a housekeeper, botanist, collector, paintress, upholsterer, Lady Bountiful, cook, dairy maid – everything but a politician, and that I do not touch'.[8] While Anne remained on stage here, and at occasional official events at the Castle, she was starting to retire to the sidelines; but although she tried to avoid politics, Lady Anne Barnard was too prominent to be ignored, and her unconventional views distanced her from the mainstream. These final years at the Cape saw a steady souring between the Barnards and the colonial establishment.

When acquaintances suggested that her husband could do more to ingratiate himself with the military by being a drinker and bon vivant, Anne would point out that the general 'treats Mr Barnard as a parvenu'.[9] But the differences between the two men went much deeper, being intrinsically those between libertarian and authoritarian spirits.

An early dispute involved the treatment of French prisoners on ships returning from India. Fifty men had died of smallpox on one vessel and Barnard argued that the rest should be allowed to disembark and convalesce at a site offshore called Robben Island.* Dundas's refusal dismayed not only Barnard but also William Pattison, head of the naval hospital, and John Pringle, the East India Company's agent, and when Barnard returned with the latter in support, the general relented.[10] Further

---

* The island in Table Bay, renowned in modern times as a political prison, has been put to various uses in the South African past, including to confine lepers, along with heretics and paupers.

disagreements arose over Dundas's readiness to issue emergency proclamations. Barnard showed reluctance to put his name to them, so the general took to bypassing him.[11]

It was proper that Dundas should be on the alert. He had lost half his forces – three regiments along with General David Baird – to India, where it appeared a French alliance with Tipu Sultan might carry Bonaparte on an invasion via Egypt. A series of fires near the Castle destroyed naval and army stores, giving rise to theories that local Jacobins were to blame. This was nonsense, but grievances among the Boers of Graaff-Reinet had resurfaced and they appeared to be seeking support from the French at Mauritius. When the hard men of the frontier rescued one of their number from arrest, Dundas sent troops under General Thomas Vandeleur to round them up for trial. A Boer insurrection, if such it could be called, was over.

At this critical juncture, Dundas followed up with an initiative to resolve a long-festering conflict between Boers and Xhosa in the region known as the Zuurveld. Vandeleur was ordered to drive the Xhosa out and across the Great Fish River. So began the first war between British soldiers and African tribesmen, between the rifle and the assegai.

The Barnards opposed war from the outset, on pragmatic and humanitarian grounds. It had been Macartney's opinion that 'rousing any warlike spirit would only be attacking the hornets nest which would not soon be quitted';[12] and early on Anne wrote in her diary:

> The Caffres [Xhosa] say, if you will let us alone we will let you ... to be sure, we were the aggressors & wrong we were for being so.[13]

Knowing that the secretary did not approve, Dundas excluded Andrew from briefings. Then, as a prolonged and messy frontier conflict dragged on and he was forced to take command in the

Zuurveld himself, his despatches were sent to Hercules Ross, the deputy secretary.[14] Of his return later that year, Anne noted with some satisfaction that Dundas had 'spent six months in *intending* to fight the Caffres, who had not stood still to be fought, and in settling a peace, when he found they would not fight, which had not been settled'.[15]

The Barnards showed other rebellious tendencies, especially over policy towards the Dutch. Soon after the Boer rebels were brought to Cape Town for trial, Dundas ordered the arrest of a moderate dissident named Horak on charges of instigating rebellion. Andrew pointed out that the allegations had been investigated and dismissed, and a furious Dundas was obliged to release him.[16] Anne then wrote to Mr and Mrs Horak, saying that although she understood they never attended English parties, she would deem it a pleasure to receive them at the Castle. Dundas's response is not recorded; but Ross 'seemed thunderstruck' at Anne's suggestion that 'the English owed Mr Horak every attention to wipe off the stain of unjust suspicion'.[17] Privately, she was angry.

Why can Englishmen not enjoy their superiority as Englishmen without eagerly marking to the Dutch how much they despise them?[18]

Barnard's good sense and dignity under trying circumstances may have been somewhat overstated by his wife, but there is still enough independent evidence to show he had thoroughly vindicated his appointment. On 18 August he drafted a forthright letter to General Dundas, pointing out that he had been placed in an impossible position – ostracised and excluded from the despatches sent to Ross, yet responsible for reporting the contents to London. 'I find myself no longer considered as Secretary to the Colony except by name ... I feel hurt to the soul at the situation in which you have placed me.'[19] Anne

persuaded him to tone the letter down, then took up her pen to
Henry Dundas.

> Mr Barnard regrets he must perform in a manner so very Inadequate
> to what you must naturally expect from the situation he fills here –
> but he cannot help it. The General I am grieved to say neither consults
> with him, nor permits any of his opinions to be advanced without that
> silencing manner which renders a man fearful of subjecting himself
> to [it].[20]

Andrew wrote to his old chief Macartney of Dundas's
contemptuous manner and his belief that the general had over-
reacted to the frontier troubles.[21] No intervention from London
was forthcoming or, indeed, likely. The Boer rebels' trial continued
for the next eighteen months and by the time it concluded with
death sentences being passed on eight men, the new governor
had arrived. Sir George Yonge proved a bad choice, but he was
at least inclined to mercy, suggesting to Barnard that in a *coup
de théâtre* the men be brought to the gallows and told at the last
minute they were to be spared. Barnard persuaded him this was
an unnecessary prolongation of agony for men already imprisoned
for more than two years.

Reports from the frontier meanwhile caused Anne alarm. For
so spirited a woman she was quite easily frightened, especially on
hearing of farmers' wives carried off by the Xhosa from burning
homesteads. 'What a shocking alternative,' she shuddered, 'death
or such lovers.'[22] Reports that the army had failed to stop an
advance on Swellendam added to her anxiety.[23] 'If the Caffres
have at their head a clever leader, what should prevent them from
coming on here & if they do, where can we fly?' she wrote in her
diary. Two weeks later another dreadful thought occurred. 'If the
black slaves here – I fancy twenty to one white – should rise, every
white person is likely to have his throat cut.'[24]

The only good news concerned the war elsewhere. In August the global position was transformed by Nelson's victory at the Nile. Despatches from India followed, carrying news of Tipu's defeat at Seringapatam. Wellesley wrote to Anne, boasting of 'my deeds of war and peace' and crowing 'our danger is converted into such strength as I think can never be shaken'.[25] She rejoiced in her diary: 'How the tide of eventful fate has turned.'[26]

By the end of 1799 the Barnards' hopes of a turn in their own fortunes rested on the new governor. Little was known of the individual concerned, Sir George Yonge, though his record in a series of minor roles at home raised questions over his ability. Anne nevertheless faced the new era with her customary optimism. 'I shall like [him] very well – he is a *well bred* Man I believe.'[27] Anyone, surely, must be an improvement on the general.

As if reflecting the Barnards' lot, Paradise fell into dilapidation. The thatch roof started to leak again, the walls leached water, and furious rainstorms made the cottage uninhabitable. Barnard, loathe to abandon the notion of a sanctuary in the country, had bought a plot of twenty acres on the Newlands estate and began building a house to be called the Vineyard.[28] For the time being, however, their only option was to move back to the Castle. On 28 May the Barnards' carriage departed from Paradise for the last time.[29]

Anne threw herself back into entertaining – and cooking: 'Twelve people to dinner. I have adopted the Dutch method of stewing the buck's flesh with wine and spice & I make it excellent.'[30] Her gripes were ironical: 'When shall I have leisure to be a Lady above the present drudgerys?'[31] And now and again an individual of real interest was brought up from an arriving ship. One such was an Indian khan, a man of fine countenance, full of fire and intelligence, dressed in purple and gold, who enthralled her with tales of oriental mythology.[32] He owned to just one wife,

Mirza Abu Taleb Khan sketched by Anne at the Cape

and though Anne fancied he must have left behind at least a hundred concubines, she gave him letters of recommendation to take on to England.* Some years later Mirza Abu Taleb Khan produced the account of his travels for which he is remembered, recalling 'the many delightful evenings I passed at the house of Lady Anne Barnet [*sic*] who was generally called the Princess of

---

* Anne was dismayed by gossip that Mirza Abu Taleb was, in fact, an imposter, fearing her endorsement would shame her, and was hugely relieved to hear he had been accepted and feted in society. (*Diaries*, vol. 2, pp. 88 and 154)

the Cape, and every week gave an entertainment and constantly did me the honour to number me among her guests'.[33]

She spent more time at her 'occupations'. Andrew remained the outdoorsman, ever a keen hunter. Yet reading between the lines of her diaries, he showed in private a growing sense of dependence as the sensual side of love turned into something more maternal. 'I hear him sigh softly at night,' she wrote, 'and sometimes a little grasp of my hand tells me he wishes I were younger – rather for the interests of his heart than those of his senses.'[34] She had started to think about death and, likely as it seemed that she would predecease him, hoped Andrew would find another wife to make up for this deficiency. For now, her pleasure at having had 'B and I tete-a-tete & by our crackling embers in the evening' was palpable.[35]

No one knows the tender gratitude that man is constantly expressing to me whenever the occasion awakens it & often when no occasion awakens it but when he looks at me & his mind speaks. 'Thou Best of human beings!' he sometimes says, & draws me to his Heart . . . What can youth or beauty create better than this? Nothing that I know of . . . Sweet B! Whenever I die I hope he will find the still unoccupied corners of his heart are filled with little Barnards, honest & mild as their father – the children of some good woman, attachd to him and worthy of his love.[36]

Their contentment was in contrast to the couple nearest to being family. Anne had never formed a close bond with Andrew's cousin, Elizabeth, being distanced by temperament as well as twenty-six years. She once confided to her diary that the younger woman was, 'cold and too disdainful ... [making] me feel the great grandmother';[37] but, as was the way in a far-off place, she provided company and advice. After two years and a good deal of courtship, Elizabeth found a husband in Colonel James Crauford of the 98th Foot. Before the marriage, Anne gave her young charge advice on sex, in a highlighted passage 'its nature very delicate & particular' from a French volume entitled *Les Confidences d'une Jolie Femme*.[38] The Craufords went on to have children but the marriage was not a happy one.[39]

The cannon fired from Lion's Head on 9 December, signalling the arrival of the governor's fleet, was seen as an auspicious omen. The Cape was returning to civilian rule precisely as a new century was dawning. A few days later Andrew drove Anne to meet Sir George Yonge at the official residence of Tuynhuys, and their optimism vanished almost immediately.

Yonge was weak and pompous, lacking the authority to bring the military to heel.[40] His flattery of Anne was embarrassing: 'He was very much pleased to see me. He fancys himself my old friend, but I am not conscious of ever having spoke to him.'[41] And it transpired that although Lady Yonge had not accompanied him, he had brought his own hostess, a Mrs Blake. Anne had no regrets. She gave a ball at the Castle for 150 people, 'particularly my Dutch friends', making it known that she would be withdrawing to the country.[42]

Nor did Yonge's arrival herald much improvement for Andrew as he also had a private secretary; and because the governor was not inclined to activity even in his official capacity, Andrew had still more time on his hands. A letter to Anne from Macartney came too late to prepare the Barnards for the new regime, but explained a good deal.

Between ourselves, I told Sir George Yonge (whenever he gave me an opportunity of talking to him) that he ought to depend upon Mr Barnard entirely for ability, diligence and integrity & that if he did not he would find himself involved in great difficulty. But tho he always received very civilly everything I said he seemd much less inquisitive than I expected, as if his own intuition were sufficient without any information.[43]

General Dundas, who had been furious on hearing that he was to be supplanted, returned to Cape Town during a lull in the frontier conflict, and promptly began feuding with Yonge. Anne and Andrew adopted a position of what she called 'armed neutrality'.[44]

Disillusionment with the governor, on top of what had already been a prolonged wait for home leave, may have precipitated the depression that followed. It was more than three years since their departure from England, and Anne longed for family and friends. 'Oh my dear Margaret,' she wrote, 'I [want] to sit down beside you for the rest of life.'[45] Looking at herself in a mirror she thought, 'I grow thin & very old,' and she worried about her health, particularly pains in her bowels.

The house in Newlands was at last ready, but the Vineyard would never take the place of Paradise. Returning to the rundown site of her bliss, Anne wandered the old garden, looking up to Table Mountain and digging up her bulbs, as if in hope that by transplanting them she might take happiness with her. Her animals had died or dispersed. (She did retain a keen interest in nature and appears to have forwarded to Sir Joseph Banks a pickled platypus despatched by Governor King from New South Wales. 'I lately sent him a mole with a duck's bill,' she wrote, 'a curious animal which I heard he disbelieved the existence of.'[46]) For months she kept her distance from the Castle and Mrs Blake's gatherings, which she likened to a kettle boiling with backbiting by various Lady Teazles.[47]

For a while even her pen failed to bring pleasure as she went back over her writings and found much wanting.

What a pity that with so much industry the use of time has been no better directed. Had I read & had I used things proper [*sic*] to enlarge and improve the mind perhaps I might have been able to have wrote & thought to some good purpose . . . but I have nothing to recommend my poor Journals except the ingenuous manner in which they are written.[48]

Anne Barnard's record of life at the Cape has proved a mine for historians. She confronted great issues, notably ethnicity and slavery. Her mischievous insights into social interplay match her observations of the London scene. Like any colonial outpost, the Cape loved a scandal and the escapades of Johanna Baumgardt, the wayward wife of a Dutch official, who bore children to General Dundas and Admiral George Elphinstone – a rare instance uniting the army and navy commanders – exercised Anne's pen, just as it did local gossip. Yet without the company of likeminded women, above all without Margaret, she was lonely. Passing ships injected an occasional shot in the arm. Lady Jane Strange, a lively fellow eccentric, charmed Anne during her short stay and sent an amusing letter from Bombay, only to die within weeks.[49] But such diversions were rare, and she was in need of stimulus.

Her diaries turn frequently to the most challenging feature of Cape life – slavery. At home William Wilberforce's campaign had gathered force to the point that a parliamentary motion proposed by Dundas in favour of a gradual abolition had been passed by 230 votes to 85. Anne's instinctive response was clear. Once in town she saw some 300 'Etruscan-looking' figures standing in a square – slaves just landed from Mozambique and about to be sold.

I sighd & thought of Wilberforce, how it would have agitated his nerves to have looked at them when it agitated mine who am not wound up as he is to vibrate to that key and who am accustomd to see slavery all day . . . I drove home full of thoughts but without power to do them any good.[50]

She had no doubt of the ruinous effect of slavery, even if her accounts jar with modern sensibilities. A case in point was one of the Barnards' slaves, Charles, 'sober & very honest' and 'a fine boy tho an idle monkey' who, it transpired, had stolen money from them more than once.[51] Anne concluded that 'the early terrible practices they see corrupts them thoroughly & I am told no slave has a chance of being honest unless he is taken a child & bred apart from his equals ... Gentleness makes no impression on them.'[52] Whatever her beliefs, she was incapable of treating anyone severely. Charles was taken before the fiscal to receive three lashes, but returned and was brought before Anne who, in a scene redolent of evangelical healing, 'gave him a little more preaching, touchd his heart for the moment & laying my hand on his head bid him go & never again be a dishonest man ... I should always be his friend & that whenever bad people desired him to steal, to tell me & I would not discover [expose] it, but would show him the danger of listening to their councils'.[53]

Women slaves were openly used for sexual purposes by British officers and civilians. So ubiquitous was the practice that even Anne took it in her stride, noting merely how Barnard's deputy, Ross, had bought a female slave, then fathered a child by her.[54]

She wrote too, with somewhat chilling sangfroid, of the dilemma she faced when her brother John Lindsay called at the Cape, homeward bound from the military service that had cost him four years a prisoner at Seringapatam. John, it became clear, was desperate for relief from 'a three-month celibacy'; Anne, with their three women slaves at hand, and in possibly the most disconcerting words ever to come from her pen, made the excuse that 'none of my black beautys are very *ragoutant* (palatable)'.[55] Lindsay dealt with the deficiency himself with a prostitute, who was probably black.

Sexuality and slavery nevertheless stimulated Anne to one remarkably bold, if abysmal, literary effort. She had recorded in her diary a dark insight into Cape society – the tale of a Dutch woman, Mrs de Waal, who gave birth to a dark-skinned child, 'its hair that of a negro'. The dead baby was later found mutilated, and the mother herself poisoned.[56] A romantic variation on this story was related to Anne by an officer on his return from the interior, of the connection between a black slave and the daughter of a Boer farmer, and their enforced separation – not by death but by the youth's exile to herding in the mountains. Anne's suggestion to Barnard that action be taken on his behalf was impractical: the colony would go up 'in flames about our ears', he said.[57] So she set the story to words and music, 'The Slave of Africa', 'commemorating his love and his misfortune'.

> Urbain was cheerful . . . patient . . . manly . . . kind
> And his young Mistress loved him . . . oh too well!
> Her shame was known . . . her furious Father
> Him banished for the space of twenty years
> Far . . . far away, to tend the Goats . . . alone.[58]

The theme aside, 'The Slave of Africa' is an ungainly work, bearing no comparison with 'Auld Robin Grey' or any of Anne's better verse. She appears to have been ashamed of it and noted its omission from her collected poems. It still bears noting as the product of an eighteenth-century mind challenging taboos and able to conceive of love between a black slave and a white woman.

16

The Court of Lilliput

1800–1802

By the start of the new century British rule had transformed the Cape from a backward agricultural settlement into a thriving mercantile hub – one, moreover, with a flavour of English sport and culture. Cape Town had a turf club, a gentlemen's drinking establishment and a coffee house, its first newspaper was about to be published and the governor lavished public spending on theatrical productions and concerts.[1] Offstage, another favourite British pastime flourished as empire-builders waged war on one another.

Anne Barnard's hopes of acting as an intelligent politician to '*bring the Nations together* on terms of good will' were but a memory.[2] She could still no more stand back than she could lay down her pen. Late in 1800 she gave a ball at the Vineyard, 'including all the new regiments . . . and a considerable number of Dutch' – a counterpoint rather than a rival to the entertainments offered by the governor's hostess, Mrs Blake. When Anne was accused of bringing ragtag and bobtail into her home, she did not deny it, merely adding: 'All I deny is that ragtag is superior to bobtail.'[3] Meanwhile, she engaged in public affairs as best she could, with letters to two men at home: Lord Macartney, who retained the ear of those in power, and Henry Dundas, second in authority only to Pitt.

Anne was starting to invest in the future. They would not always be at the Cape, talked often of where fortune might take them and, having savoured the simplicity of rustic pleasures, had concluded that happiness might not lie in the society at home. 'As for London, its amusements & dissipation,' Anne wrote to a friend, 'I do not give a wish for them.' In dreamy moments, she would suggest they could sail away to the penal colony of New South Wales where, she pointed out, she had at least one acquaintance, the former manservant convicted of stealing her jewels. Andrew liked the idea of visiting the Ottoman lands, where he had once travelled, and Greek islands.[4] Whimsical visions aside, he still wanted another position. Although they could manage quite comfortably on Anne's income, Andrew needed the dignity of employment. She would go with him wherever duty called (in other words wherever Dundas saw fit to offer him a post). 'The risk of breaking up such harmony would be too great to run.'[5]

There was, however, no escaping the paradox between her former lover's eminence and her husband's humble station. Not for the first time, she walked a fine line – on the one hand Dundas's shrewd observer at the Cape, on the other a supplicant in need of his patronage. Mostly she kept her balance with a warm yet businesslike tone, following his instructions to 'tell me when you write . . . whether you think the Colony worth keeping'.[6] Of that, naturally, she had no doubt, even if it took time for her to be vindicated.

Dundas's appreciation of Anne's diplomatic efforts came at her husband's expense. He saw her as the real force at the Cape, 'the most official person of the two', in representing the Crown and conciliating the Dutch.[7] When Anne extolled Andrew's talents, which she did not so discreetly as she imagined, it smacked to Dundas of special pleading. Like his nephew, he made no secret of his belief that Anne had married beneath herself. In attempting to remedy this defect, she showed more determination than tact. Not a letter to Dundas now passed without her returning to the field against the general. Of his contempt for Andrew she wrote: 'Mr Barnard sought his friendship at first so sincerely that it is a wonder to me why he should Hate him so.'[8] More provoking was her comment that 'when a man soars too high over the head of another he must not be surprized if the sun melts his wings & brings him down to the fair level'.[9]

One particular bone of contention was leave. While the Barnards were entitled to a visit home after more than three years at the Cape, the general had instead granted leave to Andrew's junior, his own trusted aide Hercules Ross. Anne's conclusion to one of her longest letters to Dundas, lamenting 'the politicks of our Lilliput court', was touched with despair:

> My dearest friend I did not always write you such vexed, grumbling letters, but what can I do? Oh, never, never have I felt the delay of leave of absence in the manner I do now ... Never while I had the idea that our stay might *do good*, but now that I have but too much reason to fear that there is a party *too strong* establishing itself against us at the Government house, I tremble for the ensuing twelve month. If Mr B is improperly treated by the governor *in league with the general* I really fear he will throw up the game and along with me prefer a turnip top where we are loved & respected to a life of oppression & spite ... We are not people who can gossip and tittle tattle. All must be on broad ground or sea and resignation.
>
> Be assured my best friend, *nothing shall be rashly or testily done* ... We *will endure*, even with the leave of absence in our pockets. *Support us, however. We need it and look to you for it.*[10]

The opinions and substance of what she had to report remained sound. By 1800 the frontier conflict had reached a stalemate she thought best abandoned – leaving the Zuurveld to the Xhosa: 'They will gladly furnish us with cattle in return for such articles as they want ... We should save future quarrelling, expense of men & money.'

If her writings on the Cape stand the test of time more for

their insight and vision than anything else, these reports to
Dundas did have one significant impact – the downfall of Sir
George Yonge. First impressions of 'I fear a very weak old soul'
gave way to more serious concerns, that Yonge's 'little follys will
grow up to be greater ones'.[11] So it proved. Five months after his
arrival, Anne informed Dundas that 'in some late transactions
the hands of government have not been so clean as they ought to
have been'.[12] Yonge's weakness, it appeared, was less a matter of
extravagance than corruption.

Slave auctions had been made illegal by Macartney unless
authorised from London to meet specific labour shortages. In May
1800 Anne reported to Dundas that Yonge had allowed a notorious
slaver named Michael Hogan to land 1,600 Mozambicans along
with a cargo of smuggled goods. 'It is generally believed,' she
went on, 'that a douceur of no small magnitude was given to
effect what would have put from ten to fifteen thousand pounds
in the merchant's pocket.' Barnard had warned Yonge of this
impropriety 'in the strongest terms ... but found the governor
deaf to all remonstrance or argument'.

> Being anxious to avoid all further conversation or opposition from
> Mr B, he gave the order for the landing and selling of the slaves
> himself – without bringing them through the Secretary's office.[13]

At first she could scarcely credit that a British governor would
stoop so low as to line his own pockets, but the evidence was
inescapable. Before writing her explosive letter to Dundas, she set
down a detailed account in her diary of events leading to the slave
auction and how Andrew's objection had been airily dismissed by
Yonge on the grounds that 'in all governments mercantile men
will now & then do things that are illicit ... men of eminence &
ability are not to be sacrificed to a sett of dirty low informers'.[14]

Andrew was constrained by his junior rank but still wrote

explicitly to Lord Hardwicke, who had some influence at home:

> The purpose of Sir George, or at least of those around him, is to make money by any means they can, let them be ever so foul. In short, a more corrupt administration I believe does not exist.[15]

Anne also wrote to Wellesley in Bengal setting out her concerns about Yonge, or 'the Lofty Twaddler' as she called him. Wellesley subsequently joined in her campaign. 'The imbecility and ignorance of Sir George Yonge entirely disqualify him from his situation,' he wrote to Dundas in October. 'The importance of the Cape in relation to India increases every hour.'[16] Yonge had also embroiled himself unwisely in a civil war with General Dundas over control of the army. But his fate was decided by Anne's report of the slave auction.

There she might have left it; but she could not restrain herself. Her letter to Dundas had returned with grim inevitability to his nephew: 'If the General's government was a haughty and unprosperous one, at least it was an *Incorrupt* one.'[17] Then she rushed on, to come plummeting off the tightrope she had carefully negotiated. 'What a sad pity it is that he cannot determine on anything unless he is in a passion, and then it is a great chance whether it is not in the wrong way.'[18]

The Barnards were still savouring news that their home leave had finally been approved when Anne's letter reached Henry Dundas in Cheltenham and he sat down to reply. His opening words brought reassurance that her exposure of Yonge was being taken seriously: 'You may believe that the Picture you give me of the Settlement is to me a very unpleasant one, and a radical Cure must be immediately applied to it. What that may be I shall decide when I return to London.'[19] From this point Yonge was doomed.

Dundas then turned to his nephew's treatment of Andrew.

I am perfectly aware that there are irritable parts in the General's temper, but I must do him the justice to say that I have seen no proofs of it in any part of the public proceedings which have come before me ... I am afraid from the contents of your letter that you have conceived erroneously of other parts of his conduct ... I am sure your own candour must feel how impossible it is for me not to set you right in several particulars in which you have been misinformed.[20]

Anne may have felt less injured had she known that four weeks later Dundas told the king that his friend Yonge was so wild and extravagant he would have to be recalled.[21] Her intelligence had served to bring down a corrupt regime. As it was, however, on reading Dundas's rebuke, delivered in person by Henry Wellesley on his way back to India, a chill came over her. Belatedly, she saw her candour had 'cooled Dundas as a patron to my innocent husband'. That night she lay sleepless until Andrew reached out and whispered: 'What Nanny! Not asleep yet?'

I told him the truth – that the coldness of Mr D's letter had sunk my heart so that I could not rest in peace. He bid me not to be uneasy, that he was not & that he was sure I had too much pride and too much contentment to care much for the loss of any man's favour by frankness and sincerity.[22]

Howsoever he tried to reassure her, Andrew was worried himself. In two years, he wrote to Macartney, 'I have not had one pleasant circumstance to communicate to you. Everything has gone wrong.'[23] For many at home, including Dundas, it was hard to comprehend how isolation among squabbling factions upset two peace-loving souls; Macartney at least, with his experience, understood when Anne related her efforts 'to keep [Andrew] getting too angry on some occasions & dispirited on others'.[24]

Anne drew a line with what she intended as a final despatch to Dundas, insisting that she had to be an honest friend who spoke her mind. 'I can be silent to you, but I cannot write in Shackles.'[25]

The Barnards' sense of vulnerability was reflected in their decision to forego the home leave finally approved by Dundas. Initially this had seemed a way of showing their gratitude. Now it was a case of making up to him, so that Andrew might regain approval. Had they but known, the world and everything which bore on their lives was on the verge of change.

Relatively little is recorded of Anne Barnard's last months in Africa. The diaries to which she had confided trial, joy and adventure, and which she preserved together with her sketches, came to an abrupt halt.[26] She wrote less, angered by the triviality around her, but also because of confusion over the speed of developments in Europe. Each mail packet seemed to bring momentous news which had barely been absorbed before it was overtaken by the next. During the events leading to the Treaty of Amiens and the colony's return to Holland, those at the Cape were usually the last to hear of them.

A humiliated Yonge lingered at the Castle for months, awaiting formal instruction to return home and pitied by the agent of his downfall who somehow managed to persuade herself that although corrupt, he had not intended to line his own pockets.[27] Amid reports that her old acquaintance, Lord Glenbervie, was to be appointed his successor, General Dundas was restored as acting governor.

Then came a bombshell. On 20 April a ship from Lisbon arrived with newspapers announcing that Pitt and Dundas had resigned on 6 February. The reason for an event described by Anne as 'so astonishing – so fatal I might add to the interests of poor old England' was a proposal for Catholic emancipation to which the king refused to accede.[28] The fact was, both men were utterly exhausted. But more than a month later, the cause and consequences were still unclear at the Cape and newspapers, Anne noted, were 'no very good guide'.[29]

As it transpired, a new administration under Henry Addington had taken office and peace initiatives were being extended to France. But uncertainty persisted until almost the end of the year, leaving the Cape administration in limbo and ever more susceptible to pettiness, backstabbing and mean-spiritedness.

On taking charge again General Dundas appeared willing to repair relations with the Barnards, only to be confounded by his new wife. Eliza Cumming was the daughter of minor East India Company gentry, her sweet appearance belied by a yellow smile of which it was said, ' 'Tis the venom of her tongue which has destroyd the enamel of her teeth.'[30] Once Mrs Dundas had usurped Mrs Blake as hostess, she turned on Anne, circulating a smear that a newcomer, a young man originally from Balcarres, who worked in the garden at the Vineyard, was Anne's natural son. While this risible story was dismissed by all but the windiest gossips, Anne felt obliged to cut off association with Mrs Dundas.

Malice at their Lilliput court led to further tittle-tattle, apparently by a former servant, Samuel Hudson, who had accompanied the Barnards to the Cape before going his own way and making a career in the customs department.* What he said to upset Anne is unknown. So far as she was concerned, though, Hudson was resentful 'as he cannot forget how lately he has been our servant'.[31]

---

* Samuel Hudson had been a footman at Wimpole, the home of Anne's brother-in-law, Lord Hardwicke, before embarking with the Barnards for the Cape. He kept a diary reflective of a jaundiced outlook on the world in general and about the only thing he shared with his former employers was a detestation of General Dundas. Anne recorded in her diary that Hardwicke wrote to Barnard, accusing Hudson of stealing prints from his library and urging his arrest. Barnard declined, pointing out the absence of evidence (Cape Diaries, vol. 2, pp. 255–6. Hardwicke Papers, Add. MS 35647, fo. 48, Andrew Barnard to Philip Hardwicke, 26 December 1804).

Far the most distressing and humiliating rupture, however, concerned a young artist, Samuel Daniell. A nephew of Thomas Daniell, who made his name with aquatints of India, Samuel had arrived at the Cape with Yonge and been abandoned without patronage on his departure. Anne, moved by the plight of a professional draughtsman, suggested to Andrew that they take him in and Daniell was given a room at the Vineyard with what she saw as an agreement that they might copy whatever they liked from one another's portfolios. Daniell, however, was soon seeking advice from John Barrow about what he said was an attempt to steal his work. It may be relevant that since his expedition up Table Mountain with Anne, Barrow had sided with the Castle regime against the Barnards. He, in any event, wrote to Macartney, reporting Daniell's claim that Anne had secretly traced many of his drawings and, when confronted, she had been 'confounded, ashamed and burnt them all, to an enormous amount, for she had been very industrious'.[32]

Anne's version, in her own letter to Macartney, was that she had indeed traced some of Daniell's drawings, and he some of hers, but that he became anxious, fearing his prospects might be harmed if her work 'fell into unsafe hands'. She tried to reassure him, promised to burn the copies she had made, but was unable to find one, of an antelope. That, she later claimed, was because it had been stolen by Daniell and shown at the Castle to curry favour with Mrs Dundas 'as a *bon bouche* [choice morsel] against me'.[33] As a result, Anne went on, this smear had soon started doing the rounds of the coffee house.[34]

The tone of her rambling account to Macartney suggests that mistrust may have turned to paranoia; and her claim to have destroyed all other copies of Daniell's drawings seems to have been false. Among her watercolours at Balcarres are a pair of studies titled *Caffre Equipped for War* and *Caffres on Top of Table Mountain*, both of which bear a striking similarity to images by

Daniell in the volume that made his name, *African Scenery and Animals*.[35] Anne's outlines may have been copied after the book's publication in 1805, but that is unlikely. However, her suspicion that she been a victim of spite at the Castle is credible: Daniell, thanks to his friendship with General Dundas, was appointed secretary on a mission to the interior which provided fresh inspiration for his art. Daniell went on to collaborate with Barrow (by now the general's secretary) on the second edition of his *Travels into the Interior of Southern Africa* published in 1806. Barrow dedicated the book to Henry Dundas, who made him second secretary at the Admiralty on his return to Britain.

As an example of how a colonial outpost could turn on itself in feral fury, events at the Cape in 1801 were not unique. But they also showed that an aristocratic woman – even one who did not distinguish ragtag from bobtail – was not exempt in such places from attack by those of a lower class; Daniell and Mrs Dundas had disparaged her in a way that would have been unthinkable at home. The paradox was that, as a female hobbyist who would never display her work, Anne was no artistic rival to Daniell. In London, moreover, he would have been likely to regard her interest as an endorsement, rather than a threat.

At the last, title asserted itself: Daniell was made to apologise; and General Dundas brought his wife to make *amende honorable* to Anne, which she did with an ill grace.[36] None of these gestures repaired Anne's confusion or misery. She told Macartney: 'The world went mad when you went away.'[37] To Margaret she wrote: 'This place is grown the den of faction – of abuse, calumny and jealousy. I shall quit it with joy.'[38]

The Barnards were making final preparations before sailing home on leave when Anne took up her pen to Margaret again: 'Peace! Absolutely peace! Never did any account come so unexpected!'[39] The ceasefire signed ten weeks earlier, on 30 September 1801, had transformed the world once more. The Cape was to be handed back to the Dutch.

It was, everyone agreed afterwards, a mistake, and one that might have been avoided had Henry Dundas remained in office. But while he still saw the Cape as crucial to the defence of India, the prevailing view was that British naval supremacy had rendered it superfluous. Dundas's successor, Lord Hobart, thought there was scarcely anyone 'who did not consider the Cape a burden rather than an advantage'.[40]

Anne's feelings about the loss of the Cape may be imagined and she even had mixed feelings about the peace. Writing to Wellesley the next day, she was torn between seeing it as necessary, even indispensable, and a fear – well founded, as it turned out – that 'it will not be a *lasting* peace but a cessation of hostilities to give the French time to thunder on us with redoubled force'.[41]

For the Barnards the timing could not have been worse. The *Hindostan* was already loaded with their sheep, geese and wine for the voyage home when she was ordered to sail for Ceylon. Moreover, they faced a dilemma. They could manage on Anne's resources and the house in Berkeley Square. But Andrew wanted work of his own. From the handover he would be without a position and the £3,500 a year that went with it. He had no way of obtaining another without his wife's influence; and how she would manage that now Dundas was out of government could not be ascertained while she was at the Cape.

Their decision was that Andrew should stay on because it would reflect badly on him were he to depart before the official handover to the Dutch. Anne was to proceed home in a merchantman to commence lobbying on his behalf. It evidently did not cross their minds that a whole year might pass before the Peace of Amiens led to the act of handover.

Making ready for departure, Anne reflected how five years in Africa had aged her. 'You will find me *bewitching*,' she wrote

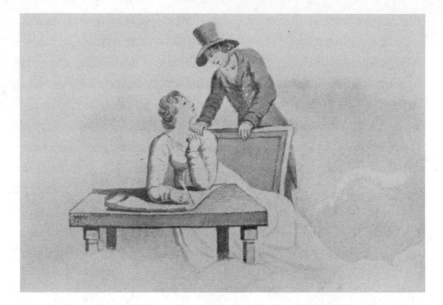

Anne wrote letters and journals throughout her life but parting from Andrew opened the way to her later literary activity as a memoirist

to Margaret, 'which is to say looking like a witch.'[42] Then the prospect of quitting the Cape once and for all brought on a flood of reflections and, her natural inclination being what it was, she found herself drawn back to the exhilaration, the endeavours, she and Barnard had shared. They *had* acted as intelligent politicians, and they *had* brought the nations together on terms of goodwill. They had ventured to the interior and savoured evenings in Paradise. These were the memories that prevailed.

On the eve of sailing, she wandered the Castle balcony looking up at Table Mountain. She had climbed it twice now, most recently with Andrew when they spent a night in a tent with 'a good bed on which two hearts reposed, grateful for all their blessings but most so for their happiness in each other'.[43] While she was on the balcony, three Khoikhoi women with shining bodies and 'little more covering than the three ladies of antiquity' came out to chant a song.[44] Her interpretation of this lament for their departure, *The*

Hottentots Farewell, found its way into her collected poems.

On 8 January 1802 Anne and Andrew went together on board the *Scarborough*. With limited space, her collection of zoological curiosities was confined to a tame antelope, a turtle, a few ducks, and a green lourie – a Cape bird also known as a turaco.[45] Andrew remained on board for one last night together, before being rowed ashore at dawn. She went straight back to her cabin desk and dashed off a final note:

> My Dearest and Best Beloved,
> Oh My B, should I never see you more do I not leave you an inestimable legacy in the full assurance that you have made me since I was in your life as Happy as it is possible to be in the world . . . To serve your future interests I leave you – the sole notice that could have persuaded me from your side . . .
>   Your Own Anne
> All is ready. They ask for my letter. Oh, God Bless You.[46]

Once at sea she reflected more deeply:

> Never can I cease to recollect (while I possess memory) the sweetness of those drivings out to Paradise, the name of our little country house half way up a stupendous mountain, hyenas and jackalls, monkeys and eagles, my neighbours, the mild expanse of pure air above my head, and the all-seeing eye to look down on the innocence of our pleasures.[47]

And another memory came of their ascending Table Mountain together . . .

> Both gay, attached to each other, blessing the Great Lord who formd the wonder before us, and equal to looking down on his world from its brow! Let no one despair, let no heart sink with despondency. Here I am, said I again. I never thought I shoud have been here atall! Africa – Africa![48]

17

Home and Away

Spring in 1802 refreshed England with hope as well as scent and bloom. Anne landed at Gravesend on 11 April after a three-month voyage to learn of the peace treaty ratified at Amiens two weeks earlier and found London in a state of rejoicing. With her Berkeley Square house being rented by the Ottoman ambassador, she took lodgings at Mollards Hotel where to start with a tremendous fuss was made of her.

'Friends have poured their civilities on me,' she wrote to Barnard. 'My levees exceed those of the minister and my invitations to dinner run at four a day. No man or woman of my former acquaintance has found himself or herself too great to have sat an hour with me.'[1] Callers included the Prince of Wales and a host of political figures, Pitt, Dundas, Windham, Fitzroy, Abercorn and various Yorkes, all coming to praise the good she had done at the Cape. Then, pricking the bubble of her own vanity, she went on: 'This makes me ask the question of Fag in the Chapter of Accidents "Am I so wery delightful?"'*

Dundas's attention was especially reassuring. As she reported it, he explained in private what he had been unable to say in writing, and the chill arising from the dispute with his nephew was set aside. Everyone else she met sympathised, asking: 'How goes on

---

* Anne seems to have been confusing a character in Sheridan's *The Rivals* with the play by Sophia Lee.

that madman General Dundas?' In the first flush of excitement there appeared a keen interest in all matters to do with the Cape, and when she showed Dundas her panorama from the Castle he, rather than an artistic work, saw a strategic diagram for another invasion. 'Guard it like the apple of your eye,' he said. 'We may not always be without the Cape.'[2] All in all, the omens could hardly have been better. 'I really think my best beloved,' she told Barnard, 'your chance of future employment is good.'

Her African creatures were spared life in the metropolis. The antelope and lourie had expired at sea and it was not long before the collection of wild fowl came to royal attention.

> The Queen, who had heard of them, was graciously pleased to send one of the Ladies of her Bedchamber to congratulate me on my safe return, and to beg that whatever birds or animals I had brought that were curious, might be sent to her villa in Frogmore, when she should be happy to shew me them in good health. The Royal Mandate was obeyed, the geese were sent, but the Goose never had the invitation renewed to her.[3]

Feminine fashion, she reported to Barnard, had taken a daring turn in their absence:

> Lady Hertford would take no denial to my appearing at her assembly t'other night and sent Lady Clive to fetch me. I was glad I went. The women are all Sir Peter Lely's beauties. The gowns are cut down behind to show bare shoulders, and before to show other bare things, and the drapery round the form is so very light that Pygmalion might chisel after nature in all her lines.[4]

Margaret's failure to join her after their five-year separation hastened the passing of euphoria. She was in Dublin with their sister Elizabeth whose husband, Lord Hardwicke, was Lord

Lieutenant of Ireland, and would not travel to a reunion, 'the journey to London being so very long'.⁵ Margaret's susceptibility to 'the blews' grew and there are signs of resentment towards Anne, who did not want to leave London because Barnard might sail home at short notice. 'Oh, no Margaret,' she wrote, 'be not vexed my best of creatures, but wait a little longer and we will come together.'⁶ The Atkinson bequest was a further source of strain. With a relatively small annuity, Margaret had been hoping to see a resolution of the case that Anne did her best to ignore. That was easy at the Cape, but she still showed no willingness to grapple with lawyers and Margaret's rebuke that 'your hatred of dispute will keep you from engaging' had an edge, as well as being true.⁷

Anne's novelty value as an informant on Africa was short-lived – indeed, indifference to the Cape now it was about to be handed back, and her efforts to remedy society's ignorance on the subject may have jarred on both sides. Unknown as she was to Henry Addington's ministers, she found the new generation of public men had 'little time for female dinners'.⁸ Close male friends, on the other hand, were no longer at the centre of national affairs. She lured an increasingly gouty Macartney from Antrim to London and found him a villa in Chiswick where she visited to administer care and humour. Dundas continued to fulminate against the peace until retreating to his estate at Dunira with the title of Viscount Melville – but not before telling her of his madness in marrying Jane Hope.

In Margaret's absence Anne made a new friend, the wife of her brother John and a fellow eccentric. Charlotte North was a sister of Frederick North, the governor of Ceylon with whom Anne formed a witty rapport when he called at the Cape. The Norths were a family of ramshackle originals. Charlotte's sister had urged Anne to 'leave your Hottentots & fly over in a balloon' to be at the wedding.⁹ Charlotte herself was a treasure.

She was not only without beauty but she might have been called very plain by anyone who could find it in their heart to say so ... but no one could refrain from loving her. Careless of censure from the extreme innocence of her heart, she said and did what she pleased and never was blamed and never deserved to be so.[10]

Artless Charlotte was the long-suffering wife of a tormented soul. John Lindsay never recovered from his years of imprisonment in India and pursued a wild career of gaming and speculation that ruined him and made regular demands on family members for help, among whom Anne was the most indulgent.

Another friend was enjoying a spell of tranquillity in her turbulent marriage to the Prince of Wales. Maria Fitzherbert had turned to Anne as peacemaker before her departure for the Cape and lamented her absence while rejoicing that 'every letter that comes to England is full of your praises'.[11]* After the prince's affair with Lady Jersey and official wedding to Princess Caroline of Brunswick, Fitz likened herself to a galley slave, telling Anne she was finished with him and wanted a financial settlement. Instead, she accepted him back at her Tilney Street house and despite his lapses into dissolution they had five years – by her own account – as merry as crickets, though she denied him her bed. 'We live like brother and sister,' she told Anne. 'I did not consent to ... live with him as his wife or his mistress.'[12] 'Both friends I love,' Anne recalled, 'both I have been obliged at times to condemn. Neither has been quite right, nor either so wrong as they have been called.'[13]

---

* Before departing Anne had continued to urge her friend against outbursts with the prince. 'Dearest Fitz be not too violent for your own sake.' After hearing the prince complaining of his misery, Anne wrote again: 'I never heard a man express himself with more attachment to a woman than he did when talking of you and the complaints he made of you ... (small ones they were) were the complaints of tenderness only.' See also *Maria Fitzherbert – The Secret Wife of George IV* by James Munson.

A renewal with William Windham was always going to be more awkward. He had written to her at the Cape that he was to wed an early love, and Anne was unimpressed, perhaps a little offended, by his choice of, 'the worthy but undistinguished Miss Forrest'. Cecilia Forrest had once been besotted with Windham's friend, Cholmondeley, and she had reached the age of forty-eight before Windham took the decisive step. Anne initially described Cecilia as 'a sick-nurse whom he could depend upon' and the match as typical of one who 'spent his life in regretting and being too late in everything'.[14] But she warmed to Mrs Windham, while her husband 'had become so little to me that to be in his company ceased to give any pain'.[15]

Hopes of a lasting peace faded as Bonaparte demonstrated that his real desire was for time to prepare for further conflict. Anne's paramount concern, however, was how delays in implementing the treaty were keeping Barnard at the Cape. Three months after her return, no Dutch officials had sailed to take over the administration and, as she told Macartney that summer, her husband could not possibly be home before the end of winter.

Andrew was not managing well without her. His letters, addressed to 'My Ever Dearest Nanny', were loving, plaintive and almost as long as hers.[16] Both dwelt on their lost happiness at the Cape and, as months went by, Anne suggested she might actually sail back to him, 'which from such a coward is saying a great deal'.[17] This set off whimsical flights of fancy as they renewed ideas for further adventure, sailing on to the Pacific or Mediterranean. As Andrew pointed out, they could be free.

> I have great comfort My Love in what at a former time I rather wished otherwise – that we have no children. You and I can make ourselves happy anywhere – in Africa, Wales, Russia. Had we children in the

present position of the times our hearts would bleed for them. I feel now for you only. I can face any ill with you.[18]

She agreed: 'There is not one part of the world makes any difference except you are in it … How comfortable we shall be when we have our nice roast leg of mutton, potatoes and an apple pie, with a bit of fish on Sundays!'[19]

Comfortable they could be. Yet while Anne positively wished to live 'careless of the pomps and vanities of this wicked world', Andrew had a desperate desire to work, partly for the self-respect of providing for his wife, and partly because he was not good at living within their means.[20] Despite a handsome salary of £3,500 his purse had been constantly stretched by what Anne saw as 'his pleasure of bestowing it on others'.[21] Meanwhile, her hopes of finding him another post had clearly been too sanguine. Quite simply, time had moved on and old friends were no longer in positions of influence. As Andrew would soon be without income, she decided to raise capital by realising some assets.

Anne's property portfolio is a confusing subject and – like her activity as a landlady – one that raised eyebrows. Her first house in Manchester Square had been followed by a second in Berkeley Square; a third was built on the same site, and a fourth purchased in Hanover Square. Returns were not high to judge from the £180 per annum she received for one, and the ravages of tenants such as the Ottoman ambassador could be severe, as she discovered on returning to find 'the seven plagues of Egypt were nothing to the 700 plagues of Elphi Bey'.[22] Intending to redecorate and sell, she rented another house a short walk away in Dover Street, from where she could oversee progress. Months later two of her properties went under the hammer, only for the sales to fall through. Money remained short.

They had been a year apart when Andrew wrote a last letter before sailing:

I meet with mortification & vexation every day. Gracious God, what a twelve month I have passed since you left me Dearest. If I was to possess the wealth of Bengal I would not undergo such another ... But home, Dearest, after all these fiery trials will be the sweeter. Let me only find my love in good health when I get there and I shall forget them all.

Your Own Slave, AB[23]

Andrew was still homeward bound when Bonaparte's aggression left even the peace-loving Addington with no option but to confront him. On 18 May 1803, three weeks after Andrew landed from the *Jupiter*, Britain and France were at war again.

Over the next three years the Barnards persevered against prevailing winds. They adopted the modest premise that Andrew's experience should lead to a paid position of some sort, somewhere in Britain. That they failed and were separated again was down largely to unkind fate and William Windham; but it is still apparent that Andrew did not attract favour. Reputation was a powerful, often terrible, thing in Georgian society, and he never quite lost the taint Anne once alluded to: Barnard had been labelled an opportunist, a blackguard even.

On reaching London he was received by the prime minister in a manner Anne insisted was markedly civil.[24] That was all very well, but Addington's civility did not amount to employment. Next Henry Dundas, now Lord Melville, visited London when it was suggested he might join the government as First Lord of the Admiralty, and assured Anne of his willingness to help. But within weeks he was on his way back to Scotland after negotiations over a coalition involving Pitt collapsed.

Only now did the Barnards set off on a journey of family reunion, another year having passed since the five-year separation of the Cape, and though Anne would never have said as much, the summer they spent among relatives in Scotland and Ireland exposed how distant she had become from the mainstream of family life. Detachment began with her native land. For some time, she had perceived in Scotland an 'illiberality of thinking on every trivial point, such as to render the society quite odious to me'. (James Boswell, a fellow Scot, also developed what one biographer has called 'a repugnance for what he saw as Scottish insularity and crudeness of expression'.[25]) It was, she admitted, 'not amiable to feel disgust to the country in which one was born, but I can't help it'.[26] The gap went further. Her mother had been softened by age and infirmity to a condition of dependence and, as Anne saw it, 'seems to rely on her children with perfect confidence for their affections and care'. She herself had no part in bearing this burden, so there may have been guilt too.

More painful was being distanced from her once-inseparable sister. Margaret had experienced further misery with an unknown lover and 'a deep resentment corroded her heart' until she found comfort in religious faith.[27] She had also been provided with a refuge by the Hardwickes and, even before the Barnards joined them in Ireland, that side of the family had signalled disapproval of Anne's unconventional ways. Her brother-in-law was the epitome of propriety and Elizabeth had become quite prim. Together they urged Anne to beware the company she kept: Lady Wellesley should not be visited; as for Mrs Fitzherbert and the prince, they were to be avoided – she entirely. 'You owe it to yourself to keep clear of the liaison,' Elizabeth wrote. 'I think of you only, of your character and your interests. Both will suffer if you are not on your guard.'[28] Margaret, for her part, was now closer to their youngest sister's way of thinking. 'Lady Hardwicke tells me she has written to you to caution you about Fitz ... I believe [she] is right – prudence is necessary.'[29]

The antics of Anne's father-in-law did not help. While the Barnards were in Ireland, it became clear the seventy-six-year-old Bishop of Limerick was infatuated with twenty-two-year-old Jane Ross-Lewin, a woman of innocent demeanour and deep designs, and because the old bon viveur was 'still animated by the promethean fire of fancy, ready to be kindled into a blaze and explode on opposition', there was nothing his son could do to restrain him. 30*

Back on the mainland, they started north to Haigh Hall, the new seat of the Earl of Balcarres.† Debts on the family estate had obliged Alexander to sell Balcarres to Robert on his return in true nabob style from India, and move to his wife's home in Lancashire.31 The Barnards went on to Balcarres and Dunira, sharing Melville's contentment with his rugged landscape, and would have stayed longer but finding there was only one room with a double bed and it was to host another guest after five nights, they moved on. They remained, in Andrew's words, 'unfashionable enough to sleep in the same bed'.32

The campaign to find Andrew a position resumed on the Barnards' return to London in the spring of 1804 and continued without success to the end of 1806. Andrew had no vaulting ambition – had, indeed, been happy with the promise of a role with Hardwicke in Ireland on a salary of a mere £600 a year. The political ground, however, was shifting constantly and when

---

* Another form of Irish volatility erupted during the Barnards' visit, in the short-lived uprising led by Robert Emmet. Of the public execution of this 'young and singularly handsome young man of noble air', Anne wished to know nothing – 'the subject demolishes me' – but Andrew attended and was impressed by Emmet's 'manly and undaunted deportment'. (Memoirs, vol. 5, pp. 86–8)

† Haigh Hall, then a comparatively simple manor house, was rebuilt at vast expense by Alexander's son James from 1827. Ultimately, the Haigh estate provided the coal wealth that revived the Lindsays' fortunes. James successfully reclaimed the title of Earl of Crawford for the family in 1843. The seat of the Earls of Crawford and Balcarres returned to Balcarres in 1947.

Addington's government fell, the post went with it. At first that appeared to Barnard's advantage because Pitt returned to power and Melville with him. Both men lived in Wimbledon, a country retreat favoured by statesmen, so naturally when a house became available, Anne took it. 'It was an old Gothic house full of ghosts and goblins,' she recalled, 'with no garden to rear a cabbage in.'[33] But it was only a hundred yards from Melville's. The likes of Fox, Wilberforce and Grenville also lived near by and Andrew's optimism returned. 'Chance may promote my wishes without my saying anything,' he said cheerfully.[34]

In the event, moving to Wimbledon served no purpose other than for Andrew to ride out on the common. When Anne managed to get Pitt round, he 'came and went without even an allusion [to] our having been six years at the Cape'.[35] The prime minister's carriage would clatter by on its way to the next house, and the cry 'Drive on to Melville's' became a joke between the Barnards. She persuaded Andrew to write to Pitt, reminding him that he was the only official from the Cape left without a post.[36] Nothing came of it.

Late in 1804 Andrew returned to Ireland when his father's affairs descended into farce. The bishop – once cited by Dr Johnson as evidence for his theory that a man could improve in later life because improvement would be so easy in his case – had married the twenty-two-year-old object of his infatuation, on whom he lavished the small remains of his estate. Matters became mysterious and fraught. Jane was mortally ill, according to the bishop. In fact, she had fallen pregnant by a young lover. The bishop's eccentricity turned to dottiness. He railed against 'my ungrateful son', but when accounts revealed he was bankrupt had no option but to return with him to England. Andrew wrote to Anne: 'I will endeavour to dream of you, which will do me good.'[37]

Money remained a serious concern. Further attempts to sell

property failed after a fall in prices. To make his own ends meet, Andrew was reduced to sending Anne silver because it fetched more in London than Ireland. For little comforts, he would ask for bottles of Harveys Fish Sauce, sold by a shop in Wigmore Street.[38]

It was not until the end of 1805 that the bishop's affairs were settled and he could be brought back to spend his last weeks at Wimbledon. Anne had had one success – obtaining a cadetship for the second of Andrew's sons. She still took a maternal interest in his boys and, with Lord Hardwicke's influence, both had been set on the path to military careers.[39] But almost four years after her return from Africa, she had failed to secure so much as an offer for Andrew and her own declining status was inescapable.

> If ambition, the pride of birth or love of pre-eminence have ever led me to wish for a certain portion of superiority, my walk in life – both in fortune and rank – denys it to me now.[40]

The fact was, she had to admit, 'I am married to an amiable good man, but he is neither a nabob or a peer.'

The start of a fateful year found them back at Berkeley Square when British troops landed at the Cape of Good Hope again. The Barnards had just attended Nelson's burial at St Paul's and the struggle for world power was once more in the balance: Trafalgar may have secured British control of the seas, but Bonaparte's victory at Austerlitz had made the French masters of Europe.

Two weeks later a stunned Andrew came home to announce, 'Pitt is no more.' The death at the age of forty-six of Britain's war leader was accompanied by the political demise of his closest associate. Melville's enemies, most notably Windham, had forced his resignation over allegations of malfeasance and impeachment proceedings were in hand. Lives seemed to be shrivelling everywhere. Macartney died on 31 March, a day after the Duchess of Devonshire. Anne had seen them at Chiswick after Pitt's death and been shocked by Georgiana's appearance, her right eye sightless and swollen, but 'with rays of beauty still, and beams of goodness gleaming from the poor eye that had lost its partner, over which there descended a lock of hair to conceal the misfortune'.[41]

Melville's trial on charges of embezzling £27,000 from navy funds began four weeks later in an incongruous blaze of Westminster pageantry. Anne did not attend, hoping to spare her friend embarrassment and clear in the belief that 'a man careless of money, high in honour' had been the victim of a political conspiracy. The vast majority of his parliamentary peers agreed. After being acquitted in June, he wrote to her that 'my triumph is certainly a complete one', and inviting the Barnards to a family celebration.[42] Within days he was on his way to Scotland, leaving power behind him once and for all.

Though Anne's old suitor had been falsely accused by his foes, it was an inescapable fact that these same individuals were now in power – among them Windham, Secretary for War and the Colonies in the coalition put together after Pitt's death. Somehow, despite all that had passed between them, Anne persuaded herself that Windham, rather than seizing an opportunity to humiliate her further, would recognise his obligation. Once more she would petition a former lover on her husband's behalf, discomforting though it was.

> To take up my pen in *solicitation* to *you* seems so strange to it that if it wanders and blots do not impute it to a want of respect for the Secretary of State . . .

She wanted, she said, 'your patronage in general' to find Barnard a post, up to and including the governorship of the Cape.

Something at home would be preferable but, she added, in a strained version of the metaphor she had once used with Dundas, 'I am ready to lay my bones down at the foot of Table Mountain if my duty calls me there, as governor's wife or secretary's wife ... the whole study of his life is to make me happy.'[43]

Barnard as a colonial governor was inconceivable and when the post was awarded to the Earl of Caledon, even the secretaryship seemed beyond his reach because the young lord wanted his cousin, a Mr Alexander, in the post.[44] Anne took the case up with the Prince of Wales who spoke to his friend Fox and word came back that the foreign secretary liked Barnard and would help. 'Poor Fox,' remarked Andrew, 'something will happen to him. It has been the case with every man ready to befriend me.'[45] If Anne's account is accurate, Fox lived just long enough to intercede with Windham, dying on 13 September. Andrew was appointed secretary, the same post he had relinquished three years earlier.

Barely had her objective been achieved than Anne began to have second thoughts. She was almost fifty-six, Andrew forty-three, and they might have no more than a dozen 'comfortable years together'. She expected to die first, but his health had been poor, with a recurrence of the stomach ailment that ended his army career. Along with risk, a return to the Cape would involve all the upheaval of transporting their way of life across the world again. A position at home, however lowly, became suddenly far preferable to a highly paid one abroad.

Anne's version of what passed was coloured by the guilt and bitterness she carried to the end of her days; but subjective though her account is, the principal strands are clear. Andrew was at Wimbledon, making arrangements for his father's memorial plaque at Westminster Abbey, when he wrote suggesting how to approach the individual who held their fate in his hands:

Perhaps you may be able to see Windham and talk the matter over *confidentially* with him remembering always that you have a politician to deal with. But you may say that on *your account* I would greatly prefer a situation of less emolument at home but in case that cannot be settled I am *ready* to go. I know you will act better than I can write.[46]

Anne's account of calling on Windham as he prepared for a court levee is couched in her most dramatic style but the essentials are substantiated by other papers.[47]

He was in his robe de chambre. He received me with a chivalric manner of obsequious gallantry, when my heart was beating with agitation and anxiety.

I told him my errand. I urged my earnest but humble petition that instead of the salary of £3,500 he had given Barnard, that he would arrange some exchange to give him a third or fourth of the sum with business at home as I thought Barnard's health was too subject to bilious attacks to venture a second trip to Africa ...

'Ah,' cried he, smiling and seeming to fly, 'I know these blandishments, these powers of persuasion, but I must fortify myself against them ... I have said what I will do, but more I think ought not to be asked. I must not bend to the powers of an enchantress who waves the wand she so well knows how to use over my head!'

Silent tears were the only reply to this irony of *Coquetry* mixed with *Resentment*. He saw them fall unmoved. He rang for my carriage unbidden and called out 'Lady Anne's servants' before the door was opened.[48]

In desperation Anne wrote to Lord Wellesley, whom she saw as her last friend of influence, asking him to intervene with Lord Grenville, the prime minister. 'Neither my own health nor the health of my excellent bilious husband is stout enough to flatter myself with the hope of our returning alive and merry some years hence.'[49] Whether or not Wellesley tried to help is not clear, but his star, too, was on the wane.

The one individual to emerge with dignity intact was the subject of these negotiations. Barnard made clear that money was not his concern by declining a private offer of £1,000 a year to stand aside in favour of the governor's cousin.[50] Reasoning that he must serve at the Cape if he was to be offered another post in future, he told Anne it would be best if he went alone: he could then make it understood that if her health did not permit her to join him, he would seek leave of absence and return after a year; in the meantime she would be best placed in London to pursue other openings.

Amid tearful preparations Anne commissioned a portrait. The great Reynolds was no more, so she turned to Sir Thomas Lawrence, the artist she thought his nearest equivalent, and over three days before Christmas at a cost of fifty guineas he produced a work typical of his talent, combining likeness with a tasteful element of flattery. As she told herself, Andrew's portrait would be a gently smiling presence at Berkeley Square until his return.

18

Alone

⁓ ᏮᏮ ⁓

1807–1810

They embraced in the bedroom at Berkeley Square on a dark, bitter morning in February. Usually Anne accompanied Andrew to the door when he went away, but this departure was so fraught he could not bear to have her there. That night, from an inn at Portsmouth, he wrote: 'I am this instant arrived here Dearest and Best Beloved.' In a shaky hand he went on: 'You behaved like an angel this morning and I feel most grateful to you for sparing me the cruel pain of parting from you in the presence of post boys and servants when I know I could not have supported myself like a *man*. My heart is breaking.'[1]

Hopes for an early sailing were dispersed by gales which prevented boats getting out to the ship. Andrew's old troubles with bile returned. He asked Anne to send pills from an apothecary on the Strand, adding a few days later: 'Can't you get some that will purge melancholy?' After a week he was still moored in Portsmouth amid deepening misery. 'Had we known Dearest as we do now, we should have made our bow to Mr Windham and desired him to appoint another secretary. But, alas, it is too late and as I have engaged in the business I must go through with it.'[2] A few days later he wrote: 'I have got a cold in my loins owing to the want of something warm near them these nights.'[3]

At last, on 4 March, Caledon's party went on board and as the ship weighed anchor Andrew sent a final note:

This very hour and day four years ago I left the Cape to return to my Dearest and Beloved Nanny and I am now leaving her again . . . What a cruel thing parting is and how very unequal I feel myself to it, but it must be done, tho I swear that this shall be the last time.[4]

Over the two-month voyage he kept a journal for her, much as she had once written for Margaret. His tiny cabin had no room for a desk, being taken up largely by chests containing the governor's plate, so he seized points between meals when the dining table was clear to 'sit down quietly and chat with my Love'. After a ferocious storm off Cape Finisterre was blown away by a fresh south-westerly trade and the *Antelope* raced along at more than eight knots, he resumed: 'Well, my dearest Nanny, here we are once more conversing together.'[5]

Anne had written a special letter in anticipation of his birthday, entrusting it to his servant with instructions that it be placed for Andrew to find on 12 April. That morning, as he picked up his hat to go on deck,

a letter fell out of it at my feet. I instantly saw by the hand who the writer was and put it in my bosom until I could retire by myself to feast upon every word it contained.[6]

Back in his cabin he read: 'Where will this find you, my Best Beloved? More than half way to the Cape I dare say ... O! Barnard, if this matter were to be acted over again I should not consent to a separation.' But, parted as they were, she urged him, 'to feel as much happiness as your situation can afford you in a place where you are so much beloved, where you have so much the power of doing good, and such field sports to amuse you and keep you in health.' To this end she enclosed a note for £50, so he could buy 'the best horse in the colony, which you may have wished for but thought above your pocket'.[7]

Andrew picked up the thread in his journal:

How kind and good it was in you Dearest and Best of Creatures to think of preparing so great a treat for me long before the time arrived when I was able to enjoy it. You are always employed in devising means by which you can make those you love Happy.[8]

But his poor health continued, with a fever and agonising stomach pains which he dosed with laudanum. Before they sailed Anne had written to Caledon imploring: 'Should you see appearance of bad health or bile, oh do not let him remain but send him home, for God's sake!'[9] The governor replied that he sympathised with her anxiety, because he found himself 'so deeply interested in everything that relates to him'.[10] Caledon was genuinely caring, giving his secretary use of his sofa during the day and at one point offering to give up his cabin.

Nearing the Cape, Andrew drew comfort from the bond formed with his new chief. 'He has said many kind things on my good nature. As he remarks, many people have embarked on a long voyage the best of friends and landed the bitterest enemies.' Barnard concluded his journal in Table Bay with 'the last conversation we shall have on board the *Antelope*'.

And now My Ever Dearest and Beloved Wife, I will take my leave of you. I almost shudder when I think of what a space there is between us, nearly 8,000 miles, but what is distance between two hearts so united as ours are? They would touch were we at the Extremities of the World. Pray for me sometimes Dearest Love as I never fail to do for you in the following words:

'Almighty and most merciful Father I humbly beseech thee to hear this my prayer which I offer up to thine Divine Majesty, beseeching Thee to save and defend my Dearly Beloved Wife from all Dangers and adversities whenever they oppress her. As her virtues are manifold and her life exemplary here on earth, I humbly hope that at the last day she may be found worthy of a place in Thy Heavenly Kingdom.'[11]

Andrew Barnard was back at the Castle again after four years, dealing once more with colonial conflict and urging restraint on the frontier Boers.

Within weeks of her husband's departure for Africa, Anne celebrated what she liked to see as the downfall of the man who had sent him there. In fact, although Windham's vacillation had exasperated colleagues in the 'Ministry of all the Talents', he was not dismissed but resigned on principle – in support of Catholic emancipation. By then, however, few would have disputed Anne's judgement on 'the worst secretary of war we have ever had'.[12]

She found a sympathetic ear in Melville, who wrote: 'I have always thought [Barnard] should have been provided for at home in place of being sent back. I think it would have happened if I had remained in power or if Mr Pitt had lived a little longer. I once would have been surprised by what you say respecting Mr Windham, but any surprise respecting that quarter has long since ceased.'[13]

Anne kept Andrew informed of political affairs, such as the passing of the Slave Trade Act in March which abolished human traffic in British colonies. 'Tell me what they think at the Cape,' she wrote. 'I suppose they will not like it.' Despite unequivocally supporting the abolition movement, she was as alive as ever to human paradox. 'Certainly the slaves at the Cape appeared to us a happier set of merry-hearted people than our *triste* [sad] peasantry; but I say nothing on this subject as a word spoken of a slave's being happy would get one thought hard-hearted.'[14]

Andrew had his hands full as it was, for Caledon was entirely dependent on him in those early days. The governor was new to administrative responsibility and, at twenty-nine, young to have had it entrusted to him. Between them, they set about forming a

liberal regime that sought at the same time to assist colonists and farmers suffering more acutely than ever since Abolition from the Cape's perennial shortage of labour. Caledon's reforms would lead to the so-called 'Magna Carta of the Hottentots', an edict stipulating that Khoikhoi farm labourers be protected by law with contracts and wages.*

For the first time since serving Macartney seven years earlier, Andrew Barnard was in work that brought him satisfaction and self-respect.

> Nothing can exceed Lord Caledon's kindness to me . . . I really think he has abilities fit for any situation, for he is wise, steady and quick in business beyond his years . . . I have such constant employment that my thoughts are scarcely allowed to rest a moment.[15]

At Andrew's suggestion, Caledon revived entertaining the colonists with twice-weekly dinners – civil and military on Tuesdays, married men and their wives on Fridays. Anne's presence was much missed. 'Everybody laments extremely your having remained behind . . . I cannot say we are very gay altho' Lord C exerts himself to make us so.'[16]

The governor was trying also to reassure Anne. Having promised to keep her informed on Andrew's condition, he wrote in June, 'I have now the particular satisfaction of saying that I never saw him appear better.'[17]

The vagaries of the postal system played havoc with Anne's emotions. Letters went astray and though it was generally assumed

---

* As Noel Mostert points out in his monumental work of South African history, *Frontiers* (pp. 347–9), this initially reformist agenda, which also prevented Khoikhoi labourers, formerly a nomadic people, from leaving their employer's lands without a pass from him, laid the basis for what became South Africa's notorious pass laws, controlling the movements of the indigenous races.

that packets would take around two months to reach England, there was no consistency in the time between their despatch and their delivery; in one instance she was assured that Andrew's health was good when she had already learnt of his having suffered a subsequent relapse. Indeed, a few days after Caledon sent off his buoyant assurance, Andrew was again wracked with stomach pains that confined him to bed for weeks. And because his suffering caused her pain, he took to downplaying his condition, sending off a few lines by fast-sailing brig when his health was good. 'I am vastly well at present,' he wrote in August.[18] The unpredictability of packets and the months between deliveries still gave rise to uncertainty, on both sides of the world. After one prolonged silence from home Andrew reported the arrival of a ship 'with the richest and most valuable cargo that ever was imported' – six letters from Anne, two from Elizabeth and one from Margaret; but the most recent had still been written more than two months earlier.[19]

Anne's concern about Andrew's symptoms led her to consult London's most eminent physicians – Matthew Baillie and Sir Walter Farquhar – whose advice added to her apprehension. He must 'give up all fermented liquors' and there was to be 'no shooting, no hunting'. Even these measures might not be adequate to ensure his full recovery once the Cape summer arrived because the heat would be inimical to his condition. Suddenly it became imperative that he should return. 'Delay not a moment, my Dearest' she begged. 'We are staking too much on what is not worth it.'[20]

Then came a letter reporting that he was not only strong again, but as happy as he could be 8,000 miles from her. Caledon treated him 'like a brother' and they were about to make a journey together. Anne went weak with relief. 'Oh, what a welcome thing the sight of your hand was! . . . I feel as if the Table Mountain was taken off my breast.'[21]

Andrew passed lightly over his mission, other than to say it should be accomplished in a fortnight and ought to bring him

back with some bulbs from the interior. The purpose, in fact, was to meet Boer leaders and introduce them to the governor – he to outline his policy for the frontier, they to present a list of grievances. Andrew had recently written to the Tulbagh magistrate, denying that Caledon's edicts prohibited self-defence against raiders: the law empowered farmers to protect themselves and their property with force; what it did not permit was 'the sufferer to adopt a regular system of retaliation'.[22]

Andrew returned to matters at hand. He had sent off a plant for her, 'the loquot plum, a China fruit of an excellent flavour', and a small case of dried crayfish for Elizabeth. The letter turned nostalgic. Andrew reported that he was at the Castle, sitting just a few yards from where he used to lie 'with my love by my side'.

> I look back on those days with infinite pleasure and only regret they are past, not to come. I am a poor lone creature without you and altho everyone is good to me, yet I have no satisfaction in a society where you are not . . .

He would write to his Dear Nanny on returning from his travels. In the meantime

> I shall offer up my prayers for her health and happiness until the day comes when I shall return to her, to part no more until called away from this world, and whether we are separated or united in the next is known to God alone.[23]

This letter, dated 6 October, was especially slow in reaching Anne, being delivered on 15 January.

The next day a chaise stopped at the door and a servant announced her sister-in-law, Lady Balcarres. She brought a letter in Lord Caledon's hand: Andrew Barnard was dead.

*

He had insisted on accompanying Caledon's mission to the Boers because it was he who had proposed it and he was the only member of the new administration known to them. Besides, he said, travel in a wagon was a pleasure and the bracing air of an African trail would do him good. But he appears to have concealed a further onset of what was by now routinely spoken of as his bile disorder: he was a heavy wine drinker and the condition may have been related to cirrhosis; or it may have been cancerous. In any event his agony after leaving Cape Town was so acute that after three days he was unable to go further.

The wagons were on a northerly trail, probably near Tulbagh, some eighty miles distant, when Andrew was taken to shelter on a farm. He urged Caledon and his aide to go off and enjoy the hunting. On their return after two days, he had deteriorated. Physicians summoned from Cape Town were unable to do anything. Andrew died in the bed of his Boer hosts on 27 October, three days short of what would have been the Barnards' fourteenth wedding anniversary. He was forty-five.

Caledon wrote to Anne on 5 November and it seems to have been thanks to his awareness of its devastating impact that his letter was delivered by a relative. His account of Andrew's death went off with a covering note to Lord Castlereagh, who had replaced Windham at the War Office, suggesting how it be conveyed. These letters reached Castlereagh on 15 January, who wrote directly to her brother Bal at the Lords, 'trusting to you for breaking this melancholy event to Lady Anne. I shall in the meantime, as far as I can, prevent the intelligence from transferring through any other channels.'[24] Andrew's death of 'a bilious fever' was not announced by the *Morning Post* for another week.

On being told, Anne went into a stupor and 'could not shed any tears for some hours', her sister-in-law reported. She then collapsed completely. The following day Lady Balcarres sent a note to the Hardwickes: 'I am still with poor Lady Anne.'[25]

A decade had passed when she wrote about these events herself, but the pain burned still.

I have no language to convey the effects produced on me by this blow. What Barnard was, what Barnard was to me, what I lost in him, can only be felt, not expressed. More than all, the agony of thinking that his death had taken place in the interior of Africa, where no care, no tenderness of his wife's was at hand to soothe his last moments . . . whose last act was to send the ring to me which from the time of his father's death he had worn on his finger, as 'the last legacy of love to his dearly beloved wife'. Oh pity, pity her who then thought herself unworthy of the pity of anyone from her faulty presumption, her blindness in hoping, her want of foresight on the possibility of losing the jewel she so highly prized, but which was lost by one of those schemes of worldly wisdom which the Almighty sometimes sees fit to level in the dust to shew us their vanity and folly.[26]

She had always assumed he would outlive her – was clear too that with 'his good looks, his fine teeth, his manly bronze', he would marry a second time. As for her, 'Were I to lose him I should not care how long or how short my day was.'[27]

Caledon's letter went into the fire at Berkeley Square: 'It is too sacred, too affecting, to be placed where in the course of time it must be read with indifference,' she wrote.[28] With it went a lock of Barnard's hair, a note from his deathbed and many of his other letters. But, as she noted on the folder of those that survive, 'I have burnt many but I *cannot* burn all.' The valedictory tone of his last letters, when he knew he was mortally ill, turned Anne, who had been something of an agnostic, to regular worship. Of his prayer that her 'manifold virtues and exemplary life here on earth' secure her a place in Heaven, she wrote:

Should this meet the eye of anyone capable of being awed and affected by a solemn lesson . . . it contains a prayer *for me* put up by a heart so true, so pious and attached, that to survive it seems almost a disgrace to my own – but while I live, I will act according to it . . .

March 22, 1808, Anne Barnard.[29]

For much of that year Anne was invisible in public and silent, having withdrawn to Wimpole Hall, the Hardwickes' immense house and estate in Cambridgeshire, which was as complete a retreat as she could find and where she remained for six months. Margaret joined her and though nothing could bring consolation, both her sisters gave Anne 'the liberty to feel my own wretchedness, unobserved but not unpitied'.[30]

A brief tide of remorse passed through political circles. Lord William Bentinck, son of the prime minister, wrote to Bal of his sadness that circumstances 'prevented arrangements from being made that would have allowed of Mr Barnard remaining in England'.[31] Windham's reaction was not recorded.

After the shock and pain, Anne's enduring emotion was bitterness. 'I hate no-one and no-one's memory,' she wrote towards the end of her life, 'but were I to say whom I should be most justified in hating, it would be the king of cruel and unfeeling coquets – the pleasing, specious Windham!'[32] While raking over the agonies she suffered in having loved him, what really blackened her heart was his part in Andrew's death. Windham became a scapegoat for her loss.

Revenge was beyond her but, as the observations in these pages show, she did her best to revise the historical verdict on a man who may have lost the lustre of his early career yet remained in the front rank of politics until his death. As well as pronouncing him Britain's worst war minister, she dug up his old letters to disclose how one renowned for adopting the high moral ground could play fast and loose with principle. Windham had once confided to her his detestation of Pitt – in whose government he was then serving – by writing: 'Never was there in my opinion a person who in the greatest situation that ever man was placed acted upon such low principles.' He followed this with a line of characteristic double-speak: 'You see in what confidence I write to you, so for God's sake do not let me be supposed to have written all this, tho' I have no objections that all the world should know these to be my sentiments.'[33] As she said, the war proved Pitt brave and right and Windham a mere ditherer. He died in the summer of 1810, a disappointment to many besides Anne.

When she did start to emerge from mourning it was in order to raise a memorial to Andrew. Five months after his body was brought back to the Castle and buried at a Dutch Reformed cemetery, she wrote to their old friend, Willem van Rijneveld, asking that a plaque be erected there. A year later he reported that as well as the colony existing in a state of tranquillity and Lord Caledon being held in the highest esteem, a tablet had been placed over Andrew Barnard's grave as a tribute by 'his afflicted widow' with the legend:

Colonist! Drop a tear to his memory.
He sought the welfare of your country and he loved its inhabitants.

By then another legacy had been brought to Anne's notice. The date of the letter is unknown, as is the wording, because it was among the papers she later consigned to the flames; but it was written by Caledon soon after Andrew's death, and though the governor must have expressed himself as delicately as possible, it could only have come as another thunderbolt.

After Anne's return to England in 1802, and shortly before his own departure from the Cape, Andrew Barnard had fathered a child. She was now aged six – 'a dear little girl of colour'. Her mother was a slave.

19

A 'Protégée of a Darker Complexion'

1810–1844

In the summer of 1809 a dark-skinned child wearing a new dress and a wide-eyed expression landed in England. The ship that brought her from the Cape was evidently an Indiaman for it is recorded that the child's passage had cost £44 and 2 shillings, and just as no expense had been spared on her comfort, a further £107 had been spent on accessories and her outfit.[1] Although Meyndrina Christina Douglas – the names with which the girl had been baptised six years earlier – was bewildered and probably terrified by everything around her, she had been spared the hurricane endured by other children on the ship after sailing from Calcutta when four Indiamen were lost.* On coming ashore at Deal she was met, addressed as Christina and put into a carriage. From the time it deposited her at 21 Berkeley Square that was the name by which she was known.

Some weeks later Lady Anne Barnard wrote to her friend Willem van Rijneveld, now a senior official at the Cape:

> You know Lord Caledon at my request sent me a dear little girl of colour . . . That the child owed her birth to my dear husband I think there is likeness enough for me to be assured of, and happy am I

---

* In the sailing seasons of 1808–9, successive homeward-bound fleets were devastated by hurricanes in the worst maritime disaster ever suffered by the East India Company. See *Storm and Conquest* by the present author.

therefore in having her as I never [saw] a more promising child or one with better disposition – indeed she seems to have inherited the happy talent of making friends from her dear father.[2]

It is possible to see Anne's decision to bring Christina back to England – to rescue the child, as she saw it, and raise her – as the bravest and most defiant act of a life that flew in the face of convention. It might just as readily be pointed out that her driving spirit arose from simple humanity and compassion. But it was brave none the less.

The presence of slaves and their offspring in well-to-do London homes was not unknown. Where they were to be seen, however, the natural assumption was that they were in service. Dr Johnson took in Francis Barber, born a slave in Jamaica, who became his manservant, won his heart and was ultimately his principal beneficiary and a schoolmaster. A notable and intriguing exception was the case of Lord Mansfield, who adopted Dido Belle, the daughter of his nephew, a navy captain, by a slave woman. Mansfield's example had a special resonance for Anne. She had been on warm terms with the Chief Justice – who, it may be recalled, called her 'the best specimen Scotland ever sent to London' – and almost certainly met Dido at his Bloomsbury town house or at Kenwood.*

But it was plainly one thing for a gentleman of status to embrace enlightened ideas in the age of abolition, and quite another for a lady to acknowledge her husband's infidelity with a former slave, then bring his child into her household. Whether Anne realised fully what she was taking on may be questioned, for

---

* There were other opportunities for meetings; Dido Belle was only thirteen years younger than Anne and for some years they lived in the same parish. They were married within a month of one another at the same church, St George's, Hanover Square. Dido Belle died in 1804.

she had always been a little blind to what made her exceptional – those acts that struck others as defying convention and defined her in her own time as an eccentric or what a later age would have called bohemian – and, as always, she reacted to a moral dilemma instinctively. In this instance, however, she must have seen that embracing Christina would take her further beyond the pale. In a catalogue of her rebellions against convention it figured large. Nevertheless, 'I sent for the child from Africa to keep her virtuous and make her happy'.[3] In doing so she cited the words of Lord Ogleby in Garrick's play, *The Clandestine Marriage*: ' 'Tis a debt of honour and must be paid.'[4] But then the consequences were always going to be felt more by the child.

Christina was born some eighteen months after Anne sailed home and six months after Andrew himself left the Cape. Of her mother virtually nothing is known besides her given name, Rachel van de Caap, which suggests that she was from the Cape and possibly of Khoikhoi origin, rather than being among the slaves imported from Mozambique. Even this is not certain as Anne spoke of her in one letter as being black; Khoikhoi tended to be of lighter complexion than other indigenous Africans. Rachel was, in any event, a servant in the household of a Dutch couple, a Mr and Mrs Necker, known to the Barnards and described by Anne as 'good people in a private station of life'.[5]

It seems unlikely Andrew learnt of his third natural child until he returned to the Cape in 1807. By then Christina was four. Whatever his flaws, his careless sexual appetite, Andrew acknowledged his responsibility as usual, and appears on his deathbed to have recommended Christina to the care of a friend, Mr Horak.[6] At this point, Lord Caledon decided Anne should be advised of the child's existence.

Anne accepted Christina as what she called 'the accident of an unguarded moment after I left my poor husband a lonely widower'.[7] This sanitised apology for Andrew's errant ways was, it is fair to add, the explanation she left to posterity for her mysterious 'protégée of a darker complexion'. Whatever was said to individual members of the family, that was as much as she placed on the record. Even when infidelity, in the form of natural children, was accepted among the ruling class, the consequences were often brushed out of family history. In Christina's case the picture was of course complicated by race, and slavery – though not necessarily in a way that disgraced Andrew as it would today. Libido in the colonies – from India to the Cape and West Indies – was often ascribed to steamy climate and dark-skinned local 'Jezebels'.[8]

How Anne reconciled herself to Andrew's betrayal, only she knew. She would have gone back to the love in his letters, his longings for her during separations, reasoning perhaps that sexuality along with physical warmth was an almost unconscious aspect of his nature. Despite her experience of men, though, she must have been troubled by this evidence of his paradoxical nature, of a lust so much at variance with fidelity and affection. Still, no hint of a shadow was allowed to fall on her husband's name. Andrew's memory was sacred.

For the first three years of her life in England Christina seems to have attended a girls' school. Once again the details are unknown, the only record being an account of expenditure which shows that from 1810 to 1812 she was away for between six and nine months a year, receiving lessons from, among others, a music mistress.[9] This ended when Christina was ten, from which point she lived at Berkeley Square until Anne's death. Whatever the other benefits of her education, one legacy was the neat, precise hand in which the later volumes of her adoptive mother's memoirs were set down. Christina had by then become Anne's amanuensis.

From Anne's solitary outpouring on the subject, neither found Christina's reception in London easy. British racial attitudes depended on the ethnicity in the beholder's eye: Anglo-Indian children, for example, were relatively common and accepted as such, at least if their complexions were light – the darker-skinned offspring of Company servants were often left behind in India.[10] Africans were a different matter, and across the range of prejudice a special horrified fascination was reserved for the Khoikhoi, or 'the Hottentot'.

In 1810 another native of the Cape landed in England. Like Christina's mother, Saartjie Baartman was a Khoikhoi woman with a Dutch name. There comparisons end, for the presence of the 'Hottentot Venus' on a Piccadilly stage had no element of salvation about it. Saartjie was an early example of the freak-show phenomenon, drawing voyeurs to peer at a physique said to include not only protuberant buttocks, known as steatopygia, but prominent labia. A case brought by outraged activists for habeas corpus against her ringmaster owner, a ship's surgeon, was dismissed in November and Saartjie spent the remainder of her bleak life as a sexual grotesque, dying in Paris in 1815.*

Human exhibition of any sort discomforted Anne, particularly when it involved exploitation. Touring Indian sword-swallowers turned her stomach. 'The money these poor creatures earn is immense but alas they get a very small part of it, having sold themselves to the captain who brought them.'[11]

Her views on the Hottentot Venus are not recorded; but the condition of other Khoikhoi women nagged at her. During the hullabaloo over Saartjie Baartman, Anne wrote again to van Rijneveld requesting him to make a payment of £10 'to the black mother of the little child that came home to me, with whom I am much pleased; and also five pounds to the poor Hottentot servant who attended my dear husband in his last illness'. If either woman fell into a state of sickness or poverty, she went on, van Rijneveld

---

* Saartjie remained on display after her death, her skeleton being exhibited at the Musée de l'Homme until 1985. Her bones, along with wax casts of her genitals and bottled organs, were returned to South Africa in 2002.

was to 'administer to their real wants and to draw on me for it'.[12]

What the Lindsay family made of her actions is a matter of speculation. A silence about Christina in surviving letters from Anne's siblings, including Margaret and Elizabeth, suggests she received limited support from those closest to her. She sailed on, providing for Andrew's other illegitimate offspring, and subsequently their children as well. Love and duty in the years after his death moved Anne Barnard to begin life anew, and shaped its final direction – as the surrogate mother to a host of young spirits.

Both Andrew's natural sons owed their careers to her. She had used the old network of influence as early as 1805, obtaining for the eldest boy Henry a cadetship through her brother-in-law, Lord Hardwicke.[13] Henry and Andrew were both known by the surname of Hervey and both became officers in the native infantry in India thanks to petitions by Anne almost as persistent as those she had made for their father.

One lesson she drew from past mistakes was to approach the wives of the powerful, rather than the men themselves. A lively note to the Countess of Loudon, for example – which proceeded to the entirely deceitful admission, 'I am really ashamed, my dear good friend, to ask you what I am about to do' – was probably more beneficial to those she termed 'my two poor boys' than would have been a plea to the Governor-General of India himself.[14] At bottom, she was as brazen as ever. One request ended: 'This is the anniversary of the day I lost my Barnard. Five years this day! Old wounds still bleed. O, soften them if you can by the balm of protection to these lads.'[15]

Henry Hervey, or 'the wild Fitzroy', prospered in India, rising to a captaincy, marrying and fathering two children. On his wife's death, their daughter Margaret was sent to Anne's care, which annoyed her at first because, as she said, 'the education of children makes no part of my habits';[16] but none would be turned away, and in due course she took in another girl, a daughter of Andrew Hervey's named Anne.

Some ten years separated the oldest and youngest of Berkeley Square's three girls. How the lady of the house managed their education was not spelled out, but books lay everywhere, writing went on, and music played an important part in evenings around the pianoforte on which Anne played a hunting song 'set to a Swiss air and sung by my three young protégées, Christina Douglas, Margaret & Anne Hervey'.[17] Christina, as the eldest, was given care of the younger two.

Any assumptions that the child of Africa fitted cosily into her new landscape were dispelled in the spring of 1813, four years after Christina's arrival. Anne was writing to a friend over their common experience as adoptive mothers, for although Maria Fitzherbert had no child by the Prince of Wales, she too had taken in 'little protégées', recently a natural daughter of her brother's.* And for once, Anne felt free to pour out her heart.

> You will find his girl a treasure to you. O was my Christina but white what an unalloy'd comfort she would be to me for there would then be no mark of birth to stamp a wrong in me or a mortification on her, poor child.[18]

The fact was that while she had embraced Christina as 'a debt of honour' there was, as she put it, 'no struggling against that colour'. The stamp of race would always exclude her from the hub of London life. Anne was egalitarian, to the point of accepting that

---

* This letter may set to rest speculation that Mary Smythe was not really a child of Mrs Fitzherbert's brother, but her daughter by the prince. 'I greatly approve of your brother's daughter being your own protégée,' Anne wrote. 'I dare say it is very pretty and resembles yourself for Jack was very like you & it resembles him you say.'

love could exist across a racial divide; but, as she now saw, 'to try to introduce [colour] to society would naturally rouse everyone to sett their face against [it]' – and that could only be to Christina's disadvantage, even distress. At this point Anne's thoughts became less clear. Essentially, however, she saw the problem as one of class. Society, by which she meant the ruling class, would reject

> the levelling principle by which the whole purity of morals would be overthrown if illegitimacy of every class were to be adopted into the circles of virtue and birth.[19]

These confidences, expressed to Maria, were purged from extracts of the same letter set down in the memoirs, so even Anne found the subject too raw for family consumption.[20] Christina was a presence in her household until Anne's death, the object of her affection with a generous legacy ensuring that, at least, her future would be comfortable. In the end, Anne's 'protégée of a darker complexion' went on to do a good deal better than that for herself, without ever having been quite accepted by her surrogate mother's circle.

Anne's friendship with Maria Fitzherbert revived – as usual because the Prince of Wales's first wife was in need of advice. In 1811 the prince had, in effect, taken the throne, being sworn in as Prince Regent in February after the king's madness became permanent. Despite their ups and downs, despite his official marriage to Princess Caroline of Brunswick, he visited Fitz almost daily and at official dinners she was still at his table. Their final parting occurred that summer, and may be attributed to Anne's failure to restrain her volatile friend.

The prince was planning an official fete when he called on Maria, explaining that he wished her to attend but, now acting as monarch, needed to reserve his table 'for persons of the very highest rank'.[21] The offended spouse wrote one of her furious responses, which she brought to Anne. Her advice was to tear it up and attend Carlton House, then – preserving her dignity – withdraw before dinner. Maria refused, but agreed her letter to the prince should be couched in milder tones. The result, written by Anne in Maria's name, bears quoting:

> Much as it has been my wish during 26 years to save you Sir from any embarrassment in my power, yet there are situations where one ought not to forget what is due to ourselves. Your Royal Highness must be aware that, in your anxiety to fill your table with persons of the highest rank, you are at present excluding one from it who is not unjustly suspected of possessing a rank above that of every other present ... I cannot therefore appear at Carlton House in any place but that which from the first day of our connection you desired me to fill.[22]

This marked the final rupture. The prince, according to Anne, was alarmed. He plied Maria with notes and asked to call but was denied. She insisted 'that to be respected by him it was necessary to respect herself'. In Anne's view, her 'fierce, proud, indignant and somewhat unhappy' friend had pressed the case too far.[23]

Two years later Maria returned from Brighton, calling herself the worst-used person in the country and seeking further advice. The prince had increased her annuity from £3,000 to £6,000 but she wanted £10,000 and was threatening to go to Parliament. Anne, still hoping for reconciliation and believing Maria under the influence of others, counselled against a public confrontation.

> I think you stand highest when lowest ... You are the friend of your country and your principles when you do nothing to injure its peace or raise a flame about our ears. Let him and all his fancies alone ... Do not think of him. Think of Mary [her adopted daughter].[24]

This time she succeeded, at the expense of becoming again the scribe who would state the case in more diplomatic terms than her friend. 'My head aches & I am unfit for anything,' Maria complained. 'Be charitably disposed & make what alterations you like.'[25] From the spring of 1813 Anne wrote a series of letters in Maria's name. All were 'cut down from vulgar violence to moderation'. None had any immediate effect – although the annuity was later increased to £8,000 and ultimately £10,000. Anne did not negotiate personally with the prince, though he must have known the elegant rebukes came not from his first wife but his 'Sister Anne'. The tone is unmistakable. In one the writer speaks of her household debts:

> from which with the most rigid economy I have not been able to extricate myself. These debts Sir have never been increased by any ostentation or extravagance of mine. The whole of them were incurr'd when we were living happily together. Need I say more?[26]

Anne, while respectful of the monarchy, was among those to discern the weakness identified by George's biographer – his need to be dominated by older, authoritarian women.[27] 'I may be wrong,' Anne wrote in the memoirs, 'but I thought then, and think still, that had the Prince found in [Maria] a sensible and temperate woman, he might not only have remained attached to her for life but have made a better figure by being a better man.'[28] She did not live to see the total dissolution of his later years as George IV. One who did was the Duke of Wellington, who attended the king's body and, noticing a red ribbon around his neck, found on it a locket containing a cameo of Maria Fitzherbert.[29]

The education of children may have played no part in Anne's habits, but the role of aunt in a family abounding with them was another matter. Along with the offspring bequeathed her by

Andrew, she had plenty of Lindsays and returning to Balcarres opened a new bond.

Anne's brothers did not have a very regular place in her life. The oldest, Alexander, remained distant, and even those with whom she had been on closer terms, Charles and Hugh, were often not at hand. John, usually in dire financial trouble, was a source of strain between her and Alexander, whom she thought unkind and ungenerous to the Lindsay who had suffered much in foreign adventure.[30] At this time she was closer to Robert, now master of Balcarres, where she spent Christmases with sisters Margaret and Elizabeth, their elderly mother and 'children and all sorts of cousins and aunts and friends'.[31] The young relative to whom an animated, affectionate widow reached out instinctively was a nephew, James Lindsay, the teenage son of Robert, who was about to embark on military life. Anne said that should he find himself in London, a comfortable room awaited.

James's first taste of war as a sixteen-year-old ensign was the disastrous Walcheren Expedition to Holland in 1809 when more than 4,000 British soldiers died of fever. He came close to death himself before being evacuated and brought to Berkeley Square where he was nursed back to health; and so a bond was forged between the intelligent young officer and 'kind Aunt Barnard whose hotel takes in so many'. From 1811, when he joined Wellington's forces in Spain, James became the most regular of Anne's correspondents. She was maternal as much as aunt-like, prescribing port to medicate against further fever epidemics: 'For this purpose I have put 20 guineas in Coutts hands for your private cellar.'[32] He responded with a flow of letters that, in the years of bloodshed and anxiety to come, were her comfort. James became the son she never had.

Another relative off fighting in the Peninsular War was a second Andrew Barnard, a nephew of her late husband's. Colonel Barnard had set forth on a trail that led him via Ciudad Rodrigo,

Badajoz, Salamanca and repeated woundings to a final blaze of glory at Waterloo. His first brush with death occurred outside Cadiz in 1811, when she wrote resignedly: 'I dare say men must do as they do at Rome for approbation of their fellows.'[33] Once he started to win acclaim, at Ciudad Rodrigo, she saw there was no restraining him: 'No wonder you like your profession Dearest Andrew for it certainly likes you . . . God bless you and keep you long in it in safety and honour with a coat of mail round you . . . Adieu My Dear Boy.'[34]

Margaret had returned to London, living at Berkeley Square but spending most of her time with Charlotte Campbell, a lady of the bedchamber to Princess Caroline. The sisters led separate lives, Anne having withdrawn 'to early hours and a bounded society' while Margaret and her new friend 'delighted in the great world they were formed to brighten and enjoy'.[35] Anne admitted to pain over their lost intimacy; but that passed when, almost out of the blue, Margaret remarried.

Her second husband was the man Anne thought should have been the first. James Burges and Margaret had met in Edinburgh when she was sixteen and he, just a year older, was seen as too young and unaccomplished. Margaret's desolation then inspired Anne to write 'Auld Robin Grey', and though Burges went on to marry happily and produce a large family, he remained in touch with his first sweetheart. His musical evenings had been a source of happy activity that brought them all together, while his verse won some recognition and the friendship of Lord Byron. Soon after his wife's death, Burges sought Margaret out.

They were married in September 1812 and honeymooned at Anne's Wimbledon villa. A month later his eighteen-year-old son was killed in an assault on Burgos. 'You will feel,' Anne wrote, 'how soothing and tender Margaret is to the afflicted person she loves.'[36] She joined them at Beauport, Burges's house near Hastings, where a memorial was erected to the boy.

Margaret's late flowering – her 'contentment in its fullest extent' – was observed by Anne with unalloyed joy.[37] Back at Beauport a year later, she wrote: 'Burges's children love her, she loves them, and there is so much patriarchal hospitality and innocent mirth and dancing going forward that I fancy myself in the golden age.'[38] Yet the toll of war remained oppressive. Colonel Barnard had suffered another wound, this time in the chest and serious enough to require rehabilitation, when she wrote to him at the end of 1813:

> Let me propose as your headquarters No 21 Berkeley Square where you shall have a couple of comfortable rooms on the ground floor to receive your world and perfect liberty, uninvaded by the creeking [sic] invalid upstairs. Do what you please, My Dear Boy, but if you feel that my house could be a comfort to you, here it is, and here am I.[39]

The gallant colonel, born to battle, was one thing. Her nephew James was another. Barely twenty, yet now a captain and witness to hard fighting, he was a sensitive youth, writing every couple of weeks, straight in without preamble as intimate correspondents did. 'I often think, dearest Aunt, of our tête-a-têtes by the fireside, so far preferable to the usual talk one hears here.'[40] She responded in kind. 'I love you so tenderly & think so highly of your heart.'[41] James came close to death in Holland for a second time during an attempt to storm the garrison at Bergen-op-Zoom early in 1814, when he was wounded severely enough for a leg amputation to be considered. Anne felt her heart stop before dashing off a note: 'Oh James, what an escape you have had!'[42] She knew too many casualties – Anstruthers, Craufords and Gordons as well as young Burges – to be sanguine. 'I am like the psalmist, "Give us peace in our time, O Lord" . . . Dear James, I shall be very, very glad to see you back in our nest, wound and all.'[43]

She had meantime begun the exercise which occupied many

hours of solitude. The idea for 'a shortened sketch of my own life' had first struck Anne at the Cape. It came with all sorts of concerns, not least the whiff of vanity. Even now she continued to deny the fame that went with authorship of 'Auld Robin Grey'. Still, as she reminded herself, her life 'has had many singularities in it'.[44] Provided she addressed herself purely to young relatives like James, who expressed astonishment as well as fascination in what she had experienced over six decades, she could tell her story with propriety. And so, surrounded with piles of letters and the innumerable folios of paper she called her scraps, Anne Barnard started to compile her memoirs.

20

Legacies

_6

1814–1825

A single woman with four houses in Bloomsbury and Wimbledon, some £35,000 in capital and income from an annuity as well as her late husband's estate, had no need to stint.* The widow of Berkeley Square spent as prudently as ever, however, so her savings, far from diminishing, accumulated. Had she not been quite indifferent to money she might have been among London's richest women: thirty years after Lady Anne Lindsay inherited a paper fortune, the dispute over Richard Atkinson's estate remained unresolved.

Her habit of avoidance, she knew, was to blame. Atkinson, it may be recalled, had held bonds and securities on Anne's behalf which were declared in his will but of which she had no independent proof. Since the challenge by Atkinson's executors – his brother and former business partner – she had shied from a legal contest, preferring to be 'ill-used but at peace'.[1] Margaret, though a lesser beneficiary, was not so easily reconciled, and, after they were urged by Burges to fight the executors, two suits were brought before the courts in 1813.[2] Both were rejected, with costs of around £500. Anne decided that to proceed further would consume a great deal more money, and probably the rest of her

---

* Her capital was made up of the residue of money made on her behalf by Atkinson, amounting to about £10,000, another £10,000 left her by an old suitor, the Amsterdam banker Henry Hope, a £6,000 legacy from Barnard and £9,000 saved from the rental of her London properties during their years in Africa (Memoirs vol. 6, p. 115).

life. The severity of her next loss was a reminder of what really mattered.

Margaret had been married to James Burges for almost two years, happier than Anne had ever known, when her poor health deteriorated seriously enough for them to move to London. The symptoms – a swollen stomach and severe pain – quickly became alarming. Spells of relief were overtaken by renewed fear. Margaret was in good spirits, Anne told the family, but the swelling 'does not diminish as we wish'.3 On 3 November doctors performed surgery to remove a tumour. When, days later, Margaret said she had not been to church for weeks and wanted a service at home, the meaning was clear.

Margaret died on 4 December. She had suffered severely and it was with something close to euphoria that Anne recorded towards the end, 'no convulsion of pain was observed'. Late on in her sixty-one years, Margaret had been sustained by a faith her sister could only envy: 'The Almighty extended the arms of his mercy to the soul that confided in his goodness . . . and with one little sigh only, Margaret – oh my Margaret! – she bade adieu to a world in which she had not known happiness till she was on the eve of quitting it.'4

Losing the primordial bond of her life brought a guilt which Anne could not explain beyond saying: 'Grief invariably takes with me the hue not only of regret but of self-blame for something on which I fancy I might have acted better.'5 Only she and Margaret could have properly accounted for their slow drift from one another in those last years, so there it must be left. Among many letters of consolation Anne kept just one, to remind her of 'days of happiness when your two selves constituted a centre to which so many were attracted'.6

She turned to prayer in an effort to emulate Margaret, but was soon chastising herself as a 'parading creature, fancying from time to time that I feel virtues which I am for ever forgetting to practise with continuity'.[7] Still, she remained a quite regular worshipper at St George's, Hanover Square, and one aspect of faith that had ever been part of her philosophy became a new source of strength:

> It is a solace to the heart when a fellow creature can be benefitted by our exertions. Even when the heart is sinking under grief, if we can feel it a *duty* to bear up, we find it an Atlas to the mind.[8]

Loss served to remind her, too, of family as a life force. Reaching out to her eldest brother Alexander in an attempt to close the distance between them, Anne wrote: 'I have lost the companion and friend of my whole life, my dearest Bal, and as our numbers decrease, we must become more valuable and tender to one another.'[9] The role of conciliator found her once more championing the hapless John against their exasperated brothers when he was sent back to debtors' prison and raising funds for his relief. Then there was her part as surrogate mother to various adopted offspring and nephews. Berkeley Square – 'my hotel', she called it – had ten bedrooms and they were rarely unoccupied.

Guests that fateful spring of 1815 included Colonel Andrew Barnard, recovering from yet another injury and 'snug laid up in the room above mine', reading novels by Madame de Stael. Another regular, Captain James Lindsay, still hobbling on sticks a year after nearly losing a leg, had just returned to Scotland when the first clap was heard in the thunderous climax to an age of conflict. Days after Bonaparte's escape from Elba, Anne wrote to James: 'He is a man of such strange and wonderful resources that there is no knowing what he may be at this moment to astonish us with.'[10]

The news had a galvanising effect on Colonel Barnard. Though confined to Berkeley Square in April, he marched into Brussels at the head of his battalion a month later and saw desperate action at Quatre Bras as well as Waterloo, from where he wrote the next day to assure Anne he was safe, failing to mention he had been wounded again.

> My Dear Lady Anne, I have only just time to tell you that yesterday witnessed the most severe action probably that the annals of modern history can produce, which ended in a most complete discomforture of Bonaparte's army. Our loss has been severe, both in the greatness of numbers and the persons fallen or severely wounded. You shall hear from me very soon again.[11]

Two cataclysmic events within months – Margaret's death, and an end to the era of war that had lasted half her lifetime and cost the lives of three Lindsay brothers – resolved Anne to conclude another long-running struggle.

Early in 1816 she wrote to Alexander: 'Respecting my Atkinson claim, *I do not mean to go on with it.*'[12] With the Atkinsons' rejection of her last offer – to settle for £35,000 – she resigned her interest in favour of her nephews, Lindsay and James. While acknowledging that 'a tempting lawsuit is a dangerous legacy', she saw energy and resources were needed to pursue the case and 'I have too often had the infirmity of bending'.[13]

The legacy had evidently become a source of tension within clan Lindsay. Anne's insinuation was that Alexander had been keen to see her fight Atkinson's executors while keeping his distance, but there is evidence that her brother had mixed feelings about the case, having developed ties of his own with the Atkinson family. Robert, too, was ambiguous, grateful for 'the kind intentions of our good sister', while urging his son James not to enter 'a sea of difficulty and intricacy'.[14]

The saga dragged on. Anne might have anticipated the Dickensian folly of *Bleak House* when she wrote to Alexander: 'Instead of rubbish being swept away to simplify, everything will be thrown to *add* difficulty to obtaining truth.'[15] It was, she went on angrily, 'time for my *brothers* and *nephews* to decide how to proceed'.[16] She was convinced she would die before any settlement, and she was right.*

The prevailing image of Lady Anne Barnard in her final years was of a virtual recluse. It was one she helped to cultivate. 'I never go out unless by the greatest accident, so if you call you are sure of finding me,' she told a friend. Retreat gave her an aura of mystery, which she rather liked: 'The sagacious hinted I was turning Methodist.' In fact, the widow of Berkeley Square was usually at her occupations – writing and drawing, poring over her papers and letters, summoning treasured moments of the past. She was still a lively occasional hostess, but one who, after diverting and amusing her guests, was equally happy to leave them to themselves and retreat to her desk.

'Her house was a home to me,' her nephew James wrote many years later. 'I loved her as a mother and so did all who dwelt under her roof.'[17] He was a whiskery old general by then, recalling the aunt with 'a power of pleasing which I have never seen equalled':

A stream of genius ran sparkling through her character. She had in society a power of placing herself in sympathy with those she addressed, of drawing forth their feelings, pleasing them with themselves, and consequently with their companion. I have often seen her change a dull party into an agreeable one; she could make the dullest speak, the shyest feel happy and the witty flash fire without any apparent exertion. It were impossible to name the number who claimed her intimacy, from the Prince on the throne to the peasant at Balcarres.[18]

---

* The claim was not pursued by the Lindsays. Anne's final illness cleared the way for the Atkinson family's lawyers to have the will executed in May 1825 within weeks of her death. (The story is the subject of an upcoming book, *Mr Atkinson's Rum Contract*, by Richard Atkinson, a descendant of the financier.)

Anne had a maid of many years' standing, Kate Cooper, who served tea, then took a seat and drank it with the lady and her friends. Kate was also seen at dinners, such as one given for a large party of notable guests when, James related, a hitch occurred in the kitchen and she bustled in to warn the hostess: 'My Lady, you must tell another story – the second course won't be ready for five minutes.'[19]

Flashes of the youthful coquette were occasionally glimpsed, as in a letter to James after a naval hero came calling:

What a Prodigious Man has been to see me! Sir Philip Durham – he is a widower, you know. He came when I had a dozen friends with me. Drunk as an owl & with all its wisdom and solemnity. He is to wait on me with a diamond star tomorrow.[20]

After a Westminster dinner seated beside the Duke of Norfolk she wrote: 'The Duke is a fine, low, square building. He had a most excellent nap by my side after he had explained to me the apartments in Arundel Castle.'[21]

One by one notable figures of the past were dying – Henry Dundas in 1811, a year after Windham and the same year as another rejected suitor, the banker Henry Hope. Her first lover, Thomas Wentworth, followed in 1814, still in her debt and having gambled away his wife's fortune too. A better friend, Horatio Mann, died the same year, and, in 1815, Emma Hamilton, whom Anne believed had been shamefully treated by a country which 'owed her much . . . for aiding her husband's virtue and her lover's glory'.[22]

Among the talents of a new era, she was fascinated but also repelled by the dazzling figure who had burst on the literary scene. She was not well acquainted with George Byron, nor did she have much to say about his poetry, other than finding it 'beautiful, sombre, deceiving'. Anne was the partisan of Annabella Byron, a niece of Wentworth's whom the poet married, disastrously, in

1815.[23] They parted soon after their daughter's birth and Lady Byron was damned for posterity in the third canto of *Childe Harold* for taking the child from him – a judgement which has largely endured, thanks to Byron's hold on the romantic imagination. Anne, anticipating such an outcome, preserved one of Annabella's letters as 'a sacred record in her favour'. Byron's wife was writing of his mental state:

> He has wished to be thought partially deranged, or on the brink of it, to perplex observers, and to prevent them from tracing effects to their real causes through all the intricacies of his conduct. I was, as I told you at one time, the dupe of his acted insanity ... He is the absolute monarch of words, and uses them as Buonaparte did lives, for conquest ... In regard to his poetry, egotism is the vital principle of his imagination, which it is difficult for him to kindle on any subject with which his own character and interests are not identified ... Nothing has contributed more to the misunderstanding of his real character than the lonely grandeur in which he shrouds it, and his affectation of being above [men] when he exists almost in their voice ...
>
> But I have not thanked you, dearest Lady Anne, for your kindness in regard to rectifying false impressions. I trust you understand my wishes, which never were to injure Lord Byron in any way, for though he would not suffer me to remain his Wife, he cannot prevent me continuing his Friend, and it was from considering myself as such that I silenced accusations which might have been justified ... His allusions to me in Childe Harold are cruel and cold, with such a semblance as to make me appear so, and to attract all sympathy to himself ... I might appeal to all those who have ever heard me speak of him, and still more to my own heart to witness, that there has been no moment when I have remembered injury otherwise than affectionately and sorrowfully.[24]

Anne was out of step generally with those who excited the new age. Of Byron and Lady Caroline Lamb she reflected, 'What a queer pair they would make.' As for Caroline's 'mad book' *Glenarvon*, in which she implicitly confessed to having cuckolded her husband, it 'narrated what I never heard of any woman publishing voluntarily of herself before'.[25]

Her own writing brought pleasure because like many of advancing years Anne was happier to live in the memory than the present and going through old papers made her feel younger. 'I forget that I am 68 and if by chance I see myself in the glass looking very abominable, I do not care. When alone I am not above five and twenty.'[26] Compiling the memoirs was not, however, solitary activity. As volume succeeded on volume, Anne wrote less and instead dictated or drafted text set down 'by the pen of my young amanuensis'.

The sources were rich, for she was an inveterate hoarder, retaining the kind of material which it was standard practice to destroy. 'Pray burn my letter immediately, dearest,' Margaret once pleaded, obviously without effect, 'I often feel cramped when I write to you from your vile careless ways with papers.'[27] Margaret's thinking was akin to Cassandra Austen's, whose action in burning and scissoring a great number of Jane's letters is naturally deplored by the author's readership to this day. In the end, Anne was discreet enough to ensure that nothing very scandalous, nothing unkindly, found a place in the memoirs. But after Margaret's death other members of the family noted this literary activity with disapproval. The formidably respectable Hardwickes were most concerned about what Anne might startle them with next. In 1818 a family crisis was in the offing as – Anne explained to her nephews – the Hardwickes 'distrust my pen'.

Elizabeth is extremely uneasy at the spirit and nature of what has for 5 years amused my leisure hours – that howmuchsoever I may have enforced & impressed my trustees never to publish what I write, published it *will be* one day, and that for the benefit of some *thief* who will steal it. How will I like to suppose that family anecdotes and private sentiments, which ought never to meet the light, not even of the next generation, should be exposed to animadversion?[28]

Anne was sufficiently daunted by the Hardwickes to turn to two confidants, her nephews James and Lindsay, for backing. They rallied to her. Aunt Anne had said explicitly: 'I utterly debar now and ever publication.'[29] That should be enough to set minds at rest. Her resolve renewed, she thanked them: 'The ill is broken now I have the comfort of your support.'[30]

The memoirs' significance to Anne went beyond the simple pleasure of a pastime. They were an endeavour, an exercise of her talents, with the objective of entertaining. In this she may have been influenced by a literary phenomenon. Publication in 1811 of a novel entitled *Sense and Sensibility*, 'By a Lady' was followed two years later by *Pride and Prejudice* and by the time *Emma* came out, in 1816, avid readers of Jane Austen included the Prince Regent, to whom it was dedicated. Anne made no known references to Austen, and there would have been no question of trying to emulate her; but she was aware of the novels, perhaps felt a shy envy, and though determined that the memoirs were not to be published – 'I know my deficiencies' – desired recognition from her own kin. Ultimately, she gave up her carriage and horses to spend some two thousand pounds on the illustration and production of these sumptuous volumes.[31]

The irony at the heart of the memoirs, however, was that the closest anyone else came to Anne's account of life among eighteenth-century aristocrats and royalty was an illegitimate slave-child barely accepted in the family to whom the work was addressed.

While it bears repeating that little is known of Christina's early years, she must have cut a forlorn figure in adolescence.

This was the point at which Anne confided to Maria Fitzherbert her anxiety about how a girl 'of colour' could be integrated into society. She had begun to worry, too, that Christina might not find a husband. Efforts to assimilate her with the Lindsays were having limited success: almost the only reference in family letters dates from 1819, when Christina was sixteen and accompanied Anne on two visits to far-off Cumbria. Their hosts, chosen for their kindness, were her nephew James and his new wife, Mary-Ann, who were duly solicitous. 'I was very glad to observe how much better Christina looked on her second visit here than her first,' Mary-Ann wrote.[32]

Soon afterwards Christina took up her stepmother's pen. Her formal education, three early years of schooling, had perhaps been supplemented by private tuition, and living in a bookish and musical household must have stimulated her. It is clear too, though, that Anne did more than just encourage her protégée's learning. Christina was drawn into literary activity by acting as her companion while Anne was at her occupations, and developed a precise hand and an eye for unscrambling her hasty, demanding scrawl. When the leather volumes were delivered by the binder, Anne wrote of 'feasting my eyes [on] the clean writing of my young amanuensis, far preferable to mine'.[33]

As a pair, they invite an artist's portrayal – the setting, a desk in the drawing room at Berkeley Square, a long, dark space heavy with chintz curtains, shadowed by portraits (including Gainsborough's full-length rendering of Margaret) and seated together a slight, elderly lady, gently smiling over the piles of papers, and her dark-skinned young companion, eyes ferociously furrowed over the words unfolding under her hand.

But what did the nineteen-year-old Christina make of the world conjured up in those words? She was not merely copying Anne's text, because decoding difficult handwriting required her to comprehend the substance, so she became an observer and participant in telling the story, following Anne Lindsay's progress from the black broth of childhood to courtship, from misery to marriage, from France to Africa. That poses another question. What did Christina know of her own birth? Anne made no bones of the fact that she was a 'connection of my late husband Andrew Barnard'.[34] Little more than that can be said. Yet Christina must have sensed a distance from the Lindsay family, realised that her dark skin made her exceptional. So the desk, the drawing room, the craft of handwriting, and the company of her stepmother became sources of comfort – for both. Anne may have hoped that Christina would obtain a position as a teacher, even a governess. Concern that she would not find a husband persisted, however, and was reflected in another document in the process of being drawn up – Anne Barnard's will.

As in any titled family, seniority virtually dictated the principal beneficiaries, but Anne took the novel step of passing over the two oldest brothers, Alexander and Robert, in favour of their sons, Lindsay and James, her senior nephews. Lindsay, as the next earl, was to have the Berkeley Square houses and £3,000, James those in Manchester Square and Wimbledon and £2,000. Anne tried to ensure she treated the two even-handedly, wrote often and affectionately to Lindsay, and made both trustees of her affairs; but there can be no doubt that the deeper intimacy was with James. When she apologised for sending an unusually brief note, he was reassuring: 'Did it satisfy me, your whisper? Much! Much!'[35] Since Margaret's death, James had become her closest friend.

He married Mary-Ann Grant in 1819 after one failed courtship and a stream of advice from his aunt which might have been thought intrusive had it not been wise.

> You both are in search of happiness & you must take a candle to it and look everywhere till you can say 'There it is.' To grope in the dark

and having thought you found the diamond to find it a flint . . . God forbid![36]

Mary-Ann proved herself a diamond. Observing them together, Anne recalled what it was to feel passion in the words she and Barnard once used: 'I fancy there is enough to make the pot boil together.'[37] The union was tragically brief. Mary-Ann died within two years. With her own experience of loss, Anne was a source of comfort. 'I never, never can forget the times you have acted as a loving and judicious Mother towards me,' James wrote after the funeral, 'indeed, upon every occasion.'[38]

Almost as heart-warming for Anne was his real mother's generosity of spirit, her entire lack of jealousy. Elizabeth Lindsay spoke of 'this dear child of yours and mine', happy to accept that 'I have been his Bodily Mother but you have a large share in being his Mental Mama'.[39] When James married again two years later Elizabeth wrote to Anne: 'Our cup of happiness is *very, very full.* May we carry it with a humble and steady hand.'[40]

For another protégé she had one final service to perform. Shortly before his coronation in 1821 Anne asked George IV for a favour on behalf of Andrew Barnard, whose military heroics had earned him a knighthood, and received a personal reply a few days later that he was to be made a groom of the bedchamber: 'You should be the first to announce the appointment to him.'[41] Her last visit to the king was, however, a sombre affair.

I received a kind message from him by Sir Andrew Barnard to say that the sight of an old friend's face would do him good, that he was an *old* man and a *thing*, and therefore I must do what he required of me which was to come to him next day after breakfast . . . But when he opened the door with his poor gouty hand and crept in on feeble legs my heart was sorry for him. He shook his head and said, ah my good friend, what a changed world it is with me. When you knew the

Prince of Wales first he could do no wrong, and now the King can do nothing right. I am a poor baited creature, snarled at and snapped at by every hound in the pack.

Her own infirmity was brought home late one night when she set fire to the drawing-room curtains with a candle. As the flames ascended she tried to pull the curtain down, 'in vain. I rang the bell. No-one answered. Where to find a ladder ... water ... help?' All around, the relics of a lifetime were threatened or being consumed by flames. Smoke obliterated the volumes of memoirs laid out on sofas. At this moment, the object she instinctively reached out to save was the portrait of Margaret.

James, staying in the room above, had meanwhile noticed smoke coming through the floorboards. He raced down, roused the servants and set up a human chain to douse the flames with buckets of water. Anne watched, helpless yet strangely calm.

> My house and everything in it was uninsured – furniture, plate, jewels, pictures, all seemed gone, and we were fast losing the power of distinguishing any object. Yet I felt a self-possession that was wonderful. It taught me what that dreadful calm is, which is the result of danger beyond a certain point, and the great use it is at moments of extremity ... At last, at last, the crackling noise of the flames grew fainter ... We could see each other.[42]

The losses included a number of paintings, and damage to the house took weeks to put right; but her dread that the memoirs had been despoiled beyond repair proved unfounded. 'All are perfectly restored by care and cash,' she reported. 'The evils which I have suffered are so small compared with the good I have met, I beg to be considered a fortunate woman.'[43]

A relative silence falls over the final years. A woman whose voice had been heard in its different forms since childhood retreated once the memoirs were finished, to the point that even her correspondence slackened. She was passing into the obscurity that would surely have been her destiny, had it not been for the attention given to her first literary endeavour by the giant of Scottish letters.

Although Sir Walter Scott was a best-selling poet and author, anonymity remained the order of the day and when his novel *The Pirate* was published in 1822 the title page stated merely it to be by the author of *Waverley*. It then went on to quote a verse from 'Auld Robin Grey' while referring specifically to 'Lady Anne Lindsay's beautiful ballad'.

Fifty years on, the lyric written by Anne at twenty-one had become a cultural landmark, the single most popular ballad of the romantic period in Britain.[44] It had been published in various collections, was sung all over England as well as Scotland and had been translated into French. Joseph Haydn had arranged it twice – for piano and soprano and for piano, violin, cello and soprano. At least two authors before Scott featured 'Auld Robin Grey' in their novels, including the pioneering feminist Mary Wollstonecraft, who introduced it as a polemic against the marital exploitation of women in her final work, *The Wrongs of Women, or, Maria*. But Scott went further in identifying Anne unequivocally as the writer of 'Auld Robin Grey', demolishing claims to authorship by others, including a Somerset clergyman, and ensuring her some little immortality.*

---

* Wollstonecraft's novel, published incomplete in 1798, has the character of a 'lovely lunatic' who 'had been married against her inclination to a rich old man' in an asylum singing the 'pathetic ballad of old Robin Grey'. The poem was also included in Sir Herbert Croft's novel of 1780 *Love and Madness: A Story Too True*. See *British Women Poets of the Romantic Era* by Paula Feldman, and 'Unclaimed Territory: The Ballad of Auld Robin Grey and the Assertion of Authorial Ownership' by Jane Millgate in *The Library*, vol. 8, issue 4.

The woman who had thus far preserved her anonymity so assiduously was thrilled – all the more perhaps because seven years earlier Scott had delivered a warm verdict on Austen's fiction in *The Quarterly Review*. Anne wrote to him directly with a playful request that he express her gratitude to 'the Author of Waverley with whom I am informed you are personally acquainted', and went on to explain the history of 'Auld Robin Grey' and the old melody with 'very naughty words' that Sophy Johnston used to sing at Balcarres.[45] Scott replied warmly, recalling the Edinburgh of his youth where he was taught 'Auld Robin' by an aunt who knew Anne to be the author of 'that real pastoral which is worth all the dialogues which Corydon and Phyllis have had together from the days of Theocritus'.[46] Would Anne now agree to his next idea? He wanted to publish 'a complete copy of Robin . . . with as much or as little of its history as you think better'.

Anne, as unable as ever to answer a simple suggestion with a direct answer, started by telling herself that although she had grown weary of Robin, he was her child and she should not be denied him. Inevitably, the contrarian in her then objected that attaching her name after so long a silence would be 'inconsistent'. Her solution was to propose an anthology to include 'some beautiful poems of Margaret's' and 'some very sweet ones' by their sister, Elizabeth. Scott graciously agreed that they should have a book to themselves, edited by himself and entitled *The Lays of the Lindsays*. A proof volume duly arrived, at which point Elizabeth objected that some of Anne's later poems were 'too trivial to be admitted as companions of the original Robin'.[47]

Elizabeth, it is only fair to add, probably knew she was jeopardising publication of her own verses and Margaret's, so it seems unlikely her opinion was offered out of jealousy: 'Do not think I am pulling down the merit of your lesser poems – I am only exalting our old friend Robin over them all.'[48] But the upshot was that *The Lays of the Lindsays* had barely come off the press in 1824 than it was suppressed.* Mortified, Anne wrote to Scott: 'For all the trouble I have given you, pardon me, pardon me!' Patient, courteous, he persisted. It was purely thanks to Scott that the authentic version of 'Auld Robin Grey' was published, with attribution, for the Bannatyne Club, a Scottish heritage society, in the year of the author's death.

Her first real intimation of mortality had occurred as early as 1816 with bowel pains that confined her to bed for six weeks and convinced her, perhaps because Andrew and Margaret had suffered from similar ailments, that she was dying. Surprised and happy to find herself alive, 'sick or well', she made few further references to health until the spring of 1823 when the condition returned with a vengeance and, 'so frightened and with so much pain in my stomach', she saw the time had come to put her affairs in order.[49]

A letter was drafted, to be sent posthumously to her brother, 'My Dearest Balcarres, Friend of my Youth and my junior but one year', explaining her will in order to forestall any objections. As well as serving clan Lindsay, 'and your descendants,' she had a duty, 'to my husband whose natural children and grandchildren are entitled to my protection'.[50] In the event, Alexander probably never saw the letter, dying six weeks before his older sister.

Her last recorded public act was a tribute to the days of Paradise. In an attempt to consolidate Cape rule, the government had recruited colonists in 1820 to settle the conflict-ridden eastern frontier where some 5,000 farming and artisan families were set down without support. Early in 1824 the press reported 'calamities never equalled in any infant colony'. Far from 'the

---

*   Anne wrote of having been sent fifty copies by the printers, 'to destroy or give away as I please', but no more than three copies appear to survive. See Feldman.

country described by travellers as a second land of promise', the settlers had suffered 'drought, crop failures, cattle raids by savage natives and the ravages of beasts of prey'.[51] An appeal for relief was launched and the *Morning Chronicle* published a list of subscribers. The East India Company gave £100. Individual donors included William Wilberforce who gave £5. Among the most forthcoming was Lady Anne Barnard with £20.[52]

Her last letter was a farewell to James, brief, scratchy, and seemingly written with difficulty, reporting she had begun to destroy the personal correspondence that convention dictated ought to have been consigned to the flames long ago.

> I am beginning to burn and put my papers in order – but fear I shall not accomplish it.[53]

What happened in her final days is unclear. The *Morning Post* of 26 April 1825 reported that Lady Anne Barnard had been among the select party at a dinner given a few days earlier by the Earl of Harewood, followed, appropriately, by 'a concert of instrumental and vocal music in the Grand Gallery'.[54] Pleasing though it is to imagine the seventy-four-year-old singer and pianist savouring music to the last, the paper was almost certainly mistaken in placing her at Harewood House, hundreds of miles away in Yorkshire, within two weeks of her death. The bowel pain had become worse than ever, producing sleepless nights.

There are no first-hand accounts of the end and the press remained muddled. One paper reported that Lady Anne Barnard's death had come 'suddenly', another that it 'followed a protracted illness', while a third settled for 'suddenly after a protracted illness'. Actually, they may not have been entirely contradictory, given her condition.

Anne died at Berkeley Square on 6 May 1825. We may assume she was not alone – that those beside her bed included 'the near connections of my dear Barnard', her trio of protégées, from Anne Hervey, the youngest at twelve, to Christina, now aged twenty-two.

What would become of Christina had worried Anne to the end. Whatever the young woman's talents, race was always going to be a factor and, with no marital prospects in sight, Anne felt it necessary to make special provision for her. Margaret and Anne Hervey were left sums of £4,000 and £2,000 respectively in trust, bequests which would have been seen as generous for girls, while anticipating that they would marry. Christina was left £3,000, but with the addition of a £200 annuity for life, that would ensure she could manage on her own.

Possession of 21 Berkeley Square was duly taken by Alexander's son, the Seventh Earl of Balcarres. Christina moved to Kentish Town, a respectable but not genteel part of London, and there the story might have ended so far as the earl was concerned, but for a letter thirty years later advising him that his cousin, Lieutenant General James Lindsay, had died. It came from James's executor and added:

> I dare say you remember a young person in Lady Anne Barnard's house many years ago named Christina Douglas – she married a farmer of the name of Sloper, had a family and died. These children are now growing up. The eldest came of age and received her money some time since & another is also of age and going to be married. Her money is not to be put into settlement so the transfer of it to her need not delay the marriage.[55]

How Christina, living in London, met and married a farmer from Wiltshire, was not stated. Plainly, though, the letter shows Christina's affairs had been handled by James after Anne's death, and the £3,000 inheritance, still in trust, was being passed on to her own daughters.

Closer examination reveals further layers to the story. The 'farmer of the name of Sloper' was in fact Mark Sloper Esq., a country gentleman, prosperous landowner and horse breeder, a stalwart of the church, the hunt and the cricket pitch, and a prize-winner at Wiltshire agricultural shows.[56] Christina's introduction to this rustic figure, from a different world but evidently a suitable match, suggests an intermediary. The most likely candidate is James Lindsay; Christina's well-being had, in effect, been a torch, passed from Anne to her beloved nephew. The marriage, at Saint Pancras Church in September 1829, was an occasion of note, being widely reported in the press before the couple began life together at Manor Farm in Bishop's Cannings, near Devizes.[57]

Christina had seven children by Sloper, and died in March 1842, aged thirty-eight. Although the cause was not reported, she had given birth a few days earlier to their eighth child, whom she named Hervey after the girls who had shared her childhood at Berkeley Square – they too descendants of the father she never knew. A sickly baby, Hervey survived her by just a few days. But Christina's three daughters married local gentlemen, her trust fund serving as their dowries as it had hers.[58] Of all Lady Anne Barnard's accomplishments – as poet, hostess, traveller, artist and chronicler – her compassion in embracing the child of a husband's infidelity was the least renowned. As her final act of defiance, it was also the most enduring.

Epilogue

Recognition came posthumously and was due entirely to the efforts of Sir Walter Scott. Eight years after Anne's death and the publication of 'Auld Robin Grey', William Wordsworth called it one of 'the two best ballads perhaps of modern times'. The great literary critic William Hazlitt said that the effect of reading it was 'as if all our hopes and fears hung upon the last fibre of the heart, and we felt that giving way. What silence, what loneliness, what leisure for grief and despair!' Leigh Hunt, another influential romantic poet, thought 'Auld Robin' 'the most pathetic ballad that ever was written'.[1] Among the Victorians it gained a huge following. Thomas Hardy was impressed enough to record the first time he read it, while Francis Turner Palgrave wrote in his anthology, *The Golden Treasury*: 'There can hardly exist a poem more truly tragic in the highest sense than this: nor, except Sappho, has any Poetess known to the Editor equalled it in excellence.'[2]

What, then, of Anne Barnard's other poems? The answer is that, thanks to her decision to suppress *The Lays of the Lindsays*, none has been published. Taken together, however, they do not seem likely to earn her belated appreciation as a significant romantic poet. Even to an unlearned eye, the quality appears too uneven from, on the one hand, 'The Rose and the Thorn', an agonising meditation on her passion for Windham, to, on the other, 'The Slave of Africa', a bold but trite reflection on inter-racial love.

It is rather as a chronicler of her own life and times that Lady Anne Barnard may be remembered. The author Anthony Powell, whose knowledge of her was limited to a few of her letters to Macartney, wrote in 1928 that 'on the whole she is perhaps less well known than she deserves'.[3] It would be interesting to know what Powell would have made of her other writings, the memoirs in particular.

Like any major work, the memoirs were the source of much anxiety to their creator – over the quality, but also whether she should be writing them at all, given the need to be at the same time candid and discreet. Because these principles were irreconcilable, Anne managed to justify the work on the grounds that it was 'a tale to caution as well as to encourage'.[4] The Hardwickes' disapproval, along with a perception common at the time that authorship was not compatible with respectability, still had a restraining effect. She abandoned writing at one point and even after resuming concealed identities in the original manuscript with pseudonyms, titling it *The History of the Family of St Aubin and the Memoirs of Louisa Melford*. Only after further assurances from the nephews James and Lindsay were identities restored in two more editions, one intended for each of them. Even then she felt a need to assure her surviving siblings that 'no brother or sister of mine can ever have reason to be uneasy at what may fall from my pen, affectionately attached as I am to all'; and she may have become constrained as the last two volumes are comparatively prosaic.[5]

In large part her purpose was to explain her life, to exculpate herself from what she saw as the charge sheet levelled against her by society, but also – and more significantly – by family. Although the precise nature of these sins was not stated, we have discovered enough of her unconventional ways to see what she alluded to when writing of her attempts

to preserve the real account of some events in our family which might otherwise be handed down as traditional blame on one who (though she may have been injudicious) deserved no such sentence as has sometimes been inflicted on her.[6]

Her confidence, never robust, had become more fragile, and here the influence of family may again be discerned. Reading the memoirs, we see her evolve from a defiant young woman to an anxious older one, unable to accept compliments without embarrassment, unwilling to trust her own judgement. Her sister Elizabeth, having tried to interfere with the memoirs, had also – in effect – prevented her receiving due recognition for 'Auld Robin Grey' until Scott took matters into his own hands and had it published, with further verses added by Anne, along with his formal declaration that 'this beautiful and long-contested ballad' was hers. Whether she lived to see this final validation is not clear, but the odds are against it. Anne died less than halfway into the year it came off the press.*

Her diffidence has continued to stand in the way of further appreciation since. James Lindsay was a dutiful custodian of an archive taken to Balcarres and, under Anne's absolute prohibition on publication of her writings, preserved from outside eyes.

A slight breach of the injunction was made by the Twenty-fifth Earl of Crawford, grandson of Anne's brother Alexander, who included her Cape journal in his three-volume family history *Lives of the Lindsays*, first published in 1849. This excited subsequent interest in South Africa, and a would-be biographer presented herself. Although Dorothea Fairbridge was able to see the memoirs, the book published in 1924 contained no extracts and was essentially confined to letters from the Barnards at the

---

* It may have been a result of Scott's editing that the title was altered from 'Auld Robin Grey', as it was always referred to in Anne's hand, to 'Auld Robin Gray', by which it has since been known.

Cape to Macartney. Another South African author, Madeleine Masson, wrote a biography without any access to Anne's papers at all. By now attention had been properly roused, but though South African academics edited a series of volumes devoted to her letters, journals and diaries from the Cape, the bigger picture – the story of her extraordinary life – remained unseen. When the present author wrote to the Twenty-ninth Earl of Crawford in 2012, requesting access to Anne's papers, the memoirs were largely unexplored as a biographical and historical resource, and virtually unknown.

What then of the flaws in these lavish volumes? Prolixity is a problem. Going back on them, Anne regretted that 'I had not passed them under the eye of some merciless reviser who would have pruned them without remorse'. Another passage begins, 'I fancy I have nothing to mark down, but the pen once in my hand & the first page wrote . . .' then sets off on another ramble, before she comes back to remind herself that wordiness is 'a species of disease'.[7] She is fallible in chronology as well, especially dates. 'My memory will go,' she wrote in 1802. 'It was never a good one and it is not now worth two-pence-halfpenny.'[8]

There are other defects. She closed herself resolutely to high-society gossip and, as readers of this book will have discerned, she was too sensitive, too forgiving, to count among the sharpest chroniclers of her times. This she knew as well.

If my reader may have been disappointed on some occasions when I have told little when I have obviously known much, let my forbearance be my praise, for surely there is more merit in suppressing the foibles of poor human nature or withholding the brilliant and pointed observation one could make, than in placing error or ridicule in an incontrovertible light.[9]

The fundamental question that arises is, did she tell the truth?

Can she be trusted?

It has been suggested that, having become aware of contemporary women authors, Anne was exploring her life in the form of a novel.[10] It is true that the early volumes are especially vivid and dramatic – and when it comes to extended passages of dialogue, she was clearly drawing on memory rather than record. It may be recalled that in relating her early courtships in Edinburgh she chided herself:

> These memoirs – I speak it with shame – are becoming a mere novel I see. 'Why not?' say you . . . Indeed, I do not know why they should not, except that I had intended they should be something better. But the past is a novel.[11]

There is a novelistic aspect to the memoirs, apparent not only in her use of dialogue but her relish for a good story. She is very persuasive, and the reader, drawn in by the intimacy of address and confessional tone, needs to guard against accepting all she has to say as an absolute record. She was, after all, seeking redemption; and she is subject to the failings intrinsic to memoirists – selectiveness, subjectivity and simple camouflage.

But she avoids those other common sins of self-aggrandisement and fabrication. It is possible to go further and say that Anne may have made omissions by choice, but she did not tamper with the truth (as she remembered it), nor flinch from a degree of self-disclosure so searing as to appear from another age from that other indefatigable memoirist, Fanny Burney. Where her version of events can be checked against other records, it stands up. The stern lecturing of her own conscience obliged her to be honest.

> Dr Johnson said people propagate falsehoods in many ways without intending it. On hearing an extraordinary circumstance told he would

say, 'it is not so, do not tell this again.' He inculcated in all his friends
the importance of perpetual vigilance . . . Those who have been of his
school have a love of truth and accuracy.[12]

Biographers agree that a 'Life' cannot give a precise picture of a
life, because no individual can be reduced properly to words. The
complexity and ambiguity of human perception came into Anne's
own observations. 'How odd it is,' she noted, 'that people have
always given me credit for many good things which I have not,
and denied me others which I have.'[13] However, a desire to reach
the heart of a matter was an instinct she shared with Burney, and
it helps to account for their wordiness. One biographer of Burney
has observed that in recording her life in minute detail, she was
acknowledging that experience has a complex texture and the
truth about it is elusive.[14] Anne would have agreed; in relating
her dilemmas at length, she was reviewing her behaviour from a
range of perspectives, and addressing each of them.

Spontaneity is another quality, and here are grounds for
suggesting that although it is right to say that a 'Life' cannot
fully reveal a life, Anne provided more than the usual materials to
assist a biographer. Margaret Lenta, who brought her to a wider
audience through editions of the Cape diaries and journals, noted
Anne's 'penchant for thinking aloud on paper as she confronted
her day-to-day problems and dilemmas'.[15] It is this meditative
tone that conveys intimacy and can lead the reader to a sense that
he or she is close to understanding Anne Barnard.

The memoirs are in part a confession of Anne's need to be
loved – in effect, a final act of reaching out to those who knew her
and who she hoped would remember her fondly. They may show
too great a desire to explain herself, be too prolix for commercial
publication today. They still cast a profoundly revealing light on
an era, and on life as a painful quest for truth and vindication –
one which she was able set down, reflect upon and, unlike so many

other women of her time, bequeath to later generations. There she is to be seen, in her own words, with all her paradoxes: high-born but egalitarian, daring yet compassionate, frightened but resolute, a figure of the Georgian age who speaks to the modern world.

We may leave her at 21 Berkeley Square, pen in hand towards the end.

My friends press me to go out to amuse myself – but I should go without any interest beyond the charm of getting home again; by the side of my fire I have got into the habit of living in other days with those I loved, reflecting on the past, hoping in the future, and sometimes looking back with a sorrowful retrospect when I fear I may have erred. Together with these mental employments I have various sources of amusement – I compile and arrange my memorandums of past observations and events ... With such entertainment for my mornings and a house full of nephews and nieces, together with the near connections of my dear Barnard, all tenderly attached to me, I have great, great reason to bless God, who, in taking much from me, has left me so much! [16]

Appendix

'Auld Robin Grey'

This is the version of the poem sent by Lady Anne Barnard to Sir Walter Scott in 1823 for publication.

'Auld Robin Grey'

When the sheep are in the fauld, when the cows come hame,
When a' the weary world to quiet rest are gane,
The woes of my heart fa' in showers frae my ee
Unkent by my Gudeman wha soundly sleeps by me.

Young Jamie lov'd me well, and sought me for his bride,
But saving a crown piece he'd naething else beside,
To make the crown a pound my Jamie gaed to sea,
And the crown and the pound, O they were baith for me.

Before he had been gone a twelvemonth and a day
My Father broke his arm, our cow was sto'en away;
My Mother she fell sick, my Jamie was at sea,
And Auld Robin Grey, O! he came a'courting me.

My Father couldna work, my Mother couldna spin,
I toil'd day and night, but their bread I couldna win;
Auld Robin maintained them baith, and wi' tears in his ee,
Said 'Jenny, O! for their sakes, will you marry me?'

My heart it said Nay, and I look'd for Jamie back,
But the winds they blew hard, and his ship was a wreck;
His ship it was a wreck, why didna Jenny dee,
Oh, wherefore was she spared to cry out 'Wae is me!'

My Father argued sair, tho' my Mother didna speak,
Yet she looked in my face till my heart was like to break,
They gied him my hand, but my heart was in the sea,
And so Auld Robin Grey he was Gudeman to me.

I hadna been his wife a week but only four,
When mournfu' as I sat on the stane at my door,
I saw my Jamie's ghaist, I couldna think it he,
Till he said 'I'm come hame my love to marry thee.'

O! sair, sair did we greet, and mickle say of a'
Ae kiss we took, nae mair, I bade him gang awa',
I wish that I were dead, but I'm no like to dee,
For O! I am but young to cry out 'Wae is me!'

I gang like a ghaist, and I carena much to spin,
I dare no' think of Jamie, for that would be a sin;
But I will be my best a gude wife to be,
For O! Auld Robin Grey, he is sae kind to me!

Bibliography

Lady Anne Barnard's archive is part of the collection known as the Crawford papers and is catalogued in the *Hand-list of Personal Papers from the Muniments of the Earl of Crawford and Balcarres*, published by the John Rylands University Library of Manchester. For the present purpose, this astonishingly rich collection of papers can be divided between items held at the family home of Balcarres and those at the National Library of Scotland (NLS) in Edinburgh.

Anne compiled no fewer than three editions of her memoirs. So far as comparisons have been possible, the contents are the same, apart from pseudonyms used in the original version and the illustrations in two others. The notes cited in this book are to the six-volume typescript at the NLS. The correspondence to and from Anne cited in references from 27/1/1 up to 27/1/371 (family) and from 27/2/1 up to 27/2/325 (personal) is deposited in Edinburgh as well.

The collection at Balcarres includes seven further volumes of Anne's papers compiled by the Twenty-seventh Earl of Crawford and relating to members of her circle and listed in the footnotes as 27/4/21–27. These cover, for example, her friendship with Maria Fitzherbert and the Prince of Wales (27/4/25), her relationship with William Windham (27/4/22) and dealings with Sir Walter Scott (27/4/26). Her unpublished poems (27/4/20) are also at Balcarres.

BIBLIOGRAPHY

ADDITIONAL MANUSCRIPT SOURCES

British Library, London
    Hardwicke Papers
    Holland House Papers
    Windham Papers
    Wellesley Papers

Bodleian Library, Oxford
    Burges Papers
    Harcourt Papers

Brenthurst Library, Johannesburg
    Lord Macartney, Diary of Official Business

Cape Archives, Cape Town
    Correspondence of Andrew Barnard as Secretary to the Governor
    Correspondence within the Colony

South African Library, Cape Town
    Lady Anne Barnard, Collection of Papers

Mount Stuart Library and Archive, Isle of Bute
    Hastings family papers

EDITED COLLECTIONS OF WRITINGS
BY LADY ANNE BARNARD

Lenta, Margaret and Basil Le Cordeur (eds), *The Cape Diaries of Lady Anne Barnard, 1799–1800*, 2 vols, Cape Town, 1999

Lenta, Margaret (ed.), *Paradise, the Castle and the Vineyard: Lady Anne Barnard's Cape Diaries*, Johannesburg, 2001

Lindsay, Alexander, *The Lives of the Lindsays: A Memoir of the Houses of Crawford and Balcarres*, 3 vols, London, 1858

Robinson, A. M. Lewin (ed.), *The Letters of Lady Anne Barnard to Henry Dundas from the Cape of Good Hope, 1793–1803*, Cape Town, 1973

Robinson, A. M. Lewin with Margaret Lenta and Dorothy Driver (eds), *The Cape Journals of Lady Anne Barnard, 1797–8*, Cape Town, 1994

BIOGRAPHIES

Fairbridge, Dorothea, *Lady Anne Barnard at the Cape of Good Hope, 1797–1802*, Oxford, 1924

Masson, Madeleine, *Lady Anne Barnard: The Court and Colonial Service under George III and the Regency*, London, 1948

SELECT BIBLIOGRAPHY

Ackroyd, Peter, *London: The Biography*, London, 2001

Balderstone, Katherine (ed.), *Thraliana: The Diary of Mrs Hester Lynch Thrale, 1776–1809*, 2 vols, Oxford, 1942

Barker, Nicolas, *Lady Anne Barnard's Watercolours and Sketches: Glimpses of the Cape*, Cape Town, 2009

Barrett, Charlotte (ed.), *Diary and Letters of Madame D'Arblay, 1778–1840*, 6 vols, London, 1904

Bickley, Reginald (ed.), *Diaries of Sylvester Douglas, Lord Glenbervie*, 2 vols, London, 1928

Blunt, Reginald (ed.), *Mrs Montagu, Queen of the Blues: Her Letters and Friendships, 1762–1800*, 2 vols, London, 1923

Boucher, Maurice and Nigel Penn, *Britain at the Cape, 1795 to 1802*, Johannesburg, 1992

Bredin, Miles, *The Pale Abyssinian: The Life of James Bruce*, London, 2001

Burton, J. H., *The Life and Correspondence of David Hume*, 2 vols, Edinburgh, 1846

Butler, Iris, *The Eldest Brother: The Marquess Wellesley*, London, 1973

Byrne, Paula, *Belle: The True Story of Dido Belle*, London, 2014

Coghlan, Margaret, *Memoirs of Mrs Coghlan (Daughter of the Late Major Moncrieffe)*, 2 vols, London, 1794 (available online)

Colley, Linda, *Britons: Forging the Nation, 1707–1837*, London, 1992

——, *Captives: Britain, Empire and the World, 1600–1850*, London, 2002

Craig-Brown, T. (ed.), *Letters and Memoir of Her Own Life by Mrs Alison Rutherford or Cockburn*, Edinburgh, 1900

Devine, T. M., *To The Ends of the Earth: Scotland's Global Diaspora, 1770–2010*, London, 2012

Ellis, Annie Raine (ed.), *The Early Diaries of Frances Burney, 1768–78*, 2 vols, London, 1913

Elwin, Malcolm, *The Noels and the Milbankes: Their Letters for Twenty-Five Years, 1767–1792*, London, 1967

Feldman, Paula, *British Women Poets of the Romantic Era*, Baltimore, 2000

Foreman, Amanda, *Georgiana, Duchess of Devonshire*, London, 1998

Harman, Claire, *Fanny Burney: A Biography*, London, 2001

Harvey, A. D., *Sex in Georgian England*, London, 2001

Hemlow, Joyce, *The Journals and Letters of Fanny Burney (Madame D'Arblay)*, vol 1., 1791–1792, Oxford, 1972

Hibbert, Christopher, *George IV*, London, 1988

Ketton-Cremer, Robert (ed.), *The Early Life and Diaries of William Windham*, London, 1930

——, *Felbrigg: The Story of a House*, The National Trust, 2010

McKenzie, Kirsten, *The Making of an English Slave-owner: Samuel Hudson at the Cape*, Cape Town, 1993

Markus, Julia, *Lady Byron and Her Daughters*, New York, 2015

Marshall, P. J. (ed.), *The Oxford History of the British Empire*, vol 2, Oxford, 1998

Martin, Peter, *A Life of James Boswell*, New Haven, 2008

Matheson, Cyril, *The Life of Henry Dundas, First Viscount Melville*, London, 1933

Mitchell, L. G., *Charles James Fox*, Oxford, 1992

Mostert, Noel, *Frontiers: The Epic of South Africa's Creation*, London, 1992

Munson, James, *Maria Fitzherbert: The Secret Wife of George IV*, London, 2001

Norman, Jesse, *Edmund Burke: Philosopher, Politician, Prophet*, London, 2013

Porter, Roy, *English Society in the Eighteenth Century*, London, 1991

Pottle, Frederick (ed.), *Boswell's London Journal, 1762–1763*, London, 1950

Powell, Anthony (ed.), *Barnard Letters, 1778–1824*, London, 1928

Schama, Simon, *Citizens: A Chronicle of the French Revolution*, London, 1989

Shields, Carol, *Jane Austen*, London, 2001

Sichel, Walter, *The Life of Richard Brinsley Sheridan*, 2 vols, London, 1909

Steinbach, Susie, *Women in England, 1760–1914*, London, 2004

Streak, Michael, *The Afrikaner as Viewed by the English*, Cape Town, 1974

Taylor, Stephen, *The Caliban Shore: The Fate of the Grosvenor Castaways*, London, 2004

Uglow, Jenny, *In These Times: Living in Britain through Napoleon's Wars, 1793–1815*, London, 2014

Notes

I THE BLACK BROTH 1750–1768

1   Barrett, vol. 1, p. 244.
2   27/2/76, E. Fauquier to Anne Lindsay, undated, about 1777.
3   LoL, vol. 2, p. 311.
4   Memoirs, vol. 1, p. 47.
5   James Lindsay had fought under the banner of James Stuart, the 'Old Pretender', at the battle of Sheriffmuir in 1715, then aged twenty-four.
6   LoL, vol. 2, p. 231.
7   Ibid., p. 210.
8   Memoirs, vol. 1, p. 38. Anne's account of her parents' courtship, in Lindsay, vol. 2, p. 234, is too flippant to be convincing.
9   Ibid., p. 49.
10 Ibid., p. 44.
11 LoL, vol. 2, p. 381.
12 Ibid., p. 314.
13 Ibid., p. 315.
14 Ibid., p. 214.
15 Ibid., p. 307.
16 Memoirs, vol. 1, p. 41.
17 LoL, vol. 2, p. 214.
18 Ibid., p. 304.
19 Memoirs, vol. 2, p. 7.
20 The final collection of the Bibliotheca Lindesiana was compiled by later generations in the nineteenth century.
21 LoL, vol. 2, p. 386.
22 27/4/20, Verses by Lady Anne Lindsay.

23 LoL, vol. 2, p. 303.
24 Memoirs, vol. 1, p. 7.
25 27/1/166, James Lindsay to his daughters, undated.
26 LoL, vol. 2, p. 275.
27 Memoirs, vol. 1, p. 70.
28 Ibid., pp. 62 and 71.
29 LoL, vol. 2, p. 335.
30 Memoirs, vol. 1, p. 61.
31 LoL, vol. 2, p. 309.
32 Devine, pp. 4–5.
33 LoL, vol. 2, p. 322.
34 *Dictionary of National Biography*, see Bluestocking circle for Scottish women.
35 27/2/45, W. Cross to Anne Lindsay, 15 October 1772.
36 Memoirs, vol. 1, p. 55.
37 Ibid.
38 Ibid., p. 13.
39 27/2/44, W. Cross to Anne Lindsay, undated.
40 Memoirs, vol. 1, p. 55.
41 Ibid., p. 63.
42 Ibid., p. 64.
43 Ibid., p. 72.
44 Ibid.
45 27/1/166, James Lindsay to Anne Lindsay, undated.
46 Memoirs, vol. 1, p. 80.

2 EDINBURGH'S COQUETTE 1768–1769

1   LoL, vol. 2, p. 279.
2   Memoirs, vol. 1, p. 84.
3   Craig-Brown, p. 75.
4   Memoirs, vol. 1, p. 84.
5   *Dictionary of National Biography.*
6   27/2/167, Augustus Oughton to Anne Lindsay, 19 May 1768.
7   LoL, vol. 2, p. 334.
8   Memoirs, vol. 1, p. 69.
9   27/2/138, Lord Lindores to Anne Lindsay, 27 January 1769.
10 Memoirs, vol. 1, p. 69.
11 27/2/35, Rudolph Bentinck to Anne Lindsay, undated [1769].
12 27/2/138, Lord Lindores to Anne Lindsay, 29 January 1769.
13 Memoirs, vol. 1, p. 95.
14 Ibid., pp. 97–8.
15 27/1/111, Lady Balcarres to Anne Lindsay, undated.
16 Memoirs, vol. 1, p. 103.
17 Anne's extended and agonised account of Bentinck's courtship is contained in the Memoirs, vol. 1, pp. 86–105. It might be thought melodramatic were it not for the supporting evidence of his letters in 27/2.
18 Memoirs, vol. 1, p. 107.

19   Ibid., p. 149.
20   Ibid., p. 85.
21   27/2/45, Sheriff Cross to Anne Lindsay, 15 October 1772.
22   Memoirs, vol. 1, p. 118.
23   Ibid., p. 114.
24   Ibid., p. 149.
25   27/2/36, Rudolph Bentinck to Anne Lindsay, 10 October 1785.
26   27/2/201 and 202, Henry Swinton to Anne Lindsay, undated and 5 June 1769.
27   Memoirs, vol. 1, p. 147.
28   27/4 Poems and Prose.
29   Memoirs, vol. 1, pp. 122–4.
30   Porter, p. 57.
31   Harvey, p. 4.

3 AULD ROBIN GREY 1770–1771

1   Memoirs, vol. 1, p. 155 and 170.
2   27/1/89, Alexander Fordyce to Anne Lindsay, undated [1770].
3   Memoirs, vol. 1, p. 169.
4   Ibid., p. 170.
5   Ibid., p. 171.
6   Ibid., p. 173.
7   Ibid., p. 174.
8   Martin, p. 80.
9   Memoirs, vol. 1, p. 179.
10   Ibid., p. 183.
11   Ibid. p. 149. This note refers to an earlier period of Anne's residence at the old house but it captures perfectly her dislike of the place.
12   Shields, p. 164.
13   29/3/1, Margaret Lindsay to Anne Lindsay, 8 July 1770.
14   Memoirs, vol. 1, p. 243.
15   29/3/1, Margaret Lindsay to Anne Lindsay, 8 July 1770.
16   Memoirs, vol. 1, p. 185.
17   LoL, vol. 2, p. 332.
18   See 'Unclaimed Territory: The Ballad of Auld Robin Gray and the Assertion of Authorial Ownership' by Jane Millgate in *The Library*, December 2007.
19   Ibid.
20   Feldman.
21   LoL, vol. 2, p. 333.
22   Craig-Brown, p. 69.
23   Ibid., p. 93.
24   Memoirs, vol. 1, pp. 118, 127–9.
25   27/4/21.
26   Memoirs, vol. 1, p. 189.
27   Ibid., p. 193.
28   Ibid., p. 196.
29   Ibid., p. 189.

30 Ibid., pp. 203 and 199.
31 Ibid., p. 200.
32 Anne's prolonged, melodramatic account of the denouement is contained in Memoirs, vol. 1, pp. 207–38.
33 27/2/203, Henry Swinton to Anne Lindsay, undated [1771].
34 Mrs Cockburn's letter is quoted in full in the Memoirs, vol. 1, p. 240–2.
35 Memoirs, vol. 1, p. 225.
36 Ibid., p. 243.
37 27/1/106, Lady Balcarres to Anne Lindsay, undated.
38 Memoirs, vol. 1, p. 247.
39 Ibid.
40 Ibid., p. 241.
41 Ibid., p. 238.
42 Ibid., p. 248.
43 Ibid., pp. 243 and 245.

4 THE GREAT CRASH 1771–1772

1   Anne was mistaken in calling it Holwell Lane.
2   Memoirs, vol. 2, p. 2.
3   Ibid., p. 4.
4   Ibid., p. 32.
5   Ibid., p. 32.
6   Ibid., p. 7.
7   Ibid., p. 35.
8   *The Times*, 14 April 1824.
9   Memoirs, vol. 2, p. 4.
10 Ibid.
11 Porter, p. 227.
12 LoL, vol. 2, p. 335.
13 Sichel, vol. 1, p. 308.
14 LoL, vol. 2, p. 335.
15 Pottle, p. 300. Boswell was writing in this instance of Fordyce's circle in Edinburgh, known as the Poker Club, but the same could be said of his London associates.
16 Memoirs, vol. 2, p. 20.
17 Ibid., p. 41.
18 Ibid., p. 11.
19 27/2/45, Sheriff Cross to Anne Lindsay, 15 October 1772. Anne commented in the margin: 'It is well written and much of it is just.'
20 Memoirs, vol. 2, p. 16.
21 *Dictionary of National Biography*.
22 Memoirs, vol. 2, p. 12.
23 29/3/1, Alexander Fordyce to Anne Lindsay, 11 December 1771.
24 Memoirs, vol. 2, p. 34.
25 Ibid., pp. 21–2.
26 Ibid., pp. 42 and 78.

27   Ibid., p. 31.
28   Ibid., p. 173.
29   Ibid., p. 8.
30   British History Online, *Survey of London, vol. 40, the Grosvenor Estate in London.*
31   Online, Rootsweb, *Anecdotes of the Manners and Customs of London During the Eighteenth Century,* James Peller Malcolm.
32   Memoirs, vol. 2, pp. 36–8.
33   Ibid., p. 40.
34   27/2/118, Sophy Johnston to Anne Lindsay, 3 June 1772.
35   27/1/88, Lady Dalrymple to Anne Lindsay, 2 June 1771.
36   Memoirs, vol. 2, p. 45.
37   *Dictionary of National Biography.*
38   Memoirs, vol. 2, p. 47.
39   Ibid.
40   Yale Edition of Horace Walpole's Correspondence, online. Walpole to Horace Mann, 1 July 1772.
41   Ibid.
42   Memoirs, vol. 2, p. 56.
43   Ibid., pp. 52–3.
44   Ibid., p. 73.
45   Ibid., p. 70.
46   Ibid., p. 77.
47   The letters are quoted in full in the Memoirs, vol. 2, pp. 83–4. The originals have not survived, but as the memoirs are accurate elsewhere when correspondence is quoted, I have felt able to do so here.
48   Ibid., p. 89.

5 RETURN TO SPARTA 1772–1776

1   The journey is described in the Memoirs, vol. 2, p. 89.
2   Ibid.
3   Ibid., p. 94.
4   Ibid., p. 109.
5   Ibid., p. 96.
6   Ibid.
7   Anne related an anecdote, told by her grandmother to illustrate Hume's unswerving virtue. While still a boy he had been present in company when a vile smell offended everyone. A sleeping dog was blamed, only for Hume to volunteer, 'Oh, pray, do not hurt the beast, it is me.' Memoirs, vol. 2, p. 107.
8   Memoirs, vol. 2, pp. 107–8.
9   Memoirs, vol. 1, p. 1.
10   Ibid.
11   Memoirs, vol. 2, p. 112.
12   Ibid., p. 103.
13   Ibid., p. 127.
14   29/3/1, Margaret Lindsay to Anne Lindsay, 17 April 1774.

15   Memoirs, vol. 2, p. 103.
16   Ibid., pp. 104–5.
17   27/2/46, W. C. Cross to Anne Lindsay, 13 December 1773.
18   Memoirs, vol. 2, p. 119.
19   Bredin, p. 251.
20   Memoirs, vol. 2, pp. 119–20.
21   Masson, p. 75.
22   Memoirs, vol. 2, pp. 135–45. Anne said that this visit took place when she was twenty-one, but her memory for dates was poor and there are other indications that it was later.
23   Ibid., p. 135.
24   27/2/190, Frances Scott to Anne Lindsay, about 1775.
25   Memoirs, vol. 2, p. 137.
26   Ibid., pp. 139–40.
27   Ibid.
28   Matheson, p. 51.
29   Memoirs, vol. 3, pp. 77/9.
30   Memoirs, vol. 2, p. 223.
31   Colley, *Britons*, pp. 122/3.
32   23/1/1, Anne Lindsay to Alexander Lindsay, 2 September 1777.
33   27/1/269, Robert Lindsay to Anne Lindsay, 25 March 1776.
34   Memoirs, vol. 2, p. 159.
35   29/3/1, Margaret Lindsay to Anne Lindsay, 29 January 1775.
36   Memoirs, vol. 2, pp. 134 and 149.
37   Ibid., p. 153. Although copied into the Memoirs, this is one of those fresh and immediate passages that were evidently drawn from her 'scraps' before they were destroyed.

6 'FOLLY, FOLLY. BUT IN CHARACTER!' 1777–1780

1   Bickley, vol. 1, p. 69.
2   Ibid.
3   Ackroyd, pp. 109 and 242.
4   Memoirs, vol. 2, pp. 182–4.
5   Blunt, vol. 2, p. 281.
6   Memoirs, vol. 2, p. 183.
7   Ibid., p. 184.
8   Ibid., p. 188.
9   Bickley, p. 88.
10   Memoirs, vol. 2, p. 186.
11   Memoirs, vol. 3, p. 85.
12   27/2/76, E. Fauquier to Anne Lindsay, undated, about 1777.
13   Harcourt Papers, Anne Lindsay to Elizabeth Harcourt, 12 October 1777.
14   Ibid., Anne Lindsay to Elizabeth Harcourt, 12 August 1779.
15   Memoirs, vol. 3, p. 46.
16   Ibid.
17   Memoirs, vol. 2, p. 181.

18 Ibid., p. 192.
19 Elwin, p. 131.
20 Memoirs, vol. 2, p. 194.
21 Ibid.
22 Ibid.
23 Ibid., p. 206.
24 Ibid., p. 209.
25 27/2/95 and 96, Catherine Hampden to Anne Lindsay, 4 and 21 January 1780.
26 Memoirs, vol. 2, p. 202.
27 Ibid., p. 201.
28 27/2/157, Judith Milbanke to Anne Lindsay, 14 July 1779.
29 Elwin, p. 136.
30 Colley, *Captives*, p. 291.
31 Memoirs, vol. 2, p. 235.
32 Bickley, p. 69.
33 29/3/1, Margaret Lindsay to Anne Lindsay, about 1775.
34 Memoirs, vol. 2, p. 245.
35 Ibid., p. 244.
36 Ackroyd, p. 491.
37 Charles Gordon was a son of the third marriage of Lord William Gordon, the Second Earl of Aberdeen. George Gordon was a son of his daughter by a second marriage.
38 Memoirs, vol. 2, p. 7. The character is Captain Lismahago.
39 Elwin, p. 150.
40 Ibid., p. 187.

7 'THE DEVIL IN SCARLET' 1781–1783

1   Memoirs, vol. 2, p. 249 and vol. 3, p. 9.
2   Ibid.
3   Elwin, p. 191.
4   Memoirs, vol. 3, p. 1.
5   27/2/3, Richard Atkinson to Anne Lindsay, about 1781.
6   Memoirs, vol. 3, p. 30.
7   Ibid., p. 29.
8   Ibid.
9   Ibid., p. 30.
10 27/2/5, Richard Atkinson to Anne Lindsay, about 1781.
11 Memoirs, vol. 3, p. 29.
12 Elwin, p. 188.
13 Ibid., p. 191.
14 27/2/95, Catherine Hampden to Anne Lindsay, about 1780.
15 Memoirs, vol. 3, p. 54.
16 Elwin, p. 197.
17 Ibid., p. 241.
18 Memoirs, vol. 3, p. 17.

19 Ibid., p. 45.
20 Barrett, vol. 2, p. 121.
21 Elwin, p. 238.
22 Memoirs, vol. 3, p. 31.
23 *The Times*, 19 July 1828.
24 27/2/7, Richard Atkinson to Anne Lindsay, undated [August 1781].
25 Memoirs, vol. 3, p. 83.
26 Masson, p. 65.
27 Memoirs, vol. 3, p. 61.
28 Ibid., p. 64.
29 27/2/162, Unsigned letter, 9 January 1783.
30 Ibid. I am obliged to Richard Atkinson for identifying his ancestor, by his handwriting, as the author.
31 27/2/14 Richard Atkinson to Anne Lindsay, 9 August 1782.
32 27/2/21, Richard Atkinson to Anne Lindsay, undated [December 1782].
33 Memoirs, vol. 3, p. 29.
34 These figures are derived from Anne's papers and Atkinson's will, PROB 11/1149/399.
35 27/1/337.
36 Memoirs, vol. 3, p. 75.

8 ESCAPE TO FRANCE 1784–1785

1 Memoirs, vol. 3, p. 48.
2 Ibid., p. 79.
3 Ibid.
4 Ibid.
5 Ibid., p. 47.
6 27/1/339.
7 27/1/337.
8 Matheson, pp. 220–1.
9 Ketton-Cremer, p. 209.
10 Memoirs, vol. 4, p. 75.
11 Memoirs, vol. 3, p. 103.
12 27/4/25, vol. 2.
13 Memoirs, vol. 3, p. 89.
14 *Morning Herald*, 5 February 1783.
15 Memoirs, vol. 3, p. 89.
16 Elwin, p. 233.
17 Memoirs, vol. 3, p. 97.
18 Ibid., p. 99.
19 Ibid.
20 27/2/23, Richard Atkinson to Anne Lindsay, undated [June 1784].
21 Memoirs, vol. 3, p. 98.
22 Ibid., p. 101.
23 Anne wrongly gave the date as 9 June in her memoirs. A letter from Mrs Fitzherbert confirms it was 9 July.

24 Memoirs, vol. 3, p. 104.
25 Cecil Woodham-Smith review of *Mrs Fitzherbert* by A. Leslie in *The Sunday Times*, 17 April 1960.
26 Memoirs, vol. 3, p. 114.
27 Ibid., pp. 120–5.
28 Hardwicke Papers, Add. MS 35532, Anne Lindsay to Sir Robert Keith, 19 October 1784.
29 27/2/181, Henri Reuss to Anne Lindsay, 13 November 1784.
30 29/3/1, Anne Lindsay to Margaret Lindsay, 20 September 1784.
31 Craig-Brown, p. 219.
32 Memoirs, vol. 3, p. 164.
33 Ibid., p. 127.
34 Ibid., p. 137.
35 27/2/35, Count Bentinck to Anne Lindsay, 10 October 1785.
36 29/3/1, Anne Lindsay to Margaret Lindsay, 20 September 1784; Memoirs, vol. 3, p. 155.
37 Memoirs, vol. 3, p. 158.
38 Hibbert, p. 75.
39 Memoirs, vol. 3, p. 175.
40 Ibid.
41 Ibid.
42 Ibid., pp. 177 and 184.
43 Ibid., p. 182.
44 Ibid., p. 212.
45 Ibid., p. 190.
46 Schama, pp. 389–405.
47 Memoirs, vol. 3, p. 195.
48 Ibid., pp. 199–200.
49 Ibid., p. 206.
50 Ibid. p. 203.
51 Ibid., p. 208.
52 'The blues' is sometimes thought of as a modern figurative term for low spirits, but it dates from 1550.
53 Memoirs, vol. 3, pp. 203 and 237.
54 Ibid., p. 231.
55 Ibid., p. 249.
56 27/2/28, Richard Atkinson to Anne Lindsay, 12 October 1785.
57 Memoirs, vol. 4, pp. 4–5.
58 Ibid.
59 Ibid., p. 7. Many passages in the Memoirs were culled from journals and notes and both the tense and the immediacy of this one suggest such an instance.

9 ROYAL GO-BETWEEN 1785–1787

1 27/2/159, Thomas Noel to Anne Lindsay, 23 September 1785.
2 27/2/312, Anne Lindsay to Thomas Noel, undated [November 1785].

3 27/4/25, Maria Fitzherbert to Anne Lindsay, undated.
4 *Morning Herald*, 10 May 1786.
5 Memoirs, vol. 4, p. 39.
6 27/4/25, Maria Fitzherbert to Anne Lindsay, 9 July 1785.
7 Ibid., Prince of Wales to Anne Lindsay, 31 October 1785.
8 Memoirs, vol. 4, p. 19.
9 Masson, pp. 109–10.
10 Memoirs, vol. 4, p. 20.
11 27/4/25, Maria Fitzherbert to Anne Lindsay, undated [November 1785].
12 Ibid., Anne Lindsay to the Prince of Wales, undated [November 1785].
13 The complete account of this incident is in the Memoirs, vol. 4, pp. 39–43.
14 27/4/25, Anne Lindsay to the Prince of Wales, undated [November 1785].
15 Ibid., Prince of Wales to Anne Lindsay, 4–5 December 1785.
16 Ibid., Prince of Wales to Anne Lindsay, 1 December 1785.
17 Ibid.
18 Ibid., Anne Lindsay to Lord Mansfield, 12 December 1785.
19 Ibid., Anne Lindsay to Maria Fitzherbert, 12 December 1785. Memoirs, vol. 4, p. 39.
20 Ibid., Maria Fitzherbert to Anne Lindsay, undated [December 1785].
21 Ibid., Anne Lindsay to Maria Fitzherbert, 12 December 1785.
22 Ibid., Anne Lindsay to Lord Mansfield, 12 December 1785. A slightly amended version of this letter appears in the Memoirs, vol. 4, pp. 47–9.
23 Memoirs, vol. 4, p. 49.
24 27/4/25, Prince of Wales to Anne Lindsay, 13 December 1785.
25 Memoirs, vol. 4, pp. 51–2.
26 Ibid., p. 53.
27 27/4/25, Anne Lindsay to Maria Fitzherbert and Maria Fitzherbert to Anne Lindsay, undated [1786].
28 Memoirs, vol. 4, p. 50.
29 Elwin, p. 273.
30 Ibid., p. 268.
31 Memoirs, vol. 4, p. 18.
32 27/1/339.
33 Memoirs, vol. 4, pp. 32–3.
34 Ibid., p. 34.
35 In a simultaneous though unrelated financial dispute, it was found that a trustee, James Wills, appointed by Atkinson to shield the £150 annual pension he had obtained for Margaret from any claim by Fordyce, had used the fund for his own purposes. This case was only resolved by the Chancery Division in 1792.
36 Memoirs, vol. 4, p. 15.
37 Ibid., p. 110.
38 Masson, p. 98.
39 Foreman, p. 45.
40 Memoirs, vol. 3, p. 86.
41 23/1/139, Robert Lindsay to Alexander Lindsay, 13 August 1787.
42 Memoirs, vol. 4, p. 74.

43   Ibid.
44   Ibid., p. 85.

10 THE WEATHERCOCK 1787–1791

1   Memoirs, vol. 4, p. 85.
2   Blunt, vol. 2, p. 250.
3   Memoirs, vol. 4, pp. 87–8.
4   Ibid., p. 97.
5   27/4/27, Thomas Barnard to Anne Lindsay, 9 May 1790.
6   27/2/38, Edmund Burke to Anne Lindsay, undated [1793].
7   Memoirs, vol. 4, p. 98.
8   27/4/27, Thomas Barnard to Anne Lindsay, undated.
9   Memoirs, vol. 4, p. 88.
10   Ibid.
11   Sichel, vol. 1, p. 611.
12   Dictionary of National Biography.
13   Memoirs, vol. 4, p. 89.
14   Ibid., p. 90.
15   Ibid., p. 118.
16   Ibid.
17   Matheson, p. 131.
18   Both from Dictionary of National Biography.
19   Holland House Papers, 51710, Windham Diary, 12 August 1789.
20   Some sources put the year of their meeting as 1788 but Anne located it to September 1789.
21   Memoirs, vol. 4, p. 111.
22   Ibid., p. 127.
23   Ibid., p. 119.
24   Ibid., pp. 156–7.
25   Holland House Papers, 51710, Windham Diary, 8 September 1789.
26   Memoirs, vol. 4, p. 103.
27   Ibid., p. 118.
28   Ibid., p. 86.
29   Ibid., pp. 285–6.
30   Memoirs, vol. 4, p. 93 and vol. 3, p. 53.
31   27/4/22, vol. 1.
32   Windham Papers, Add. MSS 37921, fo. 129, 24 July 1790.
33   27/4/22, vol. 1.
34   Memoirs, vol. 4, p. 102.
35   Ibid., pp. 143 and 148.
36   Ibid., p. 110.
37   Bickley, vol. 1, p. 69.
38   29/3/1, Alexander Fordyce to Margaret Fordyce, 23 August 1789.
39   Ibid., Alexander Fordyce to Margaret Fordyce, 14 July 1785.
40   Memoirs, vol. 4, p. 158.
41   Ibid., p. 94.

42 Elwin, p. 445, refers to reports of Margaret's disappointment at the marriage.
43 27/4/27, Dr Barnard to Anne Lindsay, undated [1790].
44 Memoirs, vol. 4, pp. 138–9.
45 27/4/27, Anne Lindsay to Thomas Barnard, 2 May 1790.
46 Ibid., Thomas Barnard to Anne Lindsay, 9 May 1790.
47 Memoirs, vol. 4, p. 156.
48 Ibid., p. 157.
49 Memoirs, vol. 3, p. 79.
50 Memoirs, vol. 4, p. 162.
51 Ibid., p. 163.
52 Ibid., p. 157.
53 Ibid., p. 166.
54 Ibid., p. 158.
55 Ibid., pp. 165–6.

II A CAPTIVE IN PARIS 1791–1792

1   Memoirs, vol. 4, p. 237.
2   Schama, pp. 531, 537, 549.
3   Memoirs, vol. 4, pp. 171 and 168.
4   Ibid., p. 173.
5   National Archives, HO 42/27/254 fos 771/2, 25 December 1793.
6   29/3/1, Margaret Fordyce to Anne Lindsay, November 1791.
7   Memoirs, vol. 4, p. 174.
8   27/4/22, scrap of a letter from Anne Lindsay to an unknown recipient, 7 September 1791.
9   27/4/22, Anne Lindsay to William Windham, undated [October 1790].
10 Memoirs, vol. 4, p. 168.
11 Ibid., p. 164.
12 Ibid., p. 200.
13 Schama, p. 573.
14 Memoirs, vol. 4, p. 187.
15 Memoirs, vol. 3, p. 184.
16 Memoirs, vol. 4, p. 177.
17 Ibid., p. 204.
18 Matheson, p. 156.
19 Ibid., p. 181.
20 Holland House Papers, Add. MS 51710, April 1791.
21 27/4/22, William Windham to Anne Lindsay, undated [1793].
22 Memoirs, vol. 4, p. 183.
23 Ibid., p. 184.
24 Ibid., p. 188.
25 Ibid., p. 197.
26 Ibid., p. 206.
27 Ibid., p. 188. The tone of Emma's voice, she wrote, 'disgusted the men and frightened the women'.
28 Masson, pp. 125–6.

29 Memoirs, vol. 4, p. 206.
30 29/3/1, Margaret Fordyce to Anne Lindsay, 2 October 1791.
31 Memoirs, vol. 4, p. 207.
32 Ibid., p. 212.
33 Ibid., p. 218. The letter, dated 31 October 1791, is also included in 27/4/22, compiled by the 27th Earl of Crawford and Balcarres. Anne destroyed about 350 of Windham's letters, preserving just enough 'to show what an ignis fatuus a luminous character sometimes is'.
34 Ibid., pp. 206.
35 Ibid., p. 238.
36 Ibid., p. 231.
37 Ibid., p. 230.
38 27/4/22, Charles Lindsay to Anne Lindsay, 1 January 1792.
39 Memoirs, vol. 4, p. 243.
40 Matheson, p. 148.
41 Memoirs, vol. 4, p. 227.

12 'A BLACKGUARD LOVER' 1793–1796

1   Memoirs, vol. 4, p. 259.
2   27/1/3, Andrew Barnard to Anne Lindsay, undated [1793].
3   Memoirs, vol. 4, p. 246.
4   27/1/4, Anne Lindsay to the Prince of Wales, July 1973.
5   Memoirs, vol. 4, pp. 248–9.
6   Ibid., p. 256.
7   Cape Archives, A1657, Elizabeth Hardwicke to Anne Lindsay, June 1793.
8   Robinson, p. 4.
9   27/2/122, Anne Keith to Anne Lindsay, 20 June (?) 1793.
10 Memoirs, vol. 4, pp. 250–1.
11 29/3/1, Margaret Forsyth to Anne Lindsay, June 1793.
12 29/3/1, Andrew Barnard to Margaret Forsyth, 14 April 1795.
13 29/3/1, Margaret Forsyth to Anne Barnard, 1 November 1793. Memoirs, vol. 4, p. 272.
14 Memoirs, vol. 4, p. 256.
15 Coghlan, vol. 1, pp. 130–1.
16 Ibid., pp. 134–5, vol. 2, p. 102.
17 Memoirs, vol. 4, p. 127.
18 27/1/109, Lady Balcarres to Anne and Andrew Barnard, undated [1794].
19 27/1/5, Andrew Barnard to Anne Lindsay, 19 July 1793.
20 27/4/22, vol. 2, p. 171.
21 Memoirs, vol. 4, p. 252.
22 Ibid., p. 260.
23 Robinson, p. 7.
24 Ibid.
25 Matheson, pp. 330–1.
26 Inscription by Anne on a folder of letters from Andrew 27/1/28–53.
27 40/123, Anne Barnard to James Lindsay, 20 August 1816.

28 27/1/6, Andrew Barnard to Anne Barnard, 1 November 1794.
29 Memoirs, vol. 4, p. 260.
30 Ibid.
31 Coghlan, vol. 2, p. 98.
32 Ibid., vol. 1, pp. 133–4.
33 Memoirs, vol. 4, p. 275.
34 27/1/7 and 9, Andrew Barnard to Anne Barnard, 21 April and 11 May 1795.
35 23/1/1, Anne Barnard to Margaret Fordyce, 24 December 1800.
36 27/1/5, Andrew Barnard to Anne Lindsay, 19 July 1793.
37 Memoirs, vol. 4, p. 272.
38 Bickley, vol. 1, p. 69.
39 Robinson, p. 9.
40 Ibid., p. 15.
41 Ibid., p. 16.
42 Ibid., p. 17.
43 Memoirs, vol. 4, p. 277.
44 Robinson, pp. 19–20.
45 Memoirs, vol. 4, p. 278.
46 Ibid., p. 279.
47 Journals, pp. 25–6.
48 29/3/1, Margaret Fordyce to Anne Barnard, 24 January 1797.

13 A CAPE OF HOPE 1797–1798

1   Taylor, p. 53.
2   Journals, pp. 39 and 70.
3   Ibid., pp. 82 and 85.
4   Ibid., p. 59.
5   Ibid., p. 102.
6   Ibid., p. 109.
7   27/2/106, James Hartley to Anne Barnard, March 1799.
8   Journals, p. 108.
9   Ibid., p. 111.
10 Ibid., p. 137.
11 Journals, pp. 140–1.
12 Robinson, p. 49. Anne believed this honour belonged to Lady Anne Monson, the wife of a Bengal official, who had been at the Cape. (Journals, p. 218) In all likelihood, the mountain had previously been climbed by Khoikhoi or Dutch settler women, who had been at the Cape for almost 150 years.
13 Journals, p. 218.
14 Robinson, p. 49.
15 Ibid., pp. 43–4.
16 N. A. M. Rodger, *The Command of the Ocean* (Harmondsworth, 2004), p. 436.
17 Robinson, p. 54.
18 Ibid., p. 35.
19 27/2/65, Lord Melville to Anne Barnard, March 1802.
20 27/2/71, Jean Dundas to Anne Barnard, undated.

21 Robinson, p. 41.

22 Ibid., p. 73.

23 A comprehensive record of this era of British rule is to be found in Boucher and Penn.

24 Brenthurst Library, *Lord Macartney's Diary of Official Business at the Castle of Good Hope*, 11 November 1798.

25 Boucher and Penn, pp. 81,89 and 197..

26 Robinson, p. 38.

27 Journals, p. 212.

28 Ibid., p. 189.

29 Boucher and Penn, p. 185.

30 Ibid.

31 Cape Archives, A1415/74. Barnard's refusal to turn a blind eye to corruption was seen during the governorship of George Yonge.

32 Journals, pp. 241.

33 Ibid., pp. 173 and 193.

34 Robinson, p. 43, Journals, p. 226.

35 27/2/175, Jane Parker to Anne Barnard, 6 March 1798.

36 Journals, p. 260.

37 Butler, p. 108.

38 27/2/209, Richard Wellesley to Anne Barnard, 2 October 1800.

39 Journals, p. 293.

40 Robinson, p. 81.

41 In 27/2/206 Wellesley indulged in an extended fart joke, enclosing 'a sketch of a part of Lady Anstruther's person, the existence of which would be doubtful if it were not proved by the nature of the storms which it brews. We argue that although we can see nothing these must be very large because they are so loud, frequent and offensive.' Anne responded in kind, reporting that 'Lady A has left such an *odour* behind her as will not be forgotten. All pity Calcutta which is to contain her.' (Wellesley Papers, Add. MS 3308, fo. 146).

42 Anne was arguably too kind in commenting on his affair: 'You have enough to tease and worry you without permitting petty calumny to do so, for this calumny is but petty – there is no man's *wife* seduced by your naughty Excellency, no family peace broke up, no pure mind rendered impure by your impurity.' See Butler, p. 277.

43 *Diaries*, vol. 2, pp. 154–5.

44 Robinson, p. 21.

45 *Diaries*, vol. 2, p. 54.

46 *Diaries*, vol. 1, p. 199.

47 Journals, pp. 195 and 227.

48 Ibid., p. 121.

49 *Diaries*, vol. 1, p. 100.

14 A WHILE IN PARADISE 1797–1798

1 References to Paradise are found in the Journals, pp. 202 and 230, and

Robinson, p. 53. The cottage fell back into decay after the Barnards' departure from the Cape, but in recent years the site at Newlands has been the subject of archaeological study by researchers at the University of Cape Town.

2 Fairbridge, p. 32, Journal p. 205.

3 27/2/33, John Barrow to Anne Barnard, 12 October 1797.

4 27/2/32, John Barrow to Anne Barnard, 4 July 1797.

5 Robinson, p. 73.

6 Ibid., p. 75. The version of this denouement in the Journal, pp. 243–4 was composed later and appears less reliable.

7 Ibid., p. 91.

8 Barrow's hostility forms the basis of a study, not always even-handed, by Michael Streak, *The Afrikaner as Viewed by the English* (Struik, 1974).

9 Mostert, p. 262.

10 Robinson, p. 83.

11 Ibid., p. 91.

12 Ibid., p. 94.

13 Ibid., p. 92.

14 Ibid., p. 96. Almost identical words are contained in the Journal, p. 256, based on a letter to Margaret.

15 Ibid.

16 29/3/1, Andrew Barnard to Margaret Fordyce, 1 April 1798.

17 Journals, pp. 261–2.

18 Ibid., p. 284.

19 The custodian of Anne's papers, Robert Lindsay, the Earl of Crawford, is sceptical of the idea that the painting is by her, noting that although she often worked in watercolours, he was not aware of any oils.

20 A stone pool at the botanical gardens of Kirstenbosch known as Lady Anne Barnard's Bath, lies not far from Paradise but cannot be the right location as it was built after her departure from the Cape. The site and remains of the cottage have been identified and excavated in recent years by specialists from the nearby campus of the University of Cape Town.

21 The copy is reprinted in *The Penguin Book of South African Verse*.

22 Boucher and Penn, p. 191.

23 Journals, p. 279.

24 Ibid., p. 293.

25 Ibid., p. 294.

26 Shields, p. 159.

27 Fairbridge, pp. 50 and 52.

28 These distances are calculated on the wagon routes of the day, by some way longer than modern roads.

29 27/2/175, Jane Parker to Anne Barnard, 6 March 1798.

30 Journals, 306.

31 Ibid., p. 308.

32 Ibid., p. 341.

33 Ibid., p. 337.

34 Ibid., pp. 337–8.

35 Ibid., p. 351.

36   Ibid., p. 369.
37   William Dalrymple, *The Guardian*, 9 June 2007.
38   Students of Anne's writings in South Africa have contributed in various
        ways to an understanding of the route she followed in May 1798, among
        them Jose Burman's *In the Footsteps of Lady Anne Barnard* (Cape Town,
        1990), a general guide although inaccurate in some respects. Her own journal
        estimated the total distance covered at 700 miles. A journey by car following
        the best knowledge of the route puts it at 640 miles.

15 PARADISE LOST 1799–1800

1   Robinson, pp. 176–7.
2   Ibid., p. 179.
3   27/2/146–151. Space does not permit more than brief reference to these
        letters from Macartney but they bear testimony to the warmth that endured
        between them up to his death in 1806.
4   Robinson, p. 166.
5   *Diaries*, vol. 1, p. 98.
6   Ibid., p. 16.
7   *Diaries*, vol. 2, p. 128 and 1, p. 87. An entry for 26 March 1799 runs: 'I am
        obliged to see every bit of meat cut into proper shape myself and give
        directions for the different dishes over and over.'
8   Harcourt Papers, MS Eng d 3851, Anne Barnard to Elizabeth Harcourt, 31
        December 1798.
9   *Diaries*, vol. 1, pp. 344 and 348.
10   Ibid., pp. 125 and 135.
11   Ibid., p. 168.
12   27/4/9 Sea Journal Home, p. 10.
13   *Diaries*, vol. 1, p. 287.
14   Ibid., pp. 88 and 310.
15   27/4/9 Sea Journal Home, p. 15.
16   *Diaries*, vol. 1, p. 165.
17   Ibid., p. 209.
18   Ibid., p. 162.
19   Ibid., pp. 245–6.
20   Robinson, p. 195.
21   Cape Archives, A1415/74, Andrew Barnard to Lord Macartney, 7 July 1799.
22   *Diaries*, vol. 1, p. 239.
23   Robinson, p. 191.
24   *Diaries*, vol. 1, pp. 222 and 252.
25   27/2/207, Richard Wellesley to Anne Barnard, 29 September 1799.
26   *Diaries*, vol. 1, p. 81, entry for 22 March 1799.
27   Ibid., p. 147.
28   Ibid., pp. 2 and 74.
29   Ibid., p. 146.
30   Ibid., p. 203.
31   Ibid., p. 154.

32 Ibid., pp. 172 and 180.

33 *Travels of Mirza Abu Taleb Khan in Asia, Africa and Europe*, vol. 1, p. 89.

34 *Diaries*, vol. 2, p. 195–6.

35 Ibid., vol. 1, p. 107.

36 Ibid., p. 154.

37 Ibid., p. 325.

38 Ibid., p. 44. The passage is not identified, but Anne indicated that it concerns a conversation between a husband and 'his pretty, giddy wife' on the morning after the marriage 'upon the subject of lengthening out for ever the Honey moon by those wise and temperate restrictions which prevent many ills arising from too unbounded liberty'.

39 *Diaries*, vol. 2, p. 82.

40 Ibid., vol. 1, p. 353.

41 Ibid., p. 349.

42 Ibid., p. 360.

43 27/2/147, Lord Macartney to Anne Barnard, 14 April 1800.

44 *Diaries*, vol. 1, p. 351.

45 Ibid., vol. 1, p. 45.

46 Ibid., pp. 175 and 84.

47 *Diaries*, vol. 1, p. 235.

48 Ibid., p. 55.

49 'I am assured we have had a good passage from the Cape,' Jane wrote. 'If so, I can only say that a good passage is the very worst thing in the world except a bad passage. Truth compels me to acknowledge that Bombay is a very vile island. It is hot, ugly, wet, the ground swarms with noxious reptiles, the air with tormenting insects, while the natives are covered with vermin and very little else.' Memoirs, vol. 5, p. 27.

50 *Diaries*, vol. 2, p. 71.

51 Ibid., vol. 1, pp. 85, 101.

52 Ibid., p. 105.

53 Ibid., p. 219.

54 Ibid., p. 264.

55 Ibid., p. 60.

56 Ibid., pp. 285–6.

57 Journals, p. 214.

58 The poem is reproduced in full in the Journals, pp. 214–15.

16 THE COURT OF LILLIPUT 1800–1802

1 Boucher and Penn, p. 241.

2 Journals, pp. 178 and 293.

3 Fairbridge, p. 189.

4 Memoirs, vol. 5, p. 87.

5 Robinson, p. 205.

6 Journals, p. 293.

7 *Diaries*, vol. 1, p. 126, Fairbridge, p. 108.

8 Robinson, p. 226.

9   Ibid., p. 228.
10 Ibid., p. 220.
11 Ibid., pp. 211 and 226.
12 Ibid., p. 240. A far more detailed description of this episode is found in *Diaries*, vol. 2, pp. 101–6.
13 Ibid.
14 *Diaries*, vol. 2, p. 104.
15 Hardwicke Papers, Add. MS 35644, Andrew Barnard to Philip Hardwicke, 26 December 1800.
16 Butler, p. 245.
17 Robinson, p. 243.
18 Ibid., p. 244.
19 Ibid., p. 247.
20 Ibid., pp. 247–8.
21 *Dictionary of National Biography*, Sir George Yonge (*Later Correspondence of George III*, 3.428).
22 *Diaries*, vol. 2, p. 264.
23 Cape Archives, A1415/74, Andrew Barnard to George Macartney, 12 November 1800.
24 Fairbridge, p. 161.
25 *Diaries*, vol. 2, pp. 284–8.
26 Margaret Lenta, whose assiduous research and transcribing led to publication of two volumes of the Cape Diaries, speculated that Anne continued with them through 1801 but noted that 'no such writings have as yet come to light'. The little she did write that year is, in fact, to be found in a mixed box of scraps and pinned papers, 27/4/9, with a note: 'Mixed & imperfectly put up. To be looked over & classed if I ever have time.'
27 Robinson, p. 275.
28 Ibid., p. 267.
29 Fairbridge, p. 276.
30 *Diaries*, vol. 2, p. 179.
31 Ibid., p. 256.
32 Barker, introduction.
33 27/4/9, pp. 33–4.
34 Fairbridge, pp. 286–8.
35 The similarity has been noted by Barker.
36 Fairbridge, pp. 286–8.
37 Ibid., p. 251.
38 27/3/1, Anne Barnard to Margaret Fordyce, 5 November 1801.
39 27/3/1, Anne Barnard to Margaret Fordyce, 19 December 1801.
40 Mostert, pp. 259 and 323.
41 Robinson, p. 277.
42 23/1/1, Anne Barnard to Margaret Fordyce, 24 December 1800.
43 Journals, p. 223.
44 27/4/20, *The Hottentots Farewell*.
45 27/4/9.
46 28/1/1, Anne Barnard to Andrew Barnard, undated [1802].

47 27/4/9, Sea Journal Home, pp. 3–4.
48 *Diaries*, vol. 2, p. 236.

17 HOME AND AWAY 1802–1806

1 Memoirs, vol. 5, p. 2.
2 Ibid., p. 21.
3 Ibid., p. 21.
4 Ibid., p. 17. The Pygmalion referred to is the mythological sculptor who carved a woman out of ivory.
5 Ibid., p. 48.
6 Ibid., pp. 58–9.
7 29/3/1, Margaret Fordyce to Anne Barnard, 1 January 1805.
8 Fairbridge, p. 311.
9 27/2/96, Anne Baker-Holroyd to Anne Barnard, about 1800.
10 Memoirs, vol. 5, p. 22.
11 27/4/25, Maria Fitzherbert to Anne Barnard, about 1799.
12 Hibbert, p. 231.
13 Memoirs, vol. 5, p. 50.
14 Ibid., p. 28.
15 Ibid., p. 129.
16 Ibid., p. 48.
17 Ibid., p. 17.
18 27/3/1, Cape Journal, scrap of an undated letter.
19 Memoirs, vol. 5, p. 17.
20 Ibid., p. 48.
21 23/1/1, Anne Barnard to Margaret Fordyce, 24 December 1800.
22 Memoirs, vol. 5., p. 111.
23 27/1/14, Andrew Barnard to Anne Barnard, 4 February 1803.
24 Memoirs, vol. 5, p. 76.
25 Martin, p. 53.
26 27/4/22, Anne Lindsay to William Windham, undated [1790].
27 LoL, vol. 2, p. 338.
28 Memoirs, vol. 5, p. 61.
29 Ibid.
30 Ibid., p. 12.
31 23/1/144–166, Letters between Alexander and Robert cast light on the financial affairs of Balcarres.
32 Matheson, pp. 330–1.
33 Memoirs, vol. 5, p. 118.
34 Ibid., p. 120.
35 Ibid., p. 118.
36 Ibid., pp. 121–2.
37 *The Barnard Letters* edited by Anthony Powell contain letters from the bishop to his daughter which allude to the marriage. Letters from Andrew to Anne

in 27/1/15–28 present the other side of the story.

38 27/1/15–28. There are fourteen surviving letters from Andrew Barnard to Anne over the year he spent in Ireland.

39 See Hardwicke Papers, Add. MS 35645, Anne Barnard to Philip Hardwicke, 24 November 1805.

40 *Diaries*, vol. 2, p. 113.

41 Memoirs, vol. 5, p. 159.

42 Ibid., p. 156.

43 Windham Papers, Add. MS 37914, fo. 916, Anne Barnard to William Windham, 12 February 1806.

44 Anne also petitioned Richard Sheridan, who had turned from the playwright of first acquaintance to politician. Her scrawl in the margin indicates his waffling reply: 'A very low, very clever, very thoughtless great man.'

45 Memoirs, vol. 5, p. 149.

46 27/1/29, Andrew Barnard to Anne Barnard, June 1806.

47 Wellesley Papers, Add. MS 37309 contains a letter from Anne to Lord Wellesley dated 26 June 1806, relating the failure of her petition to Windham.

48 Memoirs, vol. 5, pp. 164–5.

49 Wellesley Papers, Add. MS 37309, Anne Barnard to Richard Wellesley, 26 June 1806.

50 Memoirs, vol. 5, p. 164.

18 ALONE 1807–1810

1 27/1/30, Andrew Barnard to Anne Barnard, 8 February 1807.

2 27/1/31, 32 and 34, Andrew Barnard to Anne Barnard, 9, 11 and 13 February.

3 27/1/36, Andrew Barnard to Anne Barnard, 1 March 1807.

4 27/1/40, Andrew Barnard to Anne Barnard, 4 March 1807.

5 27/4/44.

6 Ibid.

7 28/1/3, Anne Barnard to Andrew Barnard, 12 April 1807.

8 27/4/44.

9 Memoirs, vol. 5, p. 169.

10 27/1/38, Lord Caledon to Anne Barnard, 27 February 1807.

11 27/4/44.

12 Memoirs, vol. 4, p. 244.

13 27/2/68, Lord Melville to Anne Barnard, 6 March 1807.

14 Memoirs, vol. 5, p. 190.

15 27/1/45 and 46, Andrew Barnard to Anne Barnard, 25 May and 15 June 1807.

16 27/1/46, Andrew Barnard to Anne Barnard, 15 June 1807.

17 27/1/1, Lord Caledon to Anne Barnard, 3 June 1807.

18 27/1/48, Andrew Barnard to Anne Barnard, 6 August 1807.

19 Memoirs, vol. 5, p. 203.

20 Ibid.

21 Ibid., p. 204.

22 Cape Archives, CO 4823, Letters Despatched, November 1806–August 1807.

23 27/1/55, Andrew Barnard to Anne Barnard, 6 October 1807.
24 Hardwicke Papers, Add. MS 35647, Lord Castlereagh to Alexander Lindsay, 15 January 1808.
25 Ibid., fos 115 and 119.
26 Memoirs, vol. 5, p. 208.
27 Journals, p. 234.
28 Memoirs, vol. 5, p. 208.
29 Note on folder, 27/1/44.
30 Memoirs, vol. 5, p. 210.
31 Hardwicke Papers, Add. MS 35647, Duke of Portland to Alexander Lindsay, 26 January 1808.
32 Memoirs, vol. 4, p. 118.
33 Memoirs, vol. 5, pp. 35 and 29.

19 A 'PROTÉGÉE OF A DARKER COMPLEXION' 1810–1844

1   27/5/2, Account of expenditure for 1809.
2   27/2/318, Anne Barnard to B. W. van Rijneveld, 27 August 1809.
3   Memoirs, vol. 6, p. 114.
4   Ibid.
5   27/2/318, Anne Barnard to B. W. van Rijneveld, 27 August 1809.
6   Ibid.
7   Memoirs, vol. 6, p. 114.
8   Samuel Hudson, formerly the Barnards' servant at the Cape and a slave-owner, was known to rail against 'the cunning and artfulness' of slave women 'always ready to offer their bodies for a trifle'. McKenzie, pp. 80–1.
9   27/4/2, Account of expenditure.
10 See William Dalrymple's *White Mughals*, pp. 50–3.
11 25/1/33, Anne Barnard to James Lindsay, 29 July 1813.
12 27/2/319, Anne Barnard to B. W. van Rijneveld, February 1810.
13 27/1/295, Lord Hardwicke to Anne Barnard, 14 October 1805. This letter marked the start of Henry Hervey's army career, as a cadet.
14 Hastings Family Papers, HA/20/27, Anne Barnard to Lady Hastings, 30 January 1819.
15 Ibid., Anne Barnard to Lady Loudon, 27 October 1812.
16 Memoirs, vol. 6, p. 114.
17 27/4/20, a note among the poems.
18 27/4/25, Anne Barnard to Maria Fitzherbert, 20 April 1813.
19 Ibid.
20 The letter, without references to Christina, is found in the Memoirs, vol. 6, pp. 24–5.
21 Memoirs, vol. 6, p. 10.
22 Ibid., p. 11.
23 Ibid., p. 12.
24 Ibid., p. 24.
25 27/4/25, Maria Fitzherbert to Anne Barnard, 14 August 1814.
26 Ibid.

27 See Hibbert.

28 Memoirs, vol. 4, p. 133.

29 Blunt, vol. 2, p. 207.

30 In 1808 John was arrested over a debt of £80, at which point his older
    brothers were on the verge of giving up on him, including Robert, the only
    Lindsay with real wealth, who declared: 'He must evidently go to the Devil.'
    In what amounted to a stylish rebuke Anne sent money to Alexander 'for
    the express purpose of relieving him', adding: 'He is not the only person who
    draws hard on my purse, which goes as far as it can but stops where it must.
    I suggest that, as this is Sunday, he might be liberated today.' 23/1/228 and
    23/1/6.

31 27/2/41, Anne Barnard to Lord Mansfield, 3 January 1810.

32 40/1/10, Anne Barnard to James Lindsay, 16 September 1811.

33 Powell, p. 196.

34 Ibid., p. 206.

35 Memoirs, vol. 5, p. 222.

36 Burges Papers 16, Anne Barnard to James Burges, 19 November 1812.

37 LoL, vol. 2, p. 338.

38 Powell, p. 236.

39 Ibid.

40 27/1/194, James Lindsay to Anne Barnard.

41 40/1/24, Anne Barnard to James Lindsay, 25 September 1816.

42 40/1/11, Anne Barnard to James Lindsay, 14 March 1814.

43 40/1/12, Anne Barnard to James Lindsay, 3 April 1814.

44 *Diaries*, vol. 2, p. 112.

20 LEGACIES 1814–1825

1 27/1/339.

2 27/1/340.

3 23/1/10, Anne Barnard to Alexander Lindsay, 31 August 1814.

4 Memoirs, vol. 6, p. 41.

5 Ibid.

6 29/3/1, Elizabeth Abbot to Anne Barnard, 17 December 1814.

7 Memoirs, vol. 6, p. 41.

8 LoL, vol. 2, p. 339.

9 23/1/10, Anne Barnard to Alexander Lindsay, 31 August 1814.

10 40/1/18, Anne Barnard to James Lindsay, 29 February 1815.

11 27/1/60, Andrew Barnard to Anne Barnard, 19 June 1815.

12 23/1/19, Anne Barnard to Alexander Lindsay, 16 March 1816.

13 27/4/20, Reflections, 1 January 1816; and 40/1/14, Anne Barnard to James
    Lindsay, 17 December 1814.

14 23/1/267, Robert Lindsay to Alexander Lindsay, 9 May 1816.

15 23/1/21, Anne Barnard to Alexander Lindsay, 24 March 1816.

16 23/1/23, Anne Barnard to Alexander Lindsay, 17 January 1816.

17 LoL, vol. 2, pp. 386–7.

18 Ibid.

19 Ibid.
20 40/1/20, Anne Barnard to James Lindsay, 3 May 1816.
21 Hardwicke Papers, Add. MS 35649 Anne Barnard to Philip Hardwicke, 17 November 1811.
22 Memoirs, vol. 5, p. 141.
23 Anne's account of her friendship with Annabella, contained in the Memoirs, vol. 6, pp. 93–9, includes a conversation in which Byron's wife related how he began to abuse her immediately after their marriage, saying: 'What a dupe you have been! How is it possible a woman of your sense could form the hope of reforming me? . . . It is enough for me that you are my wife that I may hate you.'
24 This is an abbreviated version of the letter – presumably among the thousands destroyed by Anne – to be found in the Memoirs, vol. 6, pp. 98–9.
25 40/1/21, Anne Barnard to James Lindsay, 16 May 1816.
26 LoL, vol. 2, p. 388.
27 29/3/1, Margaret Fordyce to Anne Barnard, 12 March 1806. In this instance the letter contained only inconsequential gossip.
28 25/1/62, Anne Barnard to James Lindsay, 6 August 1818.
29 Memoirs, vol. 1, p. 10.
30 25/1/67, Anne Barnard to James Lindsay, 26 September 1818.
31 Memoirs, vol. 1, p. 1.
32 27/1/262, Mary-Ann Lindsay to Anne Barnard, about 1819.
33 Memoirs, vol. 1, p. 2.
34 27/1/315, Anne's will. Barnard's paternity of Christina was, of course, also spelled out in the memoirs.
35 27/1/207, James Lindsay to Anne Barnard, 10 February 1818.
36 40/1/29, Anne Barnard to James Lindsay, 12 October 1817.
37 40/1/23, Anne Barnard to James Lindsay, 20 August 1816.
38 27/1/222, James Lindsay to Anne Barnard, 6 August 1820.
39 27/1/161, Elizabeth Lindsay to Anne Barnard, 23 October 1822.
40 27/1/162, Elizabeth Lindsay to Anne Barnard, 12 December 1822.
41 27/2/85, George IV to Anne Barnard, 24 January 1821.
42 The account of the fire is contained in an address 'To the Reader' in vol. 1 of the Memoirs, pp. 2–6.
43 Ibid.
44 Feldman, p. 419.
45 Memoirs, vol. 6, p. 177.
46 Ibid., pp. 182–3. Scott also remembered the eccentric Sophy Johnston, 'her jockey coat, masculine stride, strong voice and occasionally round oath'.
47 Ibid., p. 188.
48 Ibid., p. 189.
49 25/1/67, Anne Barnard to James Lindsay, 18 May 1823.
50 23/1/26, Anne Barnard to Alexander Lindsay, 18 May 1823.
51 *Morning Chronicle*, 14 April 1824.
52 Ibid., 26 April 1824.
53 40/1/39, Anne Barnard to James Lindsay, 19 November 1824.
54 *Morning Post*, 26 April 1825.

55 25/1/27, Sir Edmund Antrobus to James Lindsay, 7 December 1855.

56 Sloper and his activities were frequently reported in the local press, notably the *Devizes and Wiltshire Gazette*.

57 In addition to the Wiltshire papers, the marriage was reported in Oxford, Bath and Leeds.

58 Christina's death was reported in the *Hampshire Advertiser* of 5 March 1842, Hervey's in the *Salisbury and Winchester Journal*, 28 March 1842, and the marriages of her daughters in a number of local journals.

EPILOGUE

1   See Feldman, pp. 415–19.

2   Jane Millgate, *Unclaimed Territory*.

3   Powell, *Barnard Letters*, introduction.

4   25/1/67, Anne Barnard to James Lindsay, 26 September 1818.

5   Memoirs, vol. 5, p. 1.

6   Ibid.

7   *Diaries*, vol. 2, p. 186.

8   Memoirs, vol. 5, p. 72.

9   Memoirs, vol. 6, p. 116.

10 Margaret Lenta, 'The Shape of a Woman's Life: Lady Anne Barnard's Memoir' in *Literator*, August 1993.

11 Memoirs, vol. 1, p. 147.

12 Memoirs, vol. 6, p. 22.

13 *Diaries*, vol. 1, p. 11.

14 Harman, p. 385.

15 *Diaries*, vol. 1, p. xi.

16 LoL, vol. 2, p. 388.

Acknowledgements

This book would not have been written without the assistance of Robert Lindsay, the Earl of Crawford and Balcarres, and for his trust in extending to me the freedom to explore Anne Barnard's papers in his library and for the hospitality he and his wife Ruth extended on my visits to Balcarres I am sincerely grateful. His knowledge of the Crawford collection and suggestions for avenues of research added to the rewards as well as the pleasure of the experience. His son Lord Balniel gave helpful assistance with the illustrations.

The main body of the Crawford archive is now held at the National Library of Scotland in Edinburgh where the helpfulness of Kenneth Dunn and the staff over three years enabled me to make the best use of my visits there. Other archivists whom I should like to thank are Jacobus van der Merwe at the Western Cape Archive in Cape Town, Jennifer Kimble of the Brenthurst Library in Johannesburg, and Alexandra Healey of the Bute Archive. Antonia Malan shared her knowledge of researching Paradise, the Barnards' cottage at the Cape.

Peter Barrett of Cape Town was extremely generous in allowing me to use paintings from his private collection; the images were provided by Philip Mould of London. I am also obliged to Esther Esmyol and Lailah Hisham of the Iziko Museums of Cape Town for their assistance with paintings from the William Fehr Collection; and to Melanie Geustyn at the National Library of South Africa for the usage of Anne Barnard's drawings.

It was slightly alarming to discover in the early days of research that another writer was at work on Lady Anne's papers. As it transpired, Richard Atkinson came to the subject from a different perspective, but his open-handedness in sharing the fruits of his own findings not only saved me time but added to my knowledge and spared me from errors. This was a rare and happy instance of cooperation between authors. Another writer, my friend Tom Fort, was as liberal as ever in reading the manuscript and with the opinions I have sought since writing my first book almost thirty years ago. Warm thanks are also due to another friend, Katherine O'Donnell, who provided a home welcome, food, wine and company on my stays in Edinburgh.

This is the fourth time I have worked with Julian Loose at Faber and Faber and Starling Lawrence at W. W. Norton, and I am acutely conscious of my fortune in having had two such stimulating and creative editors on our projects together. My sincere thanks to Anne Owen for her tireless efforts during production, and to Paula Turner.

My previous books have had what may be seen as male themes, so approaching a female biographical subject was not without its concerns. At points along the way I have sought advice from women with literary interests, starting as ever with my wife Caroline, thanks to whose own writings and research I rediscovered Anne, and who commented on successive drafts; she has been my stimulus and sounding board. Another diligent reader and friend, Judith Jenkinson, also read the manuscript. Caroline Dawnay and Sophie Scard took a degree of interest and offered comments that went well beyond the call of literary agency. To them all I am truly grateful. The reader who will always be most deeply associated in my heart with this book, however, who questioned my interpretations and challenged assumptions, who brought her own insights and came the closest as I saw it to understanding an enigma, is my beloved daughter Juliette. Thank you, my Anne.

Index